Dynamic Therapy in Brief Hospitalization

Dynamic Therapy in Brief Hospitalization

John M. Oldham, M.D.
L. Mark Russakoff, M.D.

A JASON ARONSON BOOK

ROWMAN & LITTLEFIELD PUBLISHERS, INC.
Lanham • Boulder • New York • Toronto • Plymouth, UK

A JASON ARONSON BOOK

ROWMAN & LITTLEFIELD PUBLISHERS, INC.

Published in the United States of America
by Rowman & Littlefield Publishers, Inc.
A wholly owned subsidiary of The Rowman & Littlefield Publishing Group, Inc.
4501 Forbes Boulevard, Suite 200, Lanham, Maryland 20706
www.rowmanlittlefield.com

Estover Road
Plymouth PL6 7PY
United Kingdom

Library of Congress Cataloging-in-Publication Data

Oldham, John M.
   Dynamic therapy in brief hospitalization.

   Includes bibliographies and index.
   1. Milieu therapy.   2. Therapeutic community.
3. Psychotherapy, Brief. 4. Psychiatric hospital
patients. I. Russakoff, L. Mark. II. Title. [DNLM:
1. Hospitals, Psychiatric. 2. Milieu Therapy.
3. Psychoanalytic therapy—methods. 4. Psychotherapy,
Group. WM 420 O44d]
RC489.M5043 1987   616.89'144   87-12629
ISBN 0-87668-965-9

Manufactured in the United States of America.

Contents

Foreword

The vast majority of patients who enter psychiatric hospitals nowadays are hospitalized for brief periods of time, from days to a few weeks. They are usually in a state of severe psychological regression and often evidence acute and florid psychotic symptoms. They thus present a challenge to hospital staff to arrive quickly at an adequate diagnosis, an initial treatment strategy, and the beginning of a long-range therapeutic approach. Given these circumstances, it is astonishing that the methodology of hospital treatment has remained at a relatively simple, "fireman's approach" level in integrating general medical, psychiatric, psychodynamic, and social rehabilitative aspects. The sophisticated theory of the therapeutic community, the contemporary biological and psychosocial modalities of diagnosis and treatment, have not heretofore been brought together in an effective, theoretically integrated, and practically satisfactory methodology for brief psychiatric inpatient treatment.

In this book, such an integration of general medical, psychiatric, and psychodynamic principles applied to this particular patient population has been achieved for the first time. In an original integration of the "medical model" and therapeutic community approaches to hospital milieu treatment, Oldham and Russakoff here present both a systematic theory for acute hospital treatment and its practical application, spelled out in great detail without lowering the high level of their narrative to a "cookbook" approach to treatment.

The authors have used psychoanalytic object relations theory as a theoretical frame for the study of simultaneous, multiple interactions of individual patients in formal and informal group situations in the hospital. They also use the theory as a frame of reference for studying the shifting nature of dominant fantasies and moods, regression, and work capabilities of small groups and larger social gatherings, such as community meetings. The integration of an object relations theory model with a theory that considers nonfunctional administration the key precondition for regression in groups (an integration that inspires the organizational model of hospital treatment presented in this book) articulates, in turn, object relations theory with overall hospital service organization. An exciting integration of psychodynamic theory and administrative principles permeates the entire book.

Oldham and Russakoff, through a systematic effort, remain at a comprehensive yet practical level of discourse, presenting in great detail the concrete applications of their theory without losing this focus in a too abstract discussion of the theory itself or in an excessively detailed, time-consuming focus on psychotherapeutic technique. They consistently and systematically stay at an intermediary level of theory, applied and illustrated in the dominant modalities of treatment examined.

The authors convincingly argue that the two models usually applied in organizing the short-term therapeutic milieu of a psychiatric hospital—the therapeutic community model and the medical model—each have evident advantages but also shortcomings that weaken the potential effectiveness of the short-term hospital milieu. The authors therefore propose a unified medical therapeutic community model that includes aspects of both approaches. Years of experience with this particular model have demonstrated that it can be applied in stable, flexible, empirically satisfactory ways to different patient populations, and with different administrative styles and staffing. And it is no more expensive to operate than a standard, adequately staffed acute psychiatric unit in a sophisticated academic setting.

The problems this model may present are similar to those of other therapeutic community models applied to long-term treatment programs. There is, first, the danger of excessive bureaucratization of decision making. Then, too, all therapeutic modalities may become rigid as staff insufficiently trained and educated attempts to copy treatment modalities initiated by more sophisticated leadership. A temptation exists to "overtreat" patients by including them all in every therapeutic activity, regardless of specific contraindications for individual patients. In addition, "burnout" is a common threat for all social modalities of psychiatric treatment in which the subtle, temporarily undiagnosed collective acting out of the patients greedily swallows the time available to treat them, and demands unreasonable time and energy investments on the part of staff.

All group treatment modalities are time consuming, and the greater the number of staff members participating in such activities, the greater the danger that time allocations, decision making, and priority setting will be undermined and diffused. Oldham and Russakoff are well aware of these difficulties and constraints; their therapeutic model is optimal, but they do not imply that it is flawless nor free of risks.

This book presents a clear, concise picture of the practical application of a sophisticated model of treatment. The medical therapeutic community model for brief hospital treatment presented here is an illustration of contemporary dynamic psychiatry at its best. What the authors modestly do not state is the outstanding leadership they have provided to the units in which this model was applied. Drs. Oldham and Russakoff are unusually skilled dynamic psychiatrists who combine a thorough knowledge of biological psychiatry with a solid grasp of how to apply psychoanalytic principles to individual and group psychotherapy. They have, in addition, particular expertise in therapeutic community models.

This is a book of fundamental interest for all professionals working with therapeutic community models. It is also a book for the psychoanalyst interested in applying an object relations theory model to the psychodynamically oriented modalities of treatment in brief hospitalization. This sophisticated, thorough, and practical text should be invaluable to all mental health professionals involved in the hospital treatment of acutely ill psychiatric patients.

Otto F. Kernberg, M.D.

Preface

The ideas presented in this book arose out of our experience, over several years, directing a short-term inpatient general psychiatric service at The New York Hospital–Cornell Medical Center, Westchester Division. In the course of our work, we were confronted with the complex demands that all such units present: rapid diagnostic evaluation, swift reduction of life-threatening or disorganizing psychotic dyscontrol, careful early discharge planning, and maintenance of a program and an environment therapeutic to 25 patients widely divergent in age, educational level, socioeconomic background, social support systems, psychopathology, legal status, and duration of illness. In addition, the unit served as a central training site for psychiatric residents, third-year medical students, psychology trainees, social work students, and nursing students, which greatly enriched the nature of the work but added to its complexity.

While in the process of organizing the unit into a multidisciplinary team structure, we visited several other well-established inpatient facilities. We noted that although all units we visited considered themselves engaged in providing milieu therapy, among other types of therapy, for their patients, there were widely divergent milieu therapy approaches. Some services borrowed heavily from the therapeutic community model, without always taking into account the drastic difference between the types of patients they were treating and those treated in the original therapeutic communities. Elements of medical models were at times mixed haphazardly with emphases on patient government or cathartic abreaction, often without sufficient recognition of the conflicting messages that resulted. As we developed our own approach, we came to believe that for acute inpatient work on a unit such as ours, accepting both voluntary and involuntary patients with a wide range of diagnoses, the therapeutic milieu needed to be highly structured yet could incorporate selected aspects of the therapeutic community movement.

A second observation was that, understandably, acute inpatient units generally emphasize the somatic therapies as the most important specific treatments to be used within a therapeutic milieu. Although we wholeheartedly endorse the importance of these treatment modalities, we became concerned that newer methods of approaching patients psychotherapeutically—methods that might prove effective in the right inpatient environment—might be neglected. For instance, we became interested in the concepts involved in object relations theory, as they might apply to intensive individual and group psychotherapy on an acute inpatient unit.

As we researched the recent literature, we were surprised by the paucity of material on these two aspects of current short-term inpatient care. We presented some aspects of our thinking at panels, symposia, and courses at the American Psychiatric Association and the American Group Psychotherapy Association. Our presentations were met with enthusiastic audience responses and requests for such material. In that way, this book was born. We sincerely hope that these ideas can be both stimulating and helpful to those students and staff members who work so hard to meet the many challenges in brief inpatient psychiatric care.

Acknowledgments

We are grateful to the patients and staff of 6 North, at the New York Hospital, Westchester Division: to the patients, who helped educate us and who tolerated the inevitable stresses involved in evolution and change, and to the staff, whose enthusiasm and spirit of cooperation were invaluable. Many of our teachers and supervisors will see the imprint of their efforts on our work, and we are forever indebted to them for all that they have given us. We would particularly like to thank Dr. Walter Strauser and Dr. Alan Tipermas for their clinical contributions, and Ms. Lillian Wahrow for her most generous library assistance. We also greatly appreciate the help and hard work in preparing the manuscript by the following friends and co-workers: Dorothy Chartier, Karen Geraghty, Carol Haller, June Hefferon, H. Sam McGowan, and Susan Terry.

Introduction

Recent trends in hospital-based psychiatric work include shortened lengths of stay, deinstitutionalization of chronic patients, and the application of therapeutic community principles to inpatient care. Each of these has resulted from pressures to correct injustices and improve patient care, although each in turn has had "side effects," sometimes unexpected. Thus, we have learned that lengths of hospital stay, return rates, or time out of the hospital do not suffice as predictors of outcome, and that in selected patients, better outcomes may follow not-so-brief hospitalizations. For chronic patients, deinstitutionalization has meant transinstitutionalization, with inadequate follow-up care, leading to a recent APA commission recommendation for long-term care for some patients. In addition, overzealous application of therapeutic community principles has led to a series of critiques advocating greater thoughtfulness about the differences between inpatient communities.

All of these trends have occurred against the backdrop of greatly increasing knowledge of biological psychiatry, leading to exciting renewed emphasis on the clinical laboratory and on psychopharmacotherapy. At risk of getting lost in this important shuffle is the role of the psychotherapist in an acute inpatient setting. As well, the therapeutic effects of the milieu itself, and the optimal design of the milieu for acute hospital work, may be insufficiently considered in the rush to measure and observe the patient's biological markers.

There are signs, however, of a renewed interest in milieu therapy, as it is practiced in the hospital setting. Recent reviews cite research findings that even suggest that for certain schizophrenics, milieu therapy may be more therapeutic than neuroleptic agents. Token economies are presented as improving the functioning of chronic schizophrenics. Although we hear more often the question "Which kind of milieu is best for which kind of patient?" it becomes equally important to ask which kind of milieu best serves a general, mixed diagnostic, acute inpatient population—that is, the patients to be found on the average inpatient unit.

We have addressed these issues in the first two sections of this book, presenting historical trends along with a milieu design we believe can be flexibly therapeutic for such a patient population. Included is a discussion of the role of the psychotherapist in such a setting. We propose that significant individual and group pschotherapeutic work can be done with many inpatients, some of them quite disturbed, in a brief time frame. Such a view bears some resemblance to current outpatient approaches to brief therapy—i.e., an effort to do partial "in-depth" work to produce some insight and change. We have found that, by using an object relations frame of reference in the context of a carefully structured therapeutic milieu, individual and group psychotherapy remain potent and viable techniques to be applied in combination with the well-established as well as newer forms of somatic treatment.

The final section of the book provides selected clinical examples of individual, group, and milieu therapy experiences drawn from work in our patient unit.

Dynamic Therapy in Brief Hospitalization

Part I

Historical and
Theoretical Aspects

Chapter 1
Evolution of Milieu Therapy

Hospital psychiatry involves careful attention to the hospital milieu and its therapeutic aspects. We have moved far from the day when "the other twenty-three hours," as described by Stanton and Schwartz in their landmark study published in 1954, were accorded "relatively low prestige" compared to individual psychotherapy. Significant developments in the last few decades have changed hospital psychiatry. They have occurred in the context of widespread social forces, moving us away from a nearly exclusive focus on intrapsychic dynamics of the mentally ill toward appreciation of biological, interpersonal, and environmental influences.

Maxwell Jones suggested in 1968 that "the psychoanalytic model, with its preoccupation with conflicts as it were within the individual and its stress upon a two-person treatment relationship, must be complemented by a much greater understanding of group dynamics, social therapy, and of social organization generally" (1968b, p. 14). Social psychiatry has been defined by the World Health Organization as the preventative and curative measures needed to make the individual fit for a satisfactory and useful life in terms of his own social environment. Within this broad concept, community psychiatry has developed, emphasizing continuity of care, community aftercare services, outreach and crisis intervention, and preventative psychiatry (Langsley 1985).

Milieu therapy is the inpatient counterpart of these community-based efforts (Arthur 1973, Edelson 1970a, Hyde 1957, Jones 1976,

3

Jones 1983). Attempts to differentiate among the terms *milieu therapy*, *therapeutic milieu*, and *therapeutic community* have been made (Filstead and Rossi 1973), but these terms continue to be used interchangeably. Milieu therapy generally refers to the social processes in a hospital environment that affect the patient therapeutically. Abroms (1969) points out that milieu therapy "is clearly a treatment context rather than a specific technique" (p. 556). Van Putten and May (1976) elaborate:

> "Milieu therapy" is now commonly prescribed for virtually all mental disorders as a form of inpatient treatment on the supposition that the proper environment can exert a therapeutic effect on all who are exposed to it. To this end, the patient is expected, sometimes pressured, to participate in a treatment program that includes varying degrees and combinations of occupational therapy, group activity, vocational rehabilitation, educational therapy, industrial therapy, resocialization, remotivation, total push, therapeutic community, patient government, recreational activities, formal individual and/or group psychotherapy, and so forth. Drug therapy and other somatic therapies are used, but dedicated milieu therapists customarily deemphasize the importance of the somatic treatments relative to the social therapies [p. 217].

The therapeutic community is one form of milieu therapy, but one with specific principles. Rapoport (1960) states:

> According to this approach, the hospital is seen not as a place where patients are classified, and stored, nor a place where one group of individuals (the medical staff) gives treatment to another group of individuals (the patients) according to the model of general medical hospitals; but as a place which is organized as a community in which everyone is expected to make some contribution towards the shared goals of creating a social organization that will have healing properties [p. 10].

RECENT HISTORY

Zilboorg (1941) refers to the moral treatment of psychiatric patients as the first revolution of psychiatry, a movement begun abroad by Pinel, Tuke, and others and extending to this country by the early influence of the Quakers and reformers like Dorothea Dix (Dain 1976, Maxmen et al. 1974, Wolf 1977). The early part of this century saw the second revolution of psychiatry (Zilboorg 1941), namely, the psychoanalytic movement begun by Freud and his followers. Although the principles of psychoanalysis had an enormous impact on American psychiatry, they had little influence on the vast majority of hospitalized psychiatric patients in these early years. Hospitalized patients, in the 1940s, had become largely warehoused in overcrowded, understaffed state hospitals. In spite of some enduring effects of the early moral treatment movement, strong social forces continued to relegate the mentally ill to geographically isolated, self-contained institutions. These institutions were hampered not only by understaffing, but also by the lack of effective treatment methods. Goffman (1961) has eloquently and poignantly described the state of affairs in these noisy asylums for the chronically ill. Even in hospitals treating the acutely ill, however, patients were more often contained or sedated than given definitive treatment. Traditional medical approaches were the rule until voices arose to suggest innovations in hospital treatment.

The psychoanalytic approach began to be applied to hospitalized patients at Chestnut Lodge, The Menninger Foundation, Austin Riggs Center, and other institutions (Maxmen et al. 1974). Sullivan (1931), at The Sheppard and Enoch Pratt Hospital, reported intensive treatment of a small group of schizophrenic patients, using an interpersonal approach and involving hospital personnel in the therapeutic work. Menninger (1936) recommended individualized therapeutic use of the milieu for patients, and in 1946 Thomas Main (1946) at The Menninger Foundation suggested that psychiatric patients were infantalized by traditional medical methods of treatment. He coined the phrase *the therapeutic community*, suggesting that all staff and patients in the hospital community join together to share the therapeutic task. Group methods began to evolve (Bion 1961, Maxmen et al. 1974), leading some to refer to the therapeutic community movement as the third revolution in psychiatry (Dreikurs 1955). Others would more quickly point to the advent of neuroleptic medication as the third revolution – the two developments occurred simultaneously.

The advent of neuroleptic medication had a tremendous impact on the nature of hospital psychiatry. The average length of stay for patients admitted on an emergency basis began its precipitous drop from several years to, ultimately, several weeks. Many patients who had seemed unreachable through social rehabilitation processes became responsive and improved dramatically. However, though the state hospitals became quieter, they remained understaffed, with little attention paid to the newly developing milieu therapy techniques.

Changes began to occur as the work of several clinical investigators began to have an impact. Stanton and Schwartz (1954) published their study of a mental hospital, emphasizing the influence of the environment and the staff on the manifest pathology in hospitalized patients. Cumming and Cumming (1962), using the Stanton and Schwartz study as well as the work of others, implemented principles of milieu therapy in a large state hospital system. Maxwell Jones (Jones 1956, 1957, 1968a, 1968b; Jones et al. 1953), originally working with military stress syndromes and later with chronic character disorders, developed principles of the therapeutic community that remain indelibly linked with his name. Rapoport (1960), at Belmont Hospital in England, continued Jones's work while Jones himself applied these principles at several locations in the United States.

Emphasizing ideals such as democratization, flattening of bureaucratic hierarchies, blurring of roles, and distribution of authority, these methods were embraced by the America of the 1960s. The Joint Commission on Mental Illnesses and Health published its final report, entitled *Action for Mental Health,* in 1961. This report, combined with the influence of John F. Kennedy, gave impetus to intensive reorganization of the mental health delivery system in the United States, backed by many federally funded programs. The community psychiatry movement became so popular that Jones himself stated his concern that "there may now be a danger of the pendulum swinging too far, with expectations of community care being possibly too great and with a correspondingly excessive devaluation of the scope of hospital treatment"

(1968b, p. 71). Therapeutic communities extended into new treatment settings. Residential treatment facilities for children and adolescents, as well as hospitals working with adult patients, incorporated many principles of milieu therapy.

THE THERAPEUTIC COMMUNITY PROPER

Rapoport (1960) described the four themes of a therapeutic community as democratization, permissiveness, communalism, and reality confrontation. Democratization refers to the replacement of traditional hierarchies with a system of joint patient–staff decision making. Permissiveness describes the expectation that extremes of distressing or deviant behavior will be tolerated and dealt with by group discussions rather than by disciplinary measures. Communalism denotes the importance placed on open communications; patients and staff are usually on a first-name basis, and all feelings and thoughts should be openly shared by staff members as well as patients. Reality confrontation refers to the belief that patients should be confronted with the effects they have on others and that interpersonal conflicts should not be smoothed over or denied but, rather, openly discussed.

These principles underlie descriptions of a therapeutic community such as that by Watson (Jones et al. 1953): "The therapeutic community views treatment as located not in the application by specialists of certain shocks, drugs or interpretations, but in the normal interactions of healthy community life. The doctor has a vital role, but so also do the nurses, the job supervisors, and the other patients" (p. viii). Central in the organization of any therapeutic community is a patient government, with election of officers to chair group and community meetings. The community meeting is usually the hallmark of the therapeutic milieu, and most units begin each day with a patient-led meeting. Jones (1956) said, "A community meeting epitomizes the function of a therapeutic community. The aim is to achieve the freest possible expression of feeling by both patients and staff" (p. 648). The agenda for the meeting may change from day to day but eventually will include discussions of problems of everyday living, as well as group decisions (usually by vote) about individual patients' requests for passes, privileges, and even medications. The participants may discuss discharge plans in either these or small group meetings, and decisions about when a patient may be discharged are usually arrived at by concensus vote.

In cases where there are separate staff rounds, they are usually held in an open meeting where patients may listen and participate. Doors are unlocked, and patients rely on the honor system to abide by unit procedures.

Pure therapeutic communities of the sort described here usually result in several additional features, although they are not always emphasized (Oldham and Russakoff, 1982). The unit is often highly selective regarding who is admitted for treatment. Patients who are not voluntarily willing to be admitted are screened out. Motivation for shared work in such a setting must be high, usually including willingness of family members to join selected ward activities. Usually acutely or severely psychotic patients, seriously medically ill or disabled patients, and patients with significant organic brain syndromes are not deemed appropriate for such units. As a natural consequence of these decisions, as well as the unit philosophy, somatic treatments (medications, electroconvulsive therapy) are deemphasized, as is the use of a seclusion room or restraints. Medical diagnoses are also deemphasized, and individual psychotherapy is rare. The average length of stay of patients in such units tends to be sixty days or more.

Numerous reports in the literature describe characteristics of typical therapeutic communities (Caudill 1958, Clark 1964, 1977, Davis 1977, Greenblatt et al. 1955, Jones 1956, 1957, Jones et al. 1953, Karasu et al. 1977, Kennard 1979, Main 1946, Margolis 1973, Maxmen et al. 1974, Oldham and Russakoff 1982, Rapoport 1960, Schwartz 1957, Wilmer 1958, 1981). Critics of these units contend that they are not cost effective, since many of the patients selected for treatment in these units could be treated as effectively with shorter hospitalizations or with alternate modes not requiring full hospitalization, crisis intervention followed by intensive outpatient treatment, or the like (Herz et al. 1977, Kirshner 1982). The indiscriminate application of therapeutic community principles to inpatient psychiatric units, which are fundamentally different from those where the therapeutic community principles were originally developed, poses its own set of problems.

MILIEU THERAPY WITH SCHIZOPHRENIC PATIENTS

Milieu therapy has played a role in treating hospitalized schizophrenics, at each stage of accepted therapeutic treatment over the decades – from chronic institutionalization to neuroleptic medication to deinstitutionalization. Considering the hospital treatment of the schizophrenic elucidates the distinctions between milieu therapy and the therapeutic community. There are residential treatment centers for schizophrenic patients fashioned along traditional therapeutic community lines. Notable among these programs is the Soteria House project (Mosher and Menn 1978, 1983, Wendt et al. 1983), which emphasizes psychosocial, rather than somatic, treatments. Patients selected for these programs, however, are generally young adult acute schizophrenics who may be more receptive to such techniques than chronic patients. Mosher and Keith (1979), Gunderson (1980, 1983), and Gunderson and Carroll (1983) point out the need to differentiate programs for acute schizophrenics from those for chronic schizophrenics.

Robbins (1980) defines milieu therapy as a method of treatment that

"implies the use of a total living experience and multiple approaches around which activities and relationships are consistently organized to achieve certain therapeutic objectives. Each treatment program should be based on a thorough diagnostic assessment and tailored as much as possible to the patient's individual needs" [p. 2365].

Emphasis on diagnosis and individualized treatment plans extends beyond the therapeutic community model. A pure therapeutic community, emphasizing open information sharing, joint decision making, and permissiveness might be highly inappropriate for certain schizophrenic patients (Bursten 1973, Ciompi 1983, Oldham and Russakoff 1982, Rapoport and Rapoport 1959, Wilmer 1958). The lack of emphasis on use of medication, electroconvulsive therapy, seclusion, and restraint accounts for the frequent exclusion of many schizophrenic patients from these therapeutic communities. Most references to milieu therapy with schizophrenics, however, refer to those aspects of the hospital milieu that can be individually shaped for each patient. Abroms (1969) states: "What is unique about milieu is . . . that it constitutes a metatreatment. It should not be regarded as one among other specific treatment techniques, but rather as a general method for providing these specific techniques in an effective manner" (p. 560). Psychiatric nursing intervention, occupational therapy, recreational therapy, vocational rehabilitation, and selected types of group and family therapy are among specific elements, in addition to the somatic therapies and individual psychotherapy.

Research on the efficacy of milieu therapy for schizophrenics has been difficult to assess because treatment programs for schizophrenics may differ greatly from one another, even within the same institution. Nonetheless, there is overwhelming agreement among clinicians that schizophrenic patients achieve a better level of functioning, with greater likelihood of being able to advance beyond chronic institutionalization, with combined inpatient treatment modalities in a context called milieu therapy. The devastating results of the effects of deinstitutionalization without adequate planning for continuity of care and community after-care resources (Schoonover and Bassuk 1983, Talbott 1978, 1981) have taught us that many of the elements of therapy provided by the hospital milieu must not stop when the patient leaves inpatient status. Either extreme—chronic institionalization or deinstitutionalization—for this group of patients has its pitfalls. As Strauss and Carpenter (1981) point out, "The harmful effects of chronic hospitalization used for custodial purposes should not conceal the very positive gains associated with therapeutic hospital care" (p. 165). Mosher and Keith (1979) summarize some aspects of milieu characteristics that are effective with schizophrenics: "Acute patients have been found to recover best in highly staffed, accepting, supportive, stimulus-decreasing (at least early in treatment), relatively long-stay (3–5 month) environments in which psychosocial interventions are viewed positively" (p. 627). They point out that, in contrast, "chronic patients do best when the changes sought and the procedures for bringing them about are very clearly and specifically defined" (p. 627). Some chronic schizophrenic patients may be maintained in stable control by carefully planned community-based treatment combined with ready access to briefer hospitalizations as needed (Glick et al. 1984, Herz et al. 1977). Rehospitalization for chronic schizophrenic patients may be more effective if consistent, predictable, and familiar aspects of milieu therapy are provided.

SHORT-STAY GENERAL HOSPITAL PSYCHIATRY AND MILIEU

Considerable variation, if not confusion, has resulted from the therapeutic community movement regarding acute hospital psychiatry. Here, as in all hospital treatment, milieu therapy is an important ingredient of the inpatient work. Milieu therapy encompasses the therapeutic efforts of the patients themselves and of professionals. Virtually every short-term unit has some form of community meeting, usually several per week, in addition to group therapy. Yet the theoretical basis for both the community meetings and group therapy often stems from the principles of the pure therapeutic community, which operates over a several-month average length of stay with carefully selected patients, as described above. Maxmen and colleagues (1974) refer to the therapeutic community as a "slogan" that "for some psychiatrists . . . refers to a hospital setting in which an occasional group meeting is conducted in the presence of 'home-like' furnishings" (p. 57). They add that

> most so-called "therapeutic communities" subject their patients to a random hodgepodge of activities ranging from intensive individual psychotherapy to basket weaving and basketball, the only overall guiding theoretical structure being provided by a schedule of these activities. These poorly reasoned almost non-programs have become all too common in American psychiatry [p. 57].

Maxmen and co-authors list hospitalization "of sufficient duration" as their first condition for an effective therapeutic community. Others such as Almond (1975), Raskin (1971, 1976), and White (1972a,b) argue as well for a longer length of stay if therapeutic community principles are used.

A major difficulty between general hospital acute psychiatry (thirty days or less, usually two to three weeks) and therapeutic communities is the composition of the inpatient group. Boundary control is frequently deemed essential for the success of a therapeutic community. White (1972a) lists as one of his minimal conditions for the operation of a successful milieu unit the need for "control over . . . the composition of its therapeutic community" (p. 55). In his careful analysis of the therapeutic community originated by Jones, Rapoport (1960) emphasizes the following for an effective program: "Patients' administration of therapy to one another is fraught with hazards. Its success depends on the careful selection of patients . . ." (p. 286). Zeitlyn (1967), in a more critical vein, says:

> The introduction of the therapeutic community appears, for example, to have led in some places to a new discrimination and selection of patients and to the formation of a new group of rejected ones, excluded on the grounds that their symptomatology renders them unsuitable for the permissive milieu characteristic of this form of treatment [p. 1086].

Thus two general features of acute hospital psychiatry—short length of stay and wide spectrum of diagnoses, including acutely psychotic or organic conditions—differentiate it from the setting in which the principles of therapeutic communities originated. It is therefore not surprising that numerous reports criticize the application of such techniques to acute work. Abroms (1968, 1969), Herz (1972), Oldham and Russakoff (1982), Raskin (1971, 1976), Sacks and Carpenter (1974), and others (Bursten 1973, Johnson and Parker 1983, Spadoni and Smith 1969, Steiner et al. 1982, Van Putten 1973, Van Putten and May 1976) have criticized the use of therapeutic community methods with acutely psychotic and schizophrenic patients. The usual environment of a therapeutic community, with its expectation of self-revelatory openness, may be overstimulating to some schizophrenic patients (Van Putten 1973), and acutely psychotic or organic patients may not be able to effectively participate in shared decision making or patient government (Bursten 1973, Wilmer 1981).

The use of neuroleptic medications and the need for security precautions make clear lines of authority and capacity for containment necessary. Rapoport and Rapoport (1959), Quitkin and Klein (1967),

Friedman (1969), Brodsky and Fischer (1964), and others (Crabtree and Cox 1972, Lehman and Ritzler 1976) have cited the perils of permissiveness and the need for limit setting with borderline and character-disordered patients. Herz (1979) has pointed out the usefulness of a traditional medical model when evaluating and diagnosing acutely disturbed patients in a short-term hospital setting; he has advocated the abolition of group therapy and community meetings in acute psychiatric hospital work. Recent reports, however, suggest that a "centered" model (Wilmer 1981) or "modified" model (Oldham and Russakoff 1982, Kaufman and Sporty 1983) is more appropriate for such work, borrowing principles of the therapeutic community and combining them with more familiar aspects of the medical model.

MILIEU THERAPY OUTCOME RESEARCH

In 1956, Stanton (Caudill, 1958) said:

> The statistics were interesting and important but there was little that could be done once one had the general findings; we were in the position of being against sin . . . perhaps the outstanding clinical responsibility of our generation is to try, while we are succeeding for reasons we are not clear about, to seize the chance to identify what we can, and to hold fast in the network of scientific theory the means of effective institutional treatment. If this is to be done, the generalities which have surrounded the notion of social or milieu or institutional treatment must be replaced by more clearly analyzed understanding. . . . It would follow that research in milieu therapy should be directed toward the increasingly accurate and specific identification of special patterns of interaction or transaction with other people, which characterize various types of disorder. Milieu therapy would be differentiated sharply from good custody; therapy from uninstructed humanitarian efforts [p. 343].

And not long thereafter, in 1962, Cumming and Cumming expressed concerns of their own:

Milieu therapy shares with individual therapy the latter's "unproven" status. However, the former's problems are a little different. Whereas psychotherapy sets out to make "basic"—that is, intrapsychic changes, usually expecting social improvement to follow, milieu therapy sets out to make social changes and trusts that ego growth will ensue . . . . However . . . the terms "milieu therapy" or "therapeutic community" as generally used mean nothing. Because Jones has an inventor's claim to the latter term, it sometimes refers specifically to this rather highly specialized technique, but otherwise labels seem only to mean something vaguely benign in intent. Often . . . they refer simply to the addition of one hour of group therapy a day or perhaps the addition of patient government. It is interesting, too, that many of those who have developed successful rehabilitation programs are as reluctant to describe the day-by-day process as the psychotherapists are to submit to observation. It is therefore important to develop a standard way of discussing the milieu—perhaps in terms of such things as hours of structured activity, content of ward program and allocation of decision-making authority [pp. 271-272].

In the ensuing years, painstaking efforts have been made to follow the advice of these early researchers in milieu therapy. The task has been complicated by the imprecise descriptions of the therapeutic environments being studied; as greater descriptive precision is achieved, the variables to be considered further complicate the task. Ellsworth (1983) has suggested that four categories of variables need to be considered in evaluating the effectiveness of milieu treatment programs: (1) patient input variables, (2) setting characteristics, (3) treatment process dimensions, and (4) posttreatment events. Patient input variables may include demographic factors such as age, sex, marital status, prior hospitalization history, as well as other factors such as diagnosis. Setting characteristics include the physical characteristics of the environment, administrative practices, and characteristics of the staff. Treatment variables include use of somatic therapies, psychotherapies, and milieu therapies. Posttreatment events include aftercare social and vocational arrangements, follow-up medication and treatment, and the like. Methodologies have developed as research interest has increased in this area. Moos

(1974) created assessment instruments to evaluate hospital-based treatment programs (Ward Atmosphere Scale–WAS) as well as community-based programs (Community-Oriented Programs Environment Scale–COPES). Other methods of evaluating hospital treament variables (Gurel 1974, Guttentag and Struening 1975, Lewis et al. 1971) have been proposed. Sophisticated statistical methods (Ellsworth 1983, Glick and Hargreaves 1979, Struening and Guttentag 1975) have enhanced data retrieval and relevance. Researchers themselves have become increasingly attentive to the many variables affecting outcome (Ellsworth 1983, Hargreaves and Attkisson 1978, Strauss and Carpenter 1981). Extensive reviews of the literature on research findings in milieu therapy have been published (Ellsworth 1983, Ellsworth et al. 1971, Klass et al. 1977, May and Simpson 1980, Moos 1974, Moos et al. 1973, Mosher and Keith 1979, Paul and Lentz 1977, Ullmann 1967, Van Putten and May 1976).

May and Simpson (1980), reviewing research on drugs and in-hospital milieu therapy for schizophrenics, concluded that drug therapy combined with intensive treatment milieu produce a better outcome–in terms of employment and release rate–than milieu therapy alone. However, May and associates (1981) also concluded that "overall, the follow-up outcome is far from reassuring, whatever the type of treatment" (p. 776). In a similarly discouraging vein, Van Putten and May (1976) concluded that "the evidence from controlled studies suggests that current methods of milieu therapy given in the hospital add little to the treatment of the ordinary schizophrenic patient once gross neglect is corrected and adequate chemotherapy is used" (p. 239). Mosher and Gunderson (1979) and Gunderson (1983) have critically argued, however, that these pessimistic conclusions require reevaluation, since they were based on studies that mixed acute schizophrenics and chronic schizophrenics; they were also based on some studies of ill-defined, nonintensive milieus. Mosher and Gunderson (1979) reviewed three major controlled studies on chronic schizophrenics, those by Greenblatt and colleagues (1965), Grinspoon and co-authors (1972), and Paul and Lentz (1977). They concluded that "on balance, these studies suggest that intensive milieu treatment can offer substantial advantages for chronic schizophrenic patients when it is carefully tailored to their needs" (p. 435).

Paul and Lentz (1977), in a carefully designed study, not only looked at the effectiveness of milieu therapy for chronic schizophrenics but also compared it with a social learning, token economy approach; they concluded that for this chronic population, the social learning program produced even better results than a milieu therapy approach. Gunderson (1983) reviewed three recent studies of milieu therapy with acute schizophrenics, those by Carpenter and associates (1977), Mosher and Menn (1978), and Rappaport and colleagues (1978). Carpenter and his group (1977) reported that their patients did equally well in intensive milieu therapy whether or not on drugs and did better than similar patients treated mainly with drugs. Studying the Soteria House project, Mosher and Menn (1978) reported similar results. Rappaport and co-authors (1978) found that patients did as well or better when treated with milieu therapy alone than with drugs.

These results are in marked contrast with earlier reports; May (1968) concluded that "our statistics demonstrate beyond reasonable doubt that for the general run of schizophrenic patients, milieu therapy alone is both expensive and relatively ineffective" (p. 268). It has been argued that the types of milieu therapy studied by May were ill-defined and ineffectual (Gunderson 1983, Mosher and Gunderson 1979), accounting for his negative results. However, others have reported the ineffectiveness of intensive milieu work with acute schizophrenics (Feinsilver and Gunderson 1972, Spadoni and Smith 1969); as Gunderson (1983) says, these reports "suggest caution about too readily embracing the practices used so promisingly by Rappaport et al., Carpenter et al., and Mosher and Menn" (p. 61). Frank and Gunderson (1984) have recently emphasized the importance of the therapist's attitude within the milieu. We are coming closer to an ability to define those aspects of the milieu that exert therapeutic effects on certain acute and chronic schizophrenic patients.

Carefully designed outcome research on "pure" therapeutic communities is reported infrequently in the literature. Denford and colleagues (1983) described a 5-year follow-up of 28 patients treated at Cassel Hospital; they identified several patient variables predictive of a good outcome in that setting. Unfortunately, most research studies do not differentiate the effects of therapeutic community from the effects of general milieu. Reviewing early studies of the effects of general hospital milieus (Gurel 1964, and Ullman 1967), Ellsworth and colleagues (1971) reported that "hospital size and staffing ratios are related to release rates but not necessarily to measures of program effectiveness" (p. 429). In this study, Ellsworth and colleagues (1971) utilized release rate and community tenure as outcome measures. They concluded that highest release rate units are those that do not promote patient autonomy and are perceived negatively by nursing staff, whereas units judged most effective using the community tenure measure are those where nursing staff are active participants in treatment decisions. Previous work (Ellsworth and Ellsworth 1970) indicated the importance of shared teamwork among staff members.

Moos and co-authors (1973) also utilized release rate and community tenure as measures of outcome, and they reported in a large study that "wards that kept patients out of the hospital longest were seen as emphasizing autonomy and independence, practical orientation, order and organization, and the open expression of feelings, particularly angry feelings" (p. 291). Although this study has the advantage of large numbers, unfortunately there is little discrimination among the different wards as to patient characteristics, staff characteristics, length of stay, and the like. Also, the study is based on roughly half of the inpatients, i.e., those who were either willing or able to complete the study questionnaires. Using only time out of the hospital after discharge as an outcome measure, Klass and associates (1977) attempted to control for pretreatment variables. They concluded:

> Whereas with the treatment of neurotics, psychotherapeutic lore stresses the need to "get the affect out" and loosen structure, the opposite is often stressed for psychotic patients. If "disorganized" patients arrive on highly organized wards and internalize some of the social structure of the ward, then they may stay in the community longer after discharge. The results of this study seem to be consistent with such a view [p. 1052].

Lehman and co-authors (1982) found no differences in outcome between first admissions to a therapeutic community ward and first admissions to a medically oriented psychiatric ward. More recently, Ellsworth (1983) summarized studies showing the need for more sophisticated outcome measures; he suggested four: (1) release rates, (2) return rates, (3) posttreatment psychosocial adjustment, and (4) posttreatment role functioning. After presenting a detailed review of research on milieu therapy, he provided a useful overview of research findings in this area.

In 1974, Sacks and Carpenter (1974) wrote that "if a psychiatric unit is to be effectively therapeutic, its staff must avoid the pitfalls that can turn it into a pseudotherapeutic community . . . , a psychiatric unit that subscribes to a particular treatment philosophy, but overtly functions in ways contradictory to the expressed belief" (p. 315). They suggested five situations that increase such risk: (1) absence of a therapeutic standard, (2) assignment of irresponsibility, (3) the antitherapy leader, (4) absence of therapeutic leadership, and (5) a pathogenic environment. In light of subsequent research on milieu therapy, some of these pitfalls have contributed to the confusion as to the therapeutic efficacy of the milieu. Ideas derived from one setting have been indiscriminately applied to drastically different settings. Characteristics of the patient population and of the staff have differed widely among hospital settings, called therapeutic milieus. Pathogenic environments – environments "created and maintained by patients' attempting to meet the staff's simultaneous expectations of responsibility and irresponsibility" (Sacks and Carpenter 1974, p. 318) – may have all too often been the result.

Little by little, these areas of confusion are being sorted out, clarifying not only research, but clinical goals as well. Gunderson (1983) said recently,

> Milieu therapy has grown enormously in its complexity and ambitions during the past 200 years and it is clear that within the category of milieu therapy there is now a broad diversity of programs. It is also clear that these programs can strongly influence patients either favorably or negatively, and that this influence depends on at least three factors: (1) the type of patients, (2) the length of stay, and (3) the type of milieu program" [p. 10].

The more carefully patients are defined, both in terms of diagnosis and other variables such as amount of prior treatment and level of social and vocational functioning, the better a hospital treatment program can be designed and studied. As Sederer (1984) said, "Unless the milieu is flexibly tailored to meet the needs of each individual patient, it will be too nonspecific a treatment modality. The manic patient requires a different milieu treatment plan than the withdrawn schizophrenic patient" (p. 673). In order to evaluate the elements of a therapeutic milieu, researchers need to establish measurable, reliable methods of evaluation. Their findings, in turn, must be described with ever-increasing precision. The evidence so far seems clear: for some patients, intensive milieu therapy can indeed be therapeutic. Increasing awareness of potentially serious side effects of medications makes this conclusion significant.

Chapter 2
Organization of the Short-Term Therapeutic Milieu

Current hospital psychiatry practices mandate that effective short-term inpatient care must be provided for a full spectrum of patients, including those who are acutely psychotic, those who need repeated brief rehospitalizations, and those who are admitted involuntarily. Sederer (1986), Henisz (1981), and Hertzman (1984) have written about various aspects of brief hospital psychiatric care. The drawbacks of the therapeutic community model for this type of work will be elaborated. The traditional medical model, advocated by some for acute inpatient work, needlessly sacrifices important accomplishments of the therapeutic community movement. In our view, a combined model, which we have called the unified "Medical-Therapeutic Community" (Oldham and Russakoff 1982), incorporates key features of both models, more effectively meeting the needs of a wide variety of both voluntary and involuntary inpatients.

THERAPEUTIC COMMUNITY MODEL

The principles of a therapeutic community (permissiveness, democratization, communalism, and reality confrontation) are translated into the following key ingredients of an inpatient psychiatric service: (1) selection criteria for admission—often exclusion of involuntary patients, (2) shared responsibility in administrative and clinical decision making among patients and staff, (3) open rounds, (4) maximal information sharing among all patients and all staff, i.e., no "confidentiality," (5) patient government, (6) emphasis on groups, (7) frequent community meetings, (8) no uniforms for staff, (9) average length of stay of sixty days or more, (10) deemphasis of diagnosis, (11) deemphasis of individual therapy, (12) deemphasis of use of medication or electroconvulsive therapy, and (13) unlocked doors, no seclusion room, and no restraints. As reviewed by Clark (1977), many of these concepts have become standard psychiatric practice.

These principles are best accomplished within the time frame of longer-term hospitalization. In terms of admission control, White (1972b) points out that many general units cannot control their admissions; they receive patients requiring medical care, protection from self-destructiveness, etc., for whom "a group could not genuinely be given responsibility" (p. 55). The increased number of involuntary patients further complicates the task. Bursten (1973) has argued that only staff members are competent enough to make decisions about what is "good" for a patient. Wilmer (1981), in a recent review, argues against collective voting as a decision-making technique in therapeutic communities. Karasu and associates (1977) suggest the need to "identify the particular aspects of the therapeutic community that are most functional in various types of treatment programs" (p. 440); they point out that in a setting with many acutely disturbed patients, the patients "were rarely involved in decision-making but the staff felt that the patients should be more involved" (p. 439). We would argue that this attitude represents confusion of democratization—a desirable social process—with that which is clinically desirable for acutely disturbed patients. While we fully agree that many of the critiques described above are warranted, we are concerned that they might lead to a backlash against therapeutic community principles.

MEDICAL MODEL

Ludwig and Othmer (1977) described three essential features of the medical model: "the concept of disease and diagnosis, the concept of ideology and treatment, and the nature of the doctor–patient relationship" (p. 1087). Weiner (1978) subsequently discussed these and other aspects of the medical model. Guze (1978) asserted that "the medical model focuses primarily on the illness. It is concerned principally with analyzing and understanding the nature of the illness, with the initial effort directed at trying to identify the significant symptoms, signs, and other features that define the illness" (p. 295).

The medical model refers to principles that, when applied to the organization of a psychiatric inpatient service, usually result in the following features: (1) little or no selection for admission unless selected for high suspicion of medical ("organic") illness for diagnostic work, (2) hierarchical system, with the doctor as the most expert, the other staff next, patient least, (3) decisions made by the staff (closed rounds), (4) selected information sharing between staff and each individual patient but no group discussion of patients' illnesses; high degree of confidentiality, (5) no patient governments, (6) deemphasis of group therapy, (7) deemphasis of community meetings, with little emphasis on the patients as therapists for each other, (8) medical uniforms, (9) brief length of stay (thirty days or less), (10) emphasis on individual therapy, (11) emphasis on "disease" or "illness" and its diagnosis, (12) emphasis on biological modes of therapy (pharmacotherapy, electroconvulsive therapy), and (13) security precautions—locked doors, restraints, seclusion rooms. As is obvious, such a "medical model" inpatient unit is in many ways the antithesis of the unit organized around therapeutic community principles.

Clark (1977) stated that there is

> a major difference between a therapeutic community and a traditional medical model psychiatric unit. In a therapeutic community, the patients are active agents of therapy; in a traditional unit, they are the passive recipients of treatment and active planning; diagnosing and treatment are the exclusive functions of the paid staff, especially the doctors [p. 559].

Main (1946) asserted that patients on a medical model unit are "isolated and dominated" and "robbed of their status as responsible human beings" (p. 66).

In the literature, reference occurs fairly frequently to *authoritarian* inpatient services, a term usually equated to terms such as *custodial* or even *unpleasant* (Pardes et al. 1972, Quitkin and Klein 1967). Due to the hierarchical arrangements in such units, they often conjure up images of a medical model seen in pejorative terms such as those stated by Main (1946). However, this is more descriptive of understaffed services, not to be confused with well-staffed units run along deliberate medical model lines. Bouras and colleagues (1982, 1984) reported studies in which patients tended to be more disturbed in a therapeutic community than in a medical model ward. The medical model has importance for brief inpatient work. However, such a hierarchical system could intensify the regressive influence of "patienthood," as opposed to the ego-building effect of patients acting therapeutically with each other (Goffman 1961, Maxmen 1978, 1984).

In 1979, Herz proposed a medical model for short-term inpatient work, involving staff in white uniforms, bedside medical rounds, and the abolition of group therapy and community meetings. Such a model represents a regression to a rigid and reductionistic extreme that abandons many valuable therapeutic modalities. By providing careful attention to limit-setting and structure, elements of the therapeutic community movement can be beneficial with acutely disturbed patients. We propose a unified medical-therapeutic community model for brief inpatient work, a model that retains important features of the therapeutic community, yet incorporates many structured and limit-setting features characteristic of the medical model.

UNIFIED MEDICAL-THERAPEUTIC COMMUNITY MODEL

The medical-therapeutic community model consists of a "centered" method of inpatient work. Such a model makes possible flexible and effective brief-inpatient care. Table 1 portrays the comparative features of the three models—the therapeutic community model, the medical model, and the unified medical-therapeutic model. We will present a detailed description of an inpatient unit, organized along the principles of the medical-therapeutic community model.

Description of Program

The unit is a 25-bed general inpatient unit in a university-based hospital that serves as a primary training unit for postgraduate year (PGY) II

TABLE 1
Comparison of Characteristics of the Three Therapeutic Models

Ward characteristic	Therapeutic community model	Unified medical-therapeutic community	Medical model
Admission criteria	+*	–	–
Patient–staff shared decisions	+	–	–
Open rounds	+	–	–
Open information-sharing among patients	+	Modified	–
Patient government	+	Modified	–
Group therapy	+	Modified	–
Community meetings	+	Modified	–
Staff uniforms	–	Modified	+
30-day length-of-stay or less	–	+	+
Emphasis on diagnosis	–	+	+
Individual therapy	–	+	+
Use of medication, ECT	–	+	+
Use of locked doors, restraints	–	+	+

*The positive symbol (+) connotes a major emphasis, not necessarily 100% conditions.

psychiatric residents, third-year medical students, and trainees in other disciplines. Beds are in single rooms or dormitory-type settings. The unit is locked with an additional lockable "quiet room" (seclusion room) within the confines of the nursing station, which has a safety window in the door, providing audiovisual contact between the room's occupant and the nursing staff. The median length of stay for patients on the unit is about twenty-six days. A separate Admissions Service makes admission decisions, and patients of all diagnostic categories, and ranging in age from 14 to 65, are admitted to the unit. Approximately 18 percent of patients are on involuntary status at some time during hospitalization. Staff members do not wear uniforms, but they wear identifying name tags that also state their professional disciplines.

Each patient is assigned to one of three multidisciplinary teams on admission. Within each team, he is assigned to a primary therapist, a social worker, a nursing staff member, and a medical student. Each work day begins with a combined patient–staff activity, from 8:30 A.M. until 9:15 A.M. On Monday, Wednesday, and Friday, this activity consists of small group therapy, in which all patients on each team meet with two co-therapists from the team staff. All other team staff members on duty observe their team's group therapy session as silent observers, as described in Chapter 5. Following group therapy, all patients who do not need close supervision proceed to therapeutic activities programs, the more acutely disturbed patients remaining on the unit. At the same time, each team meets for team rounds (closed rounds for staff only). Multidisciplinary treatment plans are created and updated during team rounds. Medical evaluations and medication decisions are made by the physicians during team meetings, after information about each patient's progress is gathered from all team members. Decisions about the patient's hall status, passes, and discharge dates are made by consensus among team staff.

Community meetings are held for all patients and staff on Tuesday and Thursday from 8:30 to 9:15 A.M. The structure and technique of these meetings is described in more detail in Chapter 6. Following the community meetings, all staff members meet together for rounds, beginning with a brief "rehash" of the community meeting (staff only). On Tuesday, rounds then consist of brief interviews of all patients admitted within the previous week; on Thursday, rounds involve a review of nursing notes on all patients and an in-depth discussion of existing problems. Attendance at group therapy and community meetings is expected of all patients and staff, and any absences are explained or discussed. Only on rare occasions is a patient prohibited from attending these collective meetings, and then only for a limited period of time.

Each patient is seen in individual therapy by his primary therapist, and he meets regularly with his nursing staff member. Family evaluation and therapy are arranged by the social worker and the primary therapist when indicated. Matters of confidentiality are individually tailored. When an individual patient's behavior affects the entire community, it is always discussed in open forum. Some patients will be encouraged to be self-revelatory in groups, whereas others may be encouraged to use group settings for practical discharge planning, with efforts to support defensive repression and suppression of affect-laden, disorganizing material.

We compared the unit described above with another inpatient service within our own institution, a well-respected short-term unit whose treatment program is oriented along medical model lines (deemphasis of groups, community meetings, patient government, etc.). Both units being compared are identical in size, have comparable lengths of stay, and are PGY II residency training units. Although only one of the units serves as a medical-student teaching unit, the students function as participant–observers only and do not provide direct clinical care (Oldham et al. 1983b). Patients are admitted to one unit or the other on a random basis, and the admitting service uses the same criteria for admission to both units. If there were any bias in the admission process, such a bias would have been in the direction of sending the more difficult patients to our medical-therapeutic community model. As shown in Table 2, there were significantly fewer self-inflicted injuries as well as fewer elopements and elopement attempts on our unit than on the medical model unit.

TABLE 2

Comparison of the Frequency of Suicidal and Elopement Behaviors on Medical-Therapeutic Community and Medical Units

	Medical-therapeutic community unit* (events/patient)	Medical model unit† (events/patient)		
Self-inflicted injuries	0.09	0.17	p	0.01
Elopements and elopement attempts	0.08	0.14	p	0.05

*n = 236 patients
†n = 181 patients

Discussion of the Medical-Therapeutic Community Model

We are advocating that five elements of the therapeutic community movement be retained, in modified form, for brief hospital work involving wide varieties of inpatients, including acutely psychotic and involuntary patients: (1) Open information sharing—modified to be individually tailored according to each patient's needs—versus "total sharing," which proves to be a regressive force for many psychiatric patients. (2) Patient council—modified to play a liaison and advisory function between patients and staff—instead of being a primary administrative structure for the unit. All clinical or administrative decisions about a patient's status, treatment plan, passes, etc., are made by staff only, never in patient groups. High numbers of psychotic, demented, or poorly motivated patients make the latter inappropriate. The modified arrangement, however, allows the better-functioning patients to play active roles in life on the unit, enhancing the self-esteem of the patient body as a whole. (3) Group Therapy–modified to allow for selected in-depth work, based on object relations theory (see Chapters 3 and 5). The modification also allows all staff to observe the groups immediately prior to team rounds, enhancing efficient teamwork (see Chapter 5). (4) Community meetings–modified to be chaired by a staff member with a carefully structured agenda, and run in an organized fashion (see Chapters 3 and 6). Such meetings foster reality testing and pro-social object relatedness, without producing the overstimulating and disorganizing effects described by Van Putten (1973). The meetings can also be a useful aid to diagnosis (Schaffer et al. 1983). The need for structure in such meetings is described in the literature (Abramczuk 1972, Bernard 1983, Daniels and Rubin 1968, Rubin 1979, Russakoff and Oldham 1982). (5) No staff uniforms–modified to a requirement for identification name tags to be worn at all times. Such an arrangement fosters reality testing, yet retains a more homelike environment.

These five modifications create a type of unit similar to the one described by Klass and associates (1977), which they demonstrated produced a better outcome. Gunderson (1978) proposed five therapeutic functions that can be provided by a hospital milieu (support, validation, involvement, containment, and structure); he asserted that "an ideal milieu would incorporate all five functions" (p. 333). The medical-therapeutic community model described here incorporates all five therapeutic functions better than the other two models being discussed, namely, the medical model and the therapeutic community model.

Support and validation are present in all types of units being discussed, but involvement ("those processes which cause patients to attend actively to their so-called environment and interact with it" (Gunderson 1978, p. 330)) is all too often lacking in medical-model type units. However, involvement is clearly fostered by the modifications described above in the medical therapeutic community. Ellsworth and co-authors (1971) point out that units with more involvement prove more effective. The variables of containment and structure highlight the problems of the therapeutic community model in current hospital work. With involuntary and acutely psychotic patients admitted to general inpatient units, containment is essential for protection of the patient and those around him, and it is all too often lacking in a therapeutic community. We agree with the distinction between containment and structure, the latter serving to foster reality testing, highly important with acutely psychotic patients. Herz (1979) advocated clocks, signs, and uniforms. We utilize the first two, plus identification nameplates, structured meetings, and groups, and we address patients and staff at all meetings by last names.

A flexible approach including all of these processes produces an inpatient unit corresponding to the biopsychosocial model advocated by Engel (1977) as an approach to patient care in general.

The issue of working with involuntary patients in such an inpatient model requires some consideration. Leeman and his co-workers (Leeman 1980, Leeman and Berger 1980) proposed that locked doors and extensive use of seclusion rooms would make a unit "more restrictive and threatening for all" (p. 315). While the locked door does increase restrictions, similar units have been run in our hospital with open doors, but monitored by a staff member, as Gunderson (1978) recommends. The staff found, however, that such an arrangement made for a *de facto* locked door, while tying up valuable staff time unnecessarily. Few patients complain about the locked door, while many seem reassured by it. Leeman and Berger (1980) suggested that a higher staffing pattern would be necessary to deal with involuntary patients. We recently surveyed several other institutions, and we found our nursing staff–patient ratio to be consistently lower than that of open-door facilities with no involuntary patients (0.8 versus 0.9 to 1.3). We feel that our carefully structured model uses our staff efficiently and that we are not understaffed.

Leeman and Berger (1980) also suggest that "the average length of stay would rise if definitive treatment of involuntary patients were undertaken" (p. 320). Our data do not address the question of change in length of stay following the introduction of involuntary patients on a unit. On our service, however, where the majority of both voluntary and involuntary patients receive their entire course of inpatient treatment, there is no significant difference in the length of stay of the two groups (voluntary, average 26 days; involuntary, average 32 days). Thus the medical-therapeutic community model facilitates definitive short-term therapeutic work with involuntary patients in conjunction with voluntary patients, without significantly prolonging length of stay. We have described here the specific ingredients of a model to help accomplish such work, perhaps an example of the concept recently described by Wilmer (1981) as "therapeutic communities of the center," which he believes hold the "best chance for creating an effective therapeutic community" (pp. 97–98).

USE OF STRUCTURE FOR
BRIEF REHOSPITALIZATIONS OF CHRONIC PATIENTS

Lack of insight and lack of motivation for treatment have been described in chronic schizophrenics by Van Putten and co-authors (1976), Lin and colleagues (1976), and McEvoy and associates (1981), as well as in the new young chronic patients described by Pepper and co-workers (1981), Sheets and co-authors (1982), and by Talbott (1978, 1981). Rehospitalization often results from outpatient treatment noncompliance. Flexible community support systems may enhance outpatient treatment compliance, but a significant dropout rate will persist, since many of these patients do not acknowledge the need for treatment even while actively receiving it, as reported by McEvoy and colleagues (1981). Chronic patients who do remain in treatment programs may have lower readmission rates (Dincin and Witheridge 1982), but rehospitalization will still be required at times of life stress or treatment stress such as therapist change, transference psychosis, or countertransference stalemate.

In a recent report, Harris and associates (1982) pointed out that

> a vital aspect of any Community Support Program is the role of the hospital as a part of the treatment system. . . .As much effort must be put into redefining and redeveloping the inpatient phase of treatment. Experience has shown us that hospitalization without community support is unsuccessful. The converse is also true: community support without appropriate hospitalization is doomed to failure [p. 226].

They point out that "for revolving-door patients, periodic brief hospital stays must be seen as a routine part of good treatment" (p. 226). Emphasizing continuity of care, they focus on hospital staff outreach and community contact to effect careful discharge planning. Such discharge planning is important, but the nature of the inpatient treatment needs to be equally stressed.

Chronic patients cut across diagnostic categories, including the chronic dementias, schizophrenias, affective disorders, and personality disorders. If, instead of using a categorical diagnostic system, one adopts a dimensional perspective—such as that proposed by Frances (1982)—four dimensions of chronic patients become apparent: organicity, psychosis, depression, and behavioral dyscontrol. For the model presented here, the organic dimension can be conceptualized in the broad sense, to include not just Axis I organic illness, but the chronic schizophrenias as well. We are learning more and more about neurochemical alterations in schizophrenics, and we are continuing to raise questions about cortical atrophy, ventricular enlargement, inequalities in lateralization, and memory, perceptual, and cognitive deficits in some subgroups of chronic schizophrenics. Organic factors may also play a role in some chronic character-disordered patients, either subtly, due to residual learning disabilities, or more obviously, due to chronic alcoholism or repeated toxic drug-induced organic states.

Considering the other three dimensions in a similar fashion, psychosis, depression, and behavioral dyscontrol may occur in any of these four categories of chronic illness. Demented patients, schizophrenics, patients with affective disorders, and patients with personality disorders may become psychotic or depressed; similarly, deficits in judgment resulting in socially inappropriate behavioral dyscontrol may occur in all four diagnostic categories.

Such a dimensional approach facilitates conceptualization of a short-term inpatient service to best treat these recidivistic chronic patients, and the medical-therapeutic community model can well serve such patients. The following four approaches are incorporated into the inpatient structure: (1) consistency, order, and predictability; (2) reality-orienting procedures; (3) cognitive problem-solving approaches; and (4) limit setting.

Consistency, Order, and Predictability

Due either to frank dementia or to less obvious organic factors, many of our hospitalized chronic patients are perplexed, confused, forgetful, and periodically disoriented. One thing we have learned from the hospice movement and from neurologists and internists is that patients in such states respond more quickly in predictable, consistent surroundings. As a first principle, therefore, we attempt to readmit a chronic patient to the same inpatient service and, if possible, to the same room. We then strive to maintain a stable inpatient staff and schedule of activities, so that much is familiar when the patient returns. Although psychiatric residents rotate every six months and medical students every six weeks, three attending psychiatrists, along with social workers, occupational and recreational therapists, and nursing personnel are permanent staff. All staff members wear identification name tags that indicate their professional disciplines, a practice that mitigates against disorientation in demented patients. The patient's day begins at the same time each day with an activity that includes all staff and patients; this produces an orderly routine that helps minimize states of confusion.

Reality-orienting Procedures

The second dimension, psychosis, is approached by careful planning of the therapeutic milieu. Chronic psychotic patients are treated with antipsychotic medications; however, some of these patients may be medication-refractory or may have developed untenable side effects. We have been impressed by the degree to which actively psychotic patients can respond to simple, clear, and structured staff directions, resulting in better organized and more appropriate behavior. Particularly in community meetings, as described in Chapter 6, carefully planned agendas, rules of procedure, and staff leadership produce remarkably appropriate and participatory behavior from many chronic psychotic patients. Reality testing is further strengthened by always providing a roll call each morning to explain the absences of any patients or staff.

Cognitive Problem-solving Approaches

We have found that pragmatically oriented problem-solving approaches augment the benefits of antidepressant medications or electroconvulsive therapy to reduce the depression in our chronic patients. All our patients have individual and group therapy, and family therapy as well when appropriate. Individual, group, and family work with some chronically depressed patients takes on added importance when antidepressant medications have had limited efficacy. We are especially alert to the central role played by object loss in depression (Oldham and Russakoff 1984), the clinical experimental evidence for which was reviewed by Lloyd (1980). By design, the first item on the agenda for each community meeting is a public farewell, in turn, to each patient being discharged and to any rotating staff members leaving the service; names of replacement staff are carefully announced and posted, and their arrival dates are specified. Such an approach openly addresses the reality of loss and its impact, yet securely conveys the message that loss can be tolerated and that new beginnings follow. Specific efforts are made at all times to minimize regression and dependency, such as limiting the use of maximal observation to those patients posing serious risk to self or others. Patients are expected to participate in activities, and they may even be occasionally locked out of their rooms during activity periods if necessary. Therapeutic efforts include an active discharge group, focusing on leaving the hospital with fewer stresses and more options; staff may accompany patients on home visits to help accomplish this goal.

Limit Setting

Friedman (1969), Quitkin and Klein (1967), and others (Brodsky and Fischer 1964, Crabtree and Cox 1972, Lehman and Ritzler 1976) have advocated the use of clear and firm limit setting for effective inpatient treatment of patients with severe borderline conditions as well as other personality disorders. Many young chronic patients fall into these categories and variably demonstrate loss of behavioral control resulting in aggressive antisocial, self-mutilative, or criminal acts. Although some of these acts may reflect traits more than states, periods of intensified loss of control may occur at any time. Similarly, the dimension of behavioral dyscontrol is well known during the acutely symptomatic stages of schizophrenic illness or manic-depressive illness. Abroms (1968), Herz (1972), Spadoni and Smith (1969), and Van Putten (1973) have reminded us of the need to provide firm limits for schizophrenic patients, the same recommendation made for manic patients by Bjork and colleagues (1977), Gunderson (1974), and Janowsky and co-authors (1970). We have reviewed the use of seclusion as a limit-setting intervention, which we feel is therapeutic when used appropriately (Oldham et al. 1983a); similar conclusions have been reached by others (Soloff et al. 1985). On our inpatient service, we provide an orientation handbook for each patient; it emphasizes those behaviors not allowed on the unit, such as use of illicit drugs, or sexual or assaultive behavior toward others. When such behaviors occur, staff members present this information as a major item at the community meeting, if it is not brought up by the patients themselves. All of the patients know about such rule-breaking behavior; the behavior clearly constitutes a community-wide issue needing to be dealt with. Patients also learn that repeated infractions of the rules may lead to transfer to another inpatient facility. We have found that such an approach can be conveyed with compassion, sincerity, and concern, and that patients repeatedly report relief at firm and definitive open staff decisions in these matters. All too often, chronic patients, especially the younger character-disordered ones, have come from broken or disturbed families where one of the regular failings was the lack of recognition of the need to provide protection by means of clear rules and limits. While the history of psychiatric treatment is replete with failed attempts to correct mistakes in an enduring way by providing a "corrective emotional experience," it is still not helpful to repeat earlier mistakes. Enforced limits in the context of multiple forms of psychotherapy and pharmacotherapy may indeed be helpful in many cases.

During a sample period on our unit, we had 44 patients admitted more than once. The average length of stay for this group for their first admission was 29 days, compared to 31 days for their second admission. Excluding one patient from the group of 44—an adolescent whose second admission entailed many weeks of alternate care status while awaiting placement in a residential treatment facility—the figures are 29 days for first admissions and, identically, 29 days for second admissions. Such figures, of course, include a wide diversity of patients and clinical circumstances. These are all, however, patients who received careful discharge planning during their first admission and who subsequently needed readmission. It is reassuring that readmission to the same unit does not entail longer hospitalization and is identical in the average length of stay (less than 30 days) to admissions to the entire unit. Consistency, reality orientation, cognitive problem solving, and limit setting provide an effective structure for a short-term inpatient service during the repeated hospitalizations of chronic patients.

Chapter 3
Psychodynamic Approach: An Object Relations Framework

The psychodynamic approach to psychotherapy, in individual or group work, is the subject of a vast amount of literature. We will focus on one particular approach, based on object relations theory, in an attempt to describe some basic principles and their relevance to hospital-based work. We assume that the fundamental principles of psychodynamics – psychological and emotional growth and development, intrapsychic conflict and defense, and theories of symptom formation and character pathology – are reasonably familiar to the reader, as well as basic assumptions of psychoanalytically oriented individual or group therapy, such as transference, countertransference, and resistance. Standard references providing overviews of these concepts include Brenner (1973, 1976), Cameron (1963), Colby (1951), Fenichel (1941, 1945), Fromm-Reichmann (1950), Karasu (1984), Meissner (1985), Sacks and colleagues (1984), Sandler and co-authors (1973), and Stewart (1985).

INDIVIDUAL PSYCHOTHERAPY

Object relations theories are familiar to inpatient psychotherapists. The works of Melanie Klein, Winnicott, Fairbairn, and Guntrip, among others, provide strategies for intensive psychotherapeutic work with severely disturbed inpatients. The object relations conceptual framework, based on the British object relations school, influenced the significant clinical work of various groups, including Sullivan, Searles, and Fromm-Reichmann in Washington, and Day, Semrad, and Will in Boston. The theoretical and conceptual models of these thinkers have been applied to intensive inpatient work with severely disturbed patients. In most instances, this inpatient work has been long term, with patients remaining hospitalized for one year or more. Kernberg (1976a,b) considers object relations to be a conceptual framework applicable to the intensive long-term, psychoanalytically oriented treatment of borderline patients.

Psychotherapeutic work has attempted to harness psychodynamic theories and apply them to brief, time-limited treatment strategies. Workers such as Davanloo (1978), Malan (1976), Mann and Goldman (1982), and Sifneos (1972) have written extensively about these ideas. In addition, techniques proposed by Beck (1976) for rational cognitive therapy and by Weissman (1979) and Klerman and associates (1984) for interpersonal therapy again consist of attempts to use in-depth understanding of patients for brief psychotherapeutic work. These time-limited forms of psychotherapy have been devised for outpatients who demonstrate clear ego strengths and who usually have no history of hospitalization for psychiatric conditions.

There has been little attention to the use of intensive techniques generally seen as "exploratory" or "expressive" with psychiatric patients during brief hospitalizations. We have found that by applying certain object relations concepts to strategies of brief inpatient psychotherapy, selected confrontations and interpretations of key defensive operations and transference manifestations have been beneficial for many psychotic, borderline, and character-disordered patients. We will review briefly the conceptual framework leading to this inpatient psychotherapeutic technique, clinical examples of which are included in Section III.

Summaries of object relations theories have been presented by numerous clinicians and theoreticians (Dorpat 1981, Gedo 1979, Kernberg 1976a, Spruiell 1978, Tuttman 1981). At the present time, however, there is no single, coherent, generally accepted object relations theory

(Gedo 1979, Spruiell 1978, Sternbach 1983, Tuttman 1981). An important feature of object relations theory is its applicability to severely disturbed patients: the object relations model is most suitable for describing patients admitted to psychiatric inpatient units (Kernberg 1975b, 1976a). This approach is consistent with the view presented by Gedo and Goldberg (1973) that object relations theory best applies to preoedipal phases of development. In combination with genetic and biological disorders, hospitalized patients more often have intrapsychic and interpersonal pathology presumed to relate to their very early life experiences.

Concepts of internalized self and object representations are central to object relations theory. Two versions of such internalization processes are the positive, or libidinally linked, part-self and part-object representations, and the negative, or aggressively linked, part-self and part-object representations (Kernberg 1976a, Lax 1983). Recognition of this point is of crucial importance, as is the fact that these processes coexist in a mutually contradictory way in many hospitalized patients. Such patients may show inadequate development of mature, internalized self and object representations, or regression to an earlier fragmented state. A part-self representation might clinically appear as a view of oneself that—to an outsider—would appear to be either fragmentary, incomplete, or simply concentrating on one aspect of the self (real or imagined) while disregarding other aspects of the self. A part-object representation might appear to be the implicit or explicit view of the "other" which, again, is either fragmentary or incomplete. The "part" aspect of these conceptualizations indicates that at any given time, a patient's view of himself or of others is typically distorted by primitive mental processes, such as splitting, denial of aspects of himself, projection of hostile aggressive impulses onto others, and so on (Kernberg 1976a).

Frank (1975) noted that "focusing on the feelings of such patients often increases their anxiety . . ." (p. 469), referring to psychotic patients. It is our experience, too, that focusing on *feelings in isolation* with acutely disturbed psychotic or borderline patients is counterproductive. Discussing individual psychotherapy, Adler (1979) noted that ". . . to tell the confused schizophrenic that he is angry may be heard by him as a statement that he is a murderer" (pp. 134–135). What we wish to highlight here is our view that such approaches overlook the linkage of an affect with self and object representations ("murderer and murdered"). What the object relations approach suggests is that the therapist not only deal with the *feelings* of the patient, but concomitantly with the self and object representations, too. The feelings are not focused upon in a vacuum; they are located within the field of how the person views himself and others (see Chapter 4). The realization that the fundamental dynamic unit is constituted of a part-self representation, part-object representation, and the affect linking the two, provides a new basis for understanding the dynamics of severely disturbed patients. Frank (1975) and Adler (1979) describe interventions, predicated on a simplified psychoanalytic structural model, that miss the complexity of such situations (Dorpat 1976).

Conflict in object relations terms is conceptualized as dyadic in nature, in contrast to anxiety-producing conflict resulting from unconscious oedipal, or triadic, dynamics, as formulated by classical structural theory. Conflict occurs between two fundamental units, the "positive" self-object unit versus the "negative" self-object unit. The former usually remains introjected; the latter is projected, as it typically contains aspects of the self that are experienced at the moment as being intolerable, aspects of the other that are frightening or threatening, and an affective linkage that cannot be tolerated. Just as with the introject, this project is maintained by primitive defense mechanisms. Either self-object unit can be used, alternately, to defend against anxiety related to the other. That is, what is introjected and what is projected may continuously swap places, in the service of defense; this process is evidenced by dramatic and often confusing shifts in a patient's behavior, attitudes, and feelings. The patient denies the projected parts of the self and the concomitant extreme changes in behavior. Psychotherapeutic work with such a patient requires perseverance, and the therapist must constantly monitor countertransference responses.

For example, a borderline patient in intensive treatment began by describing herself as "incapable of aggression," and she related to the therapist in a meek, deferential, idealizing fashion. This essentially positive view of herself and of the therapist served defensive functions that became evident as the transference intensified. Primitive envy and fears of merger impelled the patient to attempt to destroy her therapist, so that when not told all the specifics she wanted to know of the therapist's educational credentials, she concluded that he "had something to hide." She quickly shifted to a regular stance of contempt for the therapist, openly raging that he was the "stupidest" therapist that she had ever known. Thus the "positive" self-object unit defended against the attacking, aggressive self-object unit, which in turn kept the patient emotionally at a safe distance from the therapist. After moving to another city, the patient telephoned the therapist for many months, claiming never to have been understood by anyone but him, reflecting once again a defensive shift. The task of the therapist becomes to delineate the various components of fundamental units via clarification, confrontation, and finally interpretation. Such work, in our experience, not only is frequently indicated in many hospitalized patients, but also may be best begun in the hospital setting, even when the hospital stay is not lengthy. Continuation of such work may be necessary in intensive outpatient follow-up treatment.

GROUP PSYCHOTHERAPY

Patients admitted to psychiatric inpatient units invariably demonstrate serious disturbances in their interpersonal relationships. Most of these patients are acutely psychotic or have severe character disorders. Group psychotherapy is a commonly recommended treatment for inpatients, even on short-term treatment units (Kibel 1978, 1981, Maves and Schulz 1985, Maxmen 1978, Waxer 1977, Yalom 1983). Clearly, the special advantages of group psychotherapy, such as a sense of commonality, learning from others, and diffusion of negative transference, are available in such a setting. Rabiner and co-workers (1975), working in a municipal hospital, developed a model for assessment in group psychotherapy involving an initial period of history gathering within the group, followed by a less structured interactional period. They noted that quality of participation in group psychotherapy predicted outcome of the patients six months after hospitalization, a fact of great value for realistic disposition planning. In spite of its common use, there is little literature on short-term inpatient group psychotherapy (Kibel 1981). We shall describe an approach to the group treatment of severely disturbed patients that is conceptualized using object relations theory, and provides a means of understanding and formulating interventions in an expressive, insight-oriented mode; such an approach utilizes concepts for individual psychotherapy, but applies these concepts to the special aspects of group work (Russakoff and Oldham 1984).

The approach used in group psychotherapy has frequently been altered from the analytic-expressive mode when used with inpatients, especially with reduced lengths of stay. Some of this alteration of techniques stems from the experience (or belief) that an insight-oriented approach is inefficacious or simply unsuitable. Frank (1975) noted:

> Insight therapy is the treatment of choice for many psychotics. But quite a few already have too much insight in a sense that they cannot cope with the urges and feelings of which they are aware. . . . Other psychotics are largely incapable of verbalizing their feelings and when faced with this task by their therapist become more discouraged, frustrated, and angry [p. 469].

Continuing in this same article, Frank suggests other possible tasks for groups that may be of benefit to such patients. Other authors share the view that insight-oriented group work has only limited usefulness on short-term inpatient services. Horowitz and Weisberg (1966) described techniques for the treatment of acutely psychotic patients who, they noted, "use active, directive, even charismatic and manipulative measures" (p. 48) to help patients. Waxer (1977) suggested the use of the "hot seat," role playing, and videotape feedback, among other techniques, for short-term group psychotherapy. Maxmen (1978) proposed an "educative" model for use with inpatients.

We have been directly observing and supervising inpatient small group psychotherapy three times a week on one of our short-term units. We recognize, and others (Kibel 1981, Klein 1977, Waxer 1977) have noted, that inpatient group psychotherapy does not function in isolation—that it functions within the ward, hospital, and, if applicable, medical school systems, and may be employed to accomplish multiple tasks (enculturation, education, treatment, etc.). We restructured our small group psychotherapy program by adding silent observers, as described in Chapter 5, and our community meeting structure, as described in Chapter 6, in an attempt to fulfill some of these multiple tasks. In spite of the difficulties posed by the large turnover of patients and staff on the unit, as well as the presence of acutely psychotic and involuntary patients, we found ourselves enthusiastic about group psychotherapy. We encouraged an insight-oriented approach in group psychotherapy, not unlike what Rabiner and colleagues (1975) described in the second period of their group sessions. Our enthusiasm for an analytic-expressive approach and its application to a patient population for whom many would question its suitability lies in the application of basic object relations concepts to group psychotherapy.

In addition to individual psychotherapy, group psychotherapy with inpatients is a reasonable setting for the application of such conceptualizations. The dynamics of small groups, as described by Bion (1961), center around psychotic anxiety. Although these dynamics transcend the ontogenetic pathology of the individual patients – that is, they are applicable to staff training groups, too – they are not only generally true for inpatient groups that we describe, but specifically true in addition, since they are at the level at which our patients experience themselves.

As discussed previously in this chapter, the object relations viewpoint postulates fundamental units constituted of three elements: part-self representations, part-object representations, and the affect linking the two. Conflict can be conceptualized as producing an internally held view in opposition to an externalized view, i.e., self-object introject versus self-object project. For example, a patient may project his rage and subsequently view himself as devalued and treated with contempt by hostile others, then justifying his anger as self-protective – all in defense against (conflict with) the view of himself as needy and dependent vis-à-vis engulfing others. There may be several "layers" of such conflicts that may be activated within patients. An especially attractive feature of the object relations view is its compatibility with here-and-now behavioral observations. That is, from the behavior of the particular patient in a given situation, one can, with only a low level of inference, assess the nature of the part-self and part-object representation; the affect linking the two is often apparent. The therapist must first clarify within the group the elements that constitute the fundamental units of the (object relations) conflicts. Second, the therapist must confront the patient with the presence of these units. Sometimes – more often in borderline patients – the act of confronting the patient helps him organize his thinking more realistically, and to integrate his part-self and part-object representations (Kernberg 1976a). When such an intervention does not have as helpful an impact as the therapist would expect, fuller interpretation of both sides of the conflict – introject and project – is indicated. Typically a primitively disturbed patient reacts to a correct interpretation with either initial silence, followed by more integrated functioning, or by the venting of rage. This is true in individual or group settings.

Two aspects of this approach for group work require special attention. The approach we are describing clearly requires the therapist to be active, but in a special manner. Interventions that will cover the breadth of the material – the fundamental units – will necessarily be long statements. However, they are not directive or simply educative. We have been impressed by the ability of patients to hear and use such interventions. This ability of patients runs counter to recommendations given early in our training to make short, even elliptical statements, particularly to schizophrenic patients, since not only was their secondary process impaired, but their attention span short. The group psychotherapists must do much work in helping delineate the elements of the fundamental units for individuals within the group as well as the group as a whole. (For a clinical example of this group approach, see Chapter 10.) The therapist must also maintain a commitment to reality; that is, groups constituted of such ill patients frequently flee the therapeutic task and can engage in maladaptive processes. With the short-term nature of the patient population, it is unreasonable to expect members of the group to be able to, on their own initiative, confront such a process and attend to its work. On the other hand, it is an error to give up on the goals of insight into behavior in such groups. Patients can develop increased understanding of the way people experience others and themselves, and consequently, more realistic views of the self and others can be achieved in such groups.

The second feature of this approach that requires special attention centers on empathy and confrontation. Empathy – particularly among trainees – is confused with a sense of warmth and friendliness. Being "very empathic" is often heard as being "very supportive" and not "confronting." However, insofar as empathy involves emotionally "knowing" another person, empathy with a patient requires knowing not only the self-object introject but the self-object project too. Yet the project typically contains those aspects of the self that the patient wishes to rid himself of, the parts of himself which he experiences as intolerable. To truly empathize with a patient–or in groups, patients–one must empathize with the contents of the project, too, and help the patient try to integrate them into a cohesive whole (Kernberg 1980, 1984). The process of accomplishing this integration involves confronting the individuals and the group with the parts being projected. The initial reaction of either individuals or group members to such confrontations is frequently a venting of rage. The therapist must be able to tolerate this rage and to persevere in the task of clarifying the part-self, part-object relations and observing the affective linkage between them. The result of such activity can be a group that is stormy, but it is at the same time not experienced by the patients as being out of control. Instead, patients leave the group feeling better about themselves, no longer defending themselves so vigorously against aspects of themselves, and more able to appreciate others as people. Rather than recommending to our therapists that they be, by design, "warm" or friendly to members of the groups, we recommend that they be compassionate, yet strive for technical neutrality (Kernberg 1976a, 1984). A therapist who is too nice to feel angry or too angry to feel nice cannot function effectively. The rehashes immediately following each group indicate that the presence of observers (see Chapter 5) helps the therapist to maintain such neutrality and tolerate being the object of the patient's anger.

Finally, we would like to address the issue of the content of the group sessions. Although we were not aware of the work of Rabiner and colleagues (1975) when we developed our group program, there are striking similarities. We begin by introducing new patients, the structure of the group is described, and each new patient is requested to describe what led to his hospitalization.

Rabiner and colleagues (1975) found that the patients who immediately revealed these details did not do well, whereas patients with greater ego strengths were more withholding. Kibel (1978) has suggested that, in short-term group psychotherapy of borderline patients, group discussions of the events leading to hospitalization be avoided, arguing that they are a source of narcissistic mortification. Since hospitalization is a crisis for all patients, we feel that *not* to talk about the events leading to hospitalization is to avoid the obvious; such immediate concerns must be on each patient's mind. To avoid such issues may reinforce pathological defenses in some patients, such as omnipotent control and grandiosity. At times, a generic approach (Jacobson et al. 1968) to the issue of hospitalization is possible. It is precisely the knowledge that it is the exceptional patient who does not experience hospitalization with some loss of self-esteem that makes a generic approach possible and fruitful. More specifically, the feelings of loss of self-esteem, anger, weakness, and failure, with the concomitant overvaluation of the hospital, its staff, and what the hospitalization will accomplish, can be sought and addressed early. Since hospitalization is a crisis that all patients in the group have undergone, it is a natural point of commonality and basis for a sense of universality. Since the idealization of the hospital and its staff can become a difficult resistance to overcome as well as a focus for regression, dealing with such a resistance early can avert a bitter experience of the hospitalization. Additionally, if the events that led to hospitalization are focused upon with the aid of the therapist, the experience can be of critical importance to the patient.

THE COMMUNITY MEETING

Many psychiatrists and mental health professionals are familiar with group psychotherapy and the theories of small groups. However, when dealing with groups of 15 or more members, the dynamics change in a profound manner. Since most inpatient units have many more patients and staff than the 15 or so that alter the dynamics, it behooves the inpatient clinician to be familiar with large group dynamics. Community meetings can be held to diagnose the large group processes that will occur on the unit regardless of other meetings, as well as to intervene in such processes in a therapeutic fashion.

In small groups, members will develop a sense of intimacy, comfort, and support from other members. Participation in the group, although initially difficult for many, becomes natural and easy. Although there are always some inequalities in levels of participation, all group members can be expected to participate in the group at one point or another. A member's sense of self is usually enhanced or stabilized in small groups. It is reasonable to anticipate that a member's contribution to the group will be responded to by other members. Agreement between members about an issue is more easily obtained (Frank 1975, Rutchick 1983, Whitely 1975, Yalom 1983).

On the other hand, in large groups the nature of processes changes dramatically (Arons 1982, Main 1975, Pines 1975, Turquet 1975). Almost immediately, members feel uncertain of themselves: they are not sure if the comments they are thinking about making are appropriate (Kisch et al. 1981, Turquet 1975). If a member chooses to contribute, the member almost inevitably will feel that the group's response – if there was any – was inadequate. Many members will not participate at all; typically a few members will dominate the group (Schiff and Glassman 1969). If the group experience persists long enough, the members will become aware of very powerful and primitive feelings within themselves, feelings that can be terrifying and overwhelming. Typically these feelings include anxiety, anger, envy, suspiciousness, and the loss of sense of self.

It is important to realize that these feelings are likely to develop in normal individuals placed in large groups in which the expected activities of the membership are ambiguous (Skynner 1975). For example, when one attends a lecture, most people do not experience any of these disorganizing feelings. However, at the end of the lecture, if the lecturer opens the floor for questions, many people will experience similar affects. People often report wondering if their question is important enough, perhaps naive or stupid; if they dare to ask it, they question how well it was answered or how seriously it was taken.

Why do these changes occur in large groups? The most obvious explanation is that the individual is less important in the large group (Turquet 1975). Whatever weakness each of us has about his sense of self is exposed in the process. This exposure occurs through the primitization of mental functions and the intensification of feelings that are features of large groups. The anxiety experienced is akin to the psychotic, disintegrating anxiety seen in acutely disturbed patients. The threats to identity are profound, and, combined with the wish to establish a sense of individual uniqueness, they make the large group experience intense and disorganizing. The threats to identity can take many forms: the sense of inadequacy, feeling of fusion, and loss of sense of self. These pressures are experienced by all members of large groups and are exquisitely felt by the patients who already are suffering from over-whelming feelings of dependency and helplessness. Normal individuals with latent, well-defended conflicts over primitive anxieties and fears will find such conflicts stirred in large group experiences. Moreover, people with less mature senses of themselves—those with partial emotional developmental arrests, many of whom will constitute the in-patients—do not ordinarily tolerate intense affects well and will further disorganize. Patients with identity diffusion and poorly modulated drives—as seen in borderline personality disordered patients—are espe-cially susceptible to such forces, since they are likely to enter into the process through their social interests but are then likely to be consumed by the feelings engendered in them by the large group experience. For instance, a borderline patient may begin participation in a large group meeting exhibiting a passive, compliant, and accepting stance. As threatening issues—such as feelings of dependency upon others, including the staff—emerge in the discussion, the patient's underlying more primitive fears of fusion with concomitant annihilation anxiety will also emerge. These latter feelings are likely to be experienced un-consciously and dealt with defensively by the eruption of the patient into a paranoid, aggressive stance utilizing projective identification, the defensive shift occurring on the spot. Thus, the patient will be seen to shift from a passive, dependent attitude regarding the leadership to a devaluing, contemptuous one. The patient is likely to attempt to rally support against the staff in order to bolster himself against the percep-tion of the part-representations that are intolerable and that have been projected onto the staff.

These changes in large groups are of great significance for commu-nity meetings (Kreeger 1975, Schiff and Glassman 1969). Considering that disruptive processes are omnipresent—on the unit as well as in meetings—merely as a result of large group phenomena, experiences should be organized to contain and channel the affects in adaptive direc-tions. The simple, one-word answer to how this is to be achieved is "structure." By structure we mean the use of explicit, known boundaries for both patients and staff as well as the use of regular, reliable proce-dures so that the meetings can be experienced by the staff and patients as known quantities and not as fear-inducing, ambiguous, and uncertain exposures. Thus, the staff and patients should know what the physical arrangements are, and an agenda is used so that the overt process of the meeting can be tracked by the participants. The specifics of this structure are detailed in Chapter 6.

The purpose of the use of such structure is to contain the countertherapeutic forces of the milieu. Borderline patients often react to hospitalization and the attendant forces with claims that "no one helps you here," and they incite themselves and other patients. The community meeting can serve to define and contain such incitement processes. Likewise, the contagion of rebellion often reported in the literature may result from the threats to the loss of identity that occur on inpatient units. These threats can be diagnosed and contained in community meetings through the analysis of the process of the meeting and the use of structure, respectively.

Regular scheduling and fixed durations are important. An occasional meeting in which people are invited to openly question matters, policies, and practices is not likely to take hold of patients or staff if such a permissive atmosphere is not enculturated. The only means of doing this is to schedule meetings regularly. The fixed duration is necessary so that timing issues can be addressed and the capacity of participants is not exceeded. If meetings are of variable duration and are set in a secretive fashion, and if issues are not completely discussed but are deferred to the next meeting because of lack of time, the participants cannot know if this represents a realistic setting of a limit or an avoidance of an issue and failure to live up to the principles explicitly stated.

Whereas in traditional community meetings participants contribute as they wish and without permission from the leader, the use of rules like hand raising and recognition seems critical for short-term unit work. Acutely psychotic patients cannot track a meeting that is very fast-paced. Nor can such patients modulate their activities properly. Thus, hand raising and recognition by the leader before participating helps modulate the interactions and maintains a realistic focus.

It is not possible to rely on an unstable (rapid turnover) unit to have the emotional strength to bring dynamically important issues to the fore in an efficient and prompt manner. Thus, issues of generic dynamic importance are raised in a regular fashion by the staff with the expectation that such issues are likely to affect a significant number of patients. The introduction of new patients and the discharge of patients tap dynamic processes that affect all the patients and relate to conflicts that are universal and powerful. Although addressing these events in a formal way may seem at times to be structure without substance, often enough issues are crystallized in such discussions and are later fruitfully discussed in smaller group settings and individual psychotherapy.

Part II

General Clinical
Principles

Chapter 4
Individual Psychotherapy

The general principles of psychotherapy apply to psychotherapy with inpatients, but the special situation of being an inpatient—both the personal characteristics of patients who become inpatients and those factors that relate to the reasons for hospitalization and state of being hospitalized—produces the need to modify typical psychotherapeutic approaches as ordinarily conceptualized for outpatients. Additionally, with outpatients it is often important to emphasize transference-countertransference issues within the therapy itself, more than external factors. However, with inpatients external factors may be of even greater significance than the conditions of the psychotherapy itself.

In days when cost-effectiveness and cost-benefit analyses are central issues, and in inpatient situations where somatic treatments are widely regarded as the effective ingredients of therapy, one might ask, why do individual psychotherapy with inpatients at all? In our opinion, no matter what the reason for hospitalization, psychotherapy offers an important experience to the patient. More often than not, patients see hospitalization as an indication of personal failure. This sense of failure is sometimes projected onto others—family, outpatient therapist, or any other involved figure—in the form of suspicion or rage. Additionally, during the hospitalization there are likely to be countertherapeutic forces engendered by the hospitalization itself, such as the desire to regress and yield responsibility for one's actions and life to others. Some psychotherapeutic endeavor is required to contain and to counter such affects and forces and help guide the patient on the road to recovery. Individual psychotherapy is, then, an important aspect of treatment for all inpatients.

As mentioned in Chapter 3, we assume that the basic principles of psychoanalytically oriented psychotherapy are familiar to the reader; selected references are cited on page 35. Additional sources of information regarding more specialized forms of individual psychotherapy applicable to hospital-based work are available (Bolten 1984, Brown 1981, Carr 1982, Cooperman 1983, Greben et al. 1981, Klerman et al. 1984, Rogoff 1983, Silver et al. 1983).

The specific role for individual psychotherapy with inpatients depends upon the nature of the particular patient's pathology, the phase of hospitalization, and the motivation and ability of the patient to use such a treatment. As a supportive or adjunctive endeavor, individual psychotherapy offers the opportunity to build or maintain self-esteem throughout an experience that regularly diminishes it; as well, it offers the possibility to help the patient make sense out of an experience that may at first make little sense at all. The latter task—the cognitive and emotional integration of the patient's experience into his life story—is important, for many patients will later struggle against or resist treatment because of the failure to attain this goal. The patient invariably attempts to explain why this "misfortune" happened to him and needs to come up with an answer that is not at the expense of reality ("a conspiracy was devised to do this to me") or at the permanent expense of his self-esteem ("I'm a failure as a person and deserve this torture"). The integration of the experience in a fashion that permits continued functioning is an important goal, although difficult to achieve.

For example, a 38-year-old married mother of two children was admitted to the hospital with a chief complaint of, "I don't know. I'm a burden to my husband and children. I'm just not right." She had had a single depressive episode 20 years ago that was treated with antidepressants and individual psychotherapy on an outpatient basis. The previous episode had been preceded by an abortion. Four months before this current admission, her aunt, to whom she had been very close during her early years, died. She had seemed to mourn appropriately, but she never regained her zest and spirit. In the three weeks prior to the current admission, she was waking up early, crying during the day, becoming easily fatigued, losing weight, and having great difficulty concentrating. Physical examination revealed no abnormalities. Results of routine laboratory studies were within normal limits. The diagnostic impression was: Axis I – Major Depression, Recurrent; Axis II – Deferred; Axis III – None. Treatment was initiated with a tricyclic antidepressant. In individual sessions, the patient ruminated about her incapacities, inadequacies, and presumed failures. She had no capacity for self-observation. As a result of this inability to use psychotherapy in a mutative way, her sessions focused on her condemnatory judgments of herself, and attempts were made to assist her with supportive reality testing. That is, sessions did not deal with the precipitants of her hospitalization – she did not understand the relationship between the mourning of the loss of her aunt and her current state of depression – but instead focused on the errors of her assessments of herself and her experience of the world.

Concomitant with this assistance with reality testing was the implicit message that she was capable, worthy, and loved by her family. Within one week, she was sleeping and eating better. She gained four pounds and was no longer waking up early. After two weeks, when the antidepressant effect of the medication began to affect her psychological state, she became able to consider the effect of the death of her aunt on her. As an outpatient, eight weeks after her admission (five-and-a-half weeks after her discharge) she was able to begin to work through the meaning of the loss she experienced with the death of her aunt.

Individual psychotherapy can also be the principal means of treatment for some patients who are hospitalized. This will often be the case for patients who suffer from personality disorders. Here, intensive psychotherapy can be used with the expectation that it will be mutative. For example, these patients may have borderline personality disorders, and their hospitalizations may be precipitated by strains in important interpersonal relationships, including transference reactions occurring in outpatient treatment.

Patients with DSM-III Axis I Disorders – for example, schizophrenia, mania, and depression – also react to life stresses. Treatment of such stress reactions with psycopharmacological agents alone may be inadequate or even ill advised. No patients are immune from the vicissitudes of life, yet the responses of these patients, using the same example, are likely to be poorly modulated. It may be convenient to respond to such reactions merely by medication increases or with extra doses of medications, but this response might deny such patients the humanity of their responses as well as the opportunity to grow from such crisis.

For example, a 24-year-old single man with a history of paranoid schizophrenia was in outpatient psychotherapy with a psychiatric resident. Sessions were scheduled for once a week, although the therapist had requested twice-weekly sessions. Neither the patient nor his family valued psychotherapy sessions. Finances were not a central issue, since the patient was seen at a publicly supported clinic. One-and-a-half weeks before the therapist was scheduled to go on a one-week vacation, the patient was requested by his employer to quit his job. He became increasingly delusional. His father called the therapist to arrange for hospitalization, additionally stating that he did not want his son to know that he had called the therapist. The therapist said that he could not keep the source of information secret, but he appreciated being informed that the patient's behavior at home was deteriorating. The following day, at the next scheduled session, the patient said that he wanted to tell the therapist "face to face" that he would not be coming to therapy any more, that there was a "contract" out on him. The therapist discussed the significance of the patient's loss of his job and of the therapist's upcoming vacation, and he recommended hospitalization, but the patient refused. The therapist did not judge the patient to be imminently suicidal or homicidal, so involuntary hospitalization was not an option. Another session was already scheduled before the therapist was to leave on vacation; the therapist stated that he would hold that time for him. The night before the appointment, the patient went out with his friends and drank to the point of passing out. The next day, four days before the therapist was scheduled to go on vacation, the patient came to his session saying that he felt he should admit himself to the hospital. The therapist arranged for admission and was able to treat the patient in the hospital until the therapist left on vacation. The patient was continued on his usual dose of antipsychotic medication. The issues of the therapist's vacation and the loss of the patient's job were again discussed. The patient was able to discuss some of his feelings about having been fired, as well as his fears of dependency upon the therapist, with other hospital staff during the absence of the therapist as well as upon his return. He rapidly became nonpsychotic and was discharged three days after the therapist returned from vacation. Additionally, he agreed to come to therapy twice a week as originally requested. In this example, the patient was struggling with fears that prevented him from coming to therapy twice a week, and he was living in a rather unsupportive household. When he was forced to leave his job and his therapist was about to leave on vacation, he felt himself to be without supports. His self-esteem was diminished; he seemed to salvage some self-worth through his delusion that he was important enough to have a "contract" out on him. Admission to the hospital became necessary. Issues that could not be resolved as an outpatient were resolvable in the supportive environment of the hospital.

The type of psychotherapeutic intervention must vary with the state of the patient. Agitated, assaultive patients who cannot fix their attention on others and thus cannot be meaningfully engaged verbally must be responded to behaviorally – perhaps restrained or secluded. Often these two interventions are accompanied by the administration of psychotropic medications. Severely regressed patients – patients with whom talking seems to lack significance – should be responded to at a level they can understand. For example, an extremely psychotic woman was admitted against her will. She felt that her brain had been stolen from her, that she was being raped repeatedly by her family members, and that she was tired of being used as a guinea pig. Both nursing staff and her hospital therapist sat with her and tried to talk with her about her fears of being in the hospital, of what was occurring with her mentally, as well as other events made known to the staff by her family. However, the patient obtained no relief – even momentarily – from the talking; it seemed to fuel her fears and concerns. It was decided to discontinue attempts to engage her in verbal discourse but to remain with her, that is, in her presence. Here the intervention was more behavioral than verbal. As the patient reconstituted, she became more amenable to verbal psychotherapeutic approaches.

Similar events often transpire with other types of patients, such as those admitted in catatonic withdrawn states. Initial attempts to engage the patient verbally should be made. Failing that, contact is important, as well as explanations to the patient of any procedures that will occur, such as use of intravenous lines, tube feedings, or parenteral administration of medications. Catatonic patients, when they recover, regularly report on what occurred to them in their withdrawn state, confirming the importance of careful consideration of how they are talked to during their states of withdrawal and seeming inattentiveness. On the other hand, patients whose rational capacities are intact can be approached in a problem-solving mode of discourse. There is no need to approach such patients behaviorally or interpretively. While such patients rarely are hospitalized, there are times at which more severely disturbed patients will have areas in which they need help and are not conflicted, and that they can discuss in a rational fashion. Between these extremes, the manner in which psychotherapy sessions are conducted eludes simple, meaningful classification.

ADMISSION TO THE HOSPITAL: THE FIRST PHASE

After the decision to admit the patient has been made, several processes begin concurrently. At the level of behavior and signs and symptoms, the differential diagnosis must occur. Here, there will be greater emphasis on behavior and phenomenology, for these parameters will be linked to descriptive diagnosis (DSM-III), which serves to guide the use of somatic treatments. Psychotherapeutically, when the decision to admit the patient is made, it is best if the treating psychiatrist meets with the patient and his family immediately to initiate the formation of the therapeutic relationship and to obtain the history. If the referring therapist and the treating therapist are the same, these tasks are already accomplished. If they are not the same, a discontinuity in the therapeutic relationship caused by hospitalization and transfer to a new therapist for the duration of the hospital treatment usually adds to the stresses on the patient. The treating therapist should immediately contact the referring therapist.

Another important factor at the outset of hospital treatment is the patient's attitude toward being hospitalized. This attitude is not determined simply by the legal status of the patient (whether the admission was voluntary or involuntary). A patient who feels unduly coerced into admission or feels deceived by his family in the process ("We're just going to talk to the doctor, that's all!") will, during the initial phase of hospitalization, have much difficulty trusting a therapist and being able to use psychotherapy efficiently.

STRUCTURAL ASPECTS

In the initial few days of hospitalization, contact with the patient should be made daily. Subsequently, the frequency and duration of sessions must be balanced by the time available from the therapist and the capacity of the patient to use the time psychotherapeutically. In very structured inpatient units, where psychotherapy is expected to serve an adjunctive function, two sessions a week of half hour duration each might suffice. With such an arrangement the goal of therapy would be to provide psychological and emotional support until somatic treatments became effective. With very disorganized patients, daily sessions of short duration – three to five minutes – may be all that is tolerated. With very dependent and needy patients, scheduling very brief sessions – say, five minutes – on days in which longer sessions are not planned may be helpful.

With better-functioning patients and patients in whom the psychotherapy is expected to play a central and mutative role, three sessions a week of 45 minutes' duration seem to work well. As schizophrenic, manic, and depressed patients reconstitute, their needs for psychotherapy often converge with those of the less severely disordered and disorganized patients. For some of these patients, similar psychotherapy hours are indicated.

For patients who are being seen daily and very briefly, visits can occur in the hall or day room. It is not necessary and may even be contraindicated to take the patient off the unit or to a private office for the session. Very confused patients may feel endangered or excessively stimulated in the confines of an office. Very agitated patients dealing with aggressive impulses may miss the sense of containment provided by the presence of other staff members.

For patients who are to be seen in individual offices, how should the offices be arranged? There must be room enough for two people. This issue would not seem to need mention except that in some institutions where either psychotherapy is not valued or there is simply too little space, patients meet their therapists in space that would be barely adequate for closets. The failure to provide a reasonable space for the psychotherapy can lead to problems in the therapy itself. Psychotic and paranoid patients may be overstimulated or confused by the abnormal physical proximity. Hostile patients may be provoked into aggressive outbursts by the closeness.

The space should be adequate for two comfortable chairs that can be placed at angles to one another, not directly facing each other. The purpose of angling the chairs is to reduce the uncomfortable feeling that patients often have of being stared at, especially if they are receiving medication and are aware of feeling different about themselves physically as well as mentally. Just as excessive closeness can lead to increased hostility, so can forced eye-to-eye contact. The patient and the therapist will not feel like they are staring each other down if they are sitting at a comfortable angle.

The patient's chair should be placed so that the patient does not have the feeling that he is trapped in the office. Ordinarily, this simply means that the therapist should not be placed so that he blocks access to the door. This placement of chairs is of particular concern with hostile paranoid patients. On short-term units where the patient is not initially known to the therapist, precautions such as attention to chair placement may avoid incidents.

Therapy sessions ordinarily have fixed durations, and a clock in the office – as opposed to the use of one's wrist watch – is preferable. Ideally, the clock should be in the fields of vision of both the therapist and the patient. This arrangement permits the patient and the therapist to use temporal factors in the pacing of statements and interventions. If the patient is deprived of time cues, observations made to the patient that important issues seem to always arise at the end of the sessions may be more a product of the short duration of the session and the need to reestablish rapport with the therapist during each session than of any significant wish on the part of the patient to obtain special extensions of sessions. Additionally, since it takes time for an effectively charged issue to develop, the patient can decide whether there is sufficient time to pursue the issue. The patient is less likely to experience the therapist as rude for ending the session when the time constraints are public.

Decorations for offices are often arranged by the institutions independent of the therapists' wishes. Where therapists have say in decorations, issues of degree and kind of stimulation should be considered. Surrealistic images can be either frightening or reassuring to patients; the individual responses must be explored if they interfere with the progress of therapy. Some therapists like to have pictures of family members in their office. Such therapists should not be surprised if some patients become especially curious about their personal lives. It becomes difficult to tease apart ordinary, unconflicted interest from transferential distortion when such stimulation is provided by the therapist.

CONTENT ASPECTS

In the cases in which the treating therapist is not the referring therapist, an early exploration of the expectancies of the patient and his family is central. Expectations are fluid but nevertheless critical and must be flushed out if therapeutic work is to be successful. For example, if the patient sees hospitalization as punishment, he is inclined to respond in a fashion that will probably irritate or alienate the therapist and the staff. Rather than willingly participate in the many activities of the unit, he will resist them, even undermine them. Or, if the family views the hospitalization as a last ditch effort in which all the stops are being pulled out, and through which a personality overhaul will result, the family is likely to be impatient with the rate of progress and dissatisfied with the outcome.

As stated before, the very first contacts are for developing a relationship, history gathering, and clarification of expectations. After those sessions, the work of the psychotherapeutic endeavor begins. Some patients believe that they should talk about their past and various traumas that befell them in their childhood to the exclusion of the problems and pressures that led to their hospitalization. They will talk openly about dramatic events in their history, steadfastly avoiding attention to current distressing realities. Since this material, obviously important, will have been covered at least in broad outline in the history-taking session, the questions for the psychotherapist are: "Why is the patient telling me this now?" "What relevance does it have to the patient's current state?" If the answers to those questions are unclear, they must be pursued with the patient. Frequently, issues from the distant past are brought up either because the patient thinks he is supposed to talk about such things to a psychiatrist, or it is the patient's way of avoiding dealing with issues in the here-and-now. If the patient talks primarily about these issues because he believes that he ought to, then simple education around what the more important and immediate issues are will suffice. The patient can be told that such issues are perhaps best dealt with in outpatient psychotherapy and that during the hospitalization therapists focus more sharply on the crisis that precipitated the patient's admission.

However, if it is not a simple matter of education, then the issue is more complicated. Patients who regale therapists with details of past traumatic events are likely to be rigidly defended against other anxiety-provoking material or feelings that might emerge in the psychotherapeutic work. A corollary to this is that such patients are likely to respond to accurate interventions regarding this defense with displays of anger toward the therapist. As Fenichel (1941) noted, ". . .he who wishes to operate has to cut and must not be afraid of blood" (p. 46). Inexperienced therapists often feel that they have made a mistake when their patients respond angrily to their well-intended interventions. The situation is one of a delicate balance; both a proper and an improper intervention are likely to be responded to with angry displays. One needs experience–as well as the help of one's colleagues–to tell them apart.

The therapist needs to have some overriding concepts to guide him through the therapy sessions and help him set priorities in his interventions. We suggest the following.

The purpose of the therapy sessions is for the therapist to understand the patient and to help the patient better understand himself, not to cure him. The corollary to this principle is that the therapist should not measure the usefulness of his verbal interventions against the behavior of his patient. Nor should the therapist simply argue or try to convince the patient to change his maladaptive ways. It is presumed that these approaches have been tried by family and friends before to no avail. The more the patient experiences therapy as an attempt to change him–in the direction the therapist believes the patient ought to change–the more likely the therapist will run into major resistances.

The more the therapist accepts this principle and is able to convince the patient that the goal of the therapy is *understanding* the patient, the more the patient will trust the therapist. Clearly the therapist's task is to understand the maladaptive aspects of the patient's behavior as well as the more neutral or adaptive aspects; it is in pursuing the maladaptive parts that the therapy may be efficacious in helping the patient alter his previous unhealthy patterns of behavior. An important reason for choosing this as a central task is that, of all the tasks one might assume, the therapist can more regularly deliver on the expectation of greater understanding; only the patient can deliver on the variable change. This point may seem trivial and insignificant, but it is of central importance. The more the therapist aspires to change the patient in a specific way, the more the ground work is laid for conflict and frustration on both the patient's and the therapist's part. Properly conducted psychotherapy can be expected to provide the patient with an alternative understanding of the patient's life. The relationship between that understanding and change in the person's life is unclear; but change is definitely not in the control of the therapist. It is possible that through the approach of improving understanding, patients begin to feel that they can choose what they will do, as opposed to what they feel. Patients often initially report in psychotherapy session that their maladaptive behaviors and reactions "just happen." As psychotherapy progresses, they begin to note that what they initially experienced as immediate impulses or affective states are mediated by other affective states and thoughts. It is in the contemplation of the mediated states that the patients may see other options, or decide that they are comfortable responding in the fashion that they have responded.

The preeminent dynamic issue confronting most inpatients has to do with self-esteem and the vicissitudes of narcissism. Although issues of dependency–independence, aggression–passivity and sexuality–asexuality are common and important, in our experience the underlying dynamic leading to hospitalization often has to do with narcissistic issues. In particular, serious defects in identity and sense of self typically occur within these patients, and, in our experience, the crisis that precipitated hospitalization frequently relates to this central issue. Thus, therapeutic interventions given priority are those that address the patient's self-representations. Superficially these self-representations can be identified as statements that are direct comments about oneself or that implicitly convey meaning about oneself.

In a patient who has been aggressive, for example, the therapist should not emphasize only the need to contain the aggression, but should explore the implicit meaning the behavior had in terms of the patient's concept of himself. Typically, aggressive behavior is a way of declaring that one is a significant presence; patients make such statements when they experience a diminished sense of self. For instance, a patient who was on cigarette restriction asked for a cigarette from a staff member. The staff member refused the request in a curt manner. The patient retreated to his room, reemerging moments later, and attacked the staff member who had denied the request. In review of the incident, the insensitive manner of the staff member was experienced by the patient as disrespectful, adding to the patient's having already felt powerless due to the restriction, even though the restriction was enforced for the patient's protection.

In medical interviewing, the physician follows the *content* of what is being discussed. For example, if a patient describes chest pain, the physician is likely to ask for details about the pain, under what conditions it occurred, what relieved the pain, and what other symptoms accompanied the pain. If, on open-ended questioning, certain symptoms are not mentioned, such as radiation down the left arm or nausea, the physician will specifically inquire as to their presence.

Classically, in dynamic psychiatric interviewing, the formula has been to follow the *affect*. Thus the phrase "How did you feel about. . . ?" has been the stock and trade of the dynamically oriented psychiatrist. As affect changes or intensifies, the therapist would pursue it, independent of the logical connectedness of the material. In fact, if the logical connections were tight, one would presume that these expressions of affect represented an avoidance of dealing with some issue.

Object relations theory would suggest that in more severely disturbed patients, the formula requires yet another modification; the therapist should follow the patient's explicit or implicit sense of self and others. That is, as mentioned in Chapter 3, the therapist should clarify the *part-self and part-object representations*. In our experience, this approach is generally experienced as being more empathic than the approach of following only the affect. In fact, when the "follow the affect" approach is joined with the classical Rogerian technique of reflecting the affect, the results can be disastrous. For example, a patient told his therapist that the hospital staff was treating him poorly, that his parents were the crazy ones, and that he himself had no problems at all. The therapist said to the patient, "You seem angry." The patient became enraged with the therapist, stating, "Of course I'm angry. You'd be too if you were in my situation. Don't you understand anything?" The therapist again, following the affect, and reflecting it back to the patient, noted that the patient was becoming even angrier. With that, the patient insisted on getting a new therapist and terminating the session. Shortly thereafter, the patient required placement in seclusion as he continued to escalate in his agitation.

A different therapist handled a similar circumstance using the principles espoused here. The patient complained to the therapist that the social worker was plotting with his family to put him away in a state hospital. The patient seemed threatening to the therapist, who sensed that the patient not only believed that such a plot was evolving, but that the therapist was a party to it, too. The therapist responded by noting that it seemed that the patient viewed himself as a helpless victim. The patient stated that that was right! He was powerless in the face of his parents and the social worker and was being unfairly treated by them. The therapist further noted that the patient seemed to feel that he could trust no one, that other people did not take his concerns seriously. The patient replied that he'd been burned too often. The therapist noted that that mistrust extended to the therapist himself, that it almost didn't pay for the therapist to answer the patient's questions since the patient had already decided what the answers were. The patient relaxed noticeably and said he wasn't sure, but was certainly afraid of what he'd overheard before. He said that in the emergency room where he had been taken by the police, he had overheard a discussion between the psychiatrist and his parents about the state hospital. The therapist remarked that it must clearly have been a frightening experience for the police to have taken him to the emergency room. To have heard that conversation could only have fueled his fears. However, the therapist informed him, when the decision was made to send him to this hospital, the plans for the state hospital had been shelved.

This example demonstrates that there are demonstrable differences in approaching patients from an object relations perspective and from dynamic perspectives that focus primarily on affects alone. Additionally, education, reinforcement of reality, and other technical maneuvers must be used when appropriate. Understanding the patient from an object relations perspective and addressing the immediate issues of how he views himself permitted the therapist to establish some rapport with the patient and to be able to converse with him. Education about reality issues was also critical.

In another situation, a manic patient who was in partial remission described her weekend visit home. She noted that her parents severely restricted her activities, not permitting her to spend any appreciable time alone. She expressed annoyance with her parents for their overbearing attitude. The therapist asked what other annoying things the parents did to her. The patient reported that her parents had rearranged her room and that she was "pretty pissed" at them for that, too. In supervision, the therapist noted that he was irritated with the parents' actions. When the therapist's attitude was explored, the therapist realized that, for countertransference reasons, he had ignored the recent history of impulsive and potentially dangerous behavior of the patient prior to her admission four weeks earlier. The patient's anger at the infantilization by her parents seemed to be predicated upon the patient's denial of her prehospitalization behaviors—behaviors her parents were not likely to have forgotten and could not be convinced would not recur. On the other hand, the patient was experiencing her parents' actions as demeaning; the patient experienced her parents as controlling, intrusive, and infantilizing and saw herelf as capable, responsible, and cooperative. These part-object and part-self representations were in conflict with the part representation of her parents as caring, concerned, and interested and herself as ill and in need of protection and care. In the subsequent therapy sessions, the therapist was able to explore the narcissistic implications of the patient's complaints about her family and was able to help the patient better integrate her view of herself as having been seriously ill but now well on the road to recovery and proper functioning.

SPECIAL ISSUES

Following Up Questions

How and when to follow up a question is a central issue in therapy. A frequent error is the failure to follow up a question adequately. Typically, the interviewer will accept as the answer a glib, superficial response that only has the appearance of relevance to the issue, or, on reflection, is clearly a partial response. Sometimes therapists feel awkward asking for more information regarding an issue, perhaps feeling it impolite to ask for detail, particularly about issues that are uncomfortable. However, if the therapist is to understand the patient, such following up is crucial.

For example, a patient was talking about problems at work and concluded that he was a "shit." The therapist immediately sensed that the patient clearly felt worthless and defective. The therapist said nothing for a brief period and then asked the patient if the side effects from the medication were troublesome. Here, the therapist assumed that he fully understood what being a "shit" meant to the patient. Although it is likely that worthlessness was a component, the therapist did not explore the possibility that the patient's feelings were linked to a sense of grandiosity, that the patient should be seen as more highly valued, and that he was not defective, but misunderstood and mistreated. Later psychotherapy session confirmed that these fantasies were present. Of course it is possible to follow up excessively, in an obsessive fashion. It is not possible simply to delimit the degree of follow up. The guideline for the therapist, and something he might say to the patient, is, "I need to know just what the experience is like for you, as if I had to act your part in a play. I need to understand what thoughts you would be thinking." One would permit the patient to go into other areas if it led to learning more about what made the patient "tick." Understandably, this is a rather loose guideline. Clearly, rote or mechanical exploration of any issue is not likely to be fruitful.

Importance of History

Nothing should be inferred that would suggest a disregard for the need for an accurate history of the patient, including the history of phenomenology, vocational performance, social effectiveness, and past treatments and results. Many patients can recover from acute exacerbations of illness and look reasonably good. Only the patient's history will tell you whether or not the patient is likely to persevere with treatment or be able to maintain the state attained in the hospital phase of treatment. Some patients simply don't comply; others comply but don't seem to be able to sustain their efforts at maintaining control. These patients may look good on a superficial level. In certain circumstances, such as in the hospital, they seem to be able to function at a high level. However, their histories suggest chronic incapacity at a much lower functional level than what appears to be the case. This situation is likely to provoke a response from the therapist and treatment team that they are being used and manipulated by the patient. Once the team members feel that they are being manipulated, they respond with controlled anger, typically in the form of the denial of certain requests. Our understanding is that the team members are correct in the perception of being used by these patients, but incorrect in the presumption that this manipulation is deliberate or even part of a pathological process that should be frustrated. Our experience is that there is a group of chronic patients who have the ability to maintain a veneer of social and vocational capacity in a structured setting, but it is just a veneer. This capacity does them a disservice, for others respond to them as if they can perform more adequately than they can. Thus, these patients constantly seek and are pushed into situations in which they inevitably fail, due primarily to failure to make or accept an accurate assessment of their true performance capabilities (as revealed in a detailed history).

Working Through

The working-through process involves repeated efforts to clarify the part-self and part-object representations as revealed in the patients' statements. Although on occasion with some outpatients, discussion of an issue can be expected to bring an issue to closure, this rapid resolution is uncommon and highly unlikely to occur in hospital treatment. Thus, therapists should not be surprised when an issue resurfaces for continued discussion. Therapists are not alone in their confusion around this fact. Patients often are frustrated when they find themselves talking about the same thing over and over again. Here, delineation of nuances of differences is important for both the therapist and the patient. There is yet another aspect of the working-through process that is apparent when the object relations perspective is used. With almost all inpatients, an integrated sense of self is lacking. The fragmentary images that are held are split-off from one another, and the contradictory images are maintained by the mechanisms of splitting and denial (Akhtar and Byrne 1983, Kernberg 1975b). The psychotherapeutic work consists, in part, of repeatedly clarifying the fragmentary view and confronting the split-off aspects. That is, the therapist will be repeatedly clarifying the part-self and part-object representations, both the introjects and the projects. What makes this aspect of the work deserve special attention is that the patient has these aspects of himself split off in consciousness, so the work has the appearance of dealing with the obvious, both to the patient and to the inexperienced therapist. Here the therapist must have a sophisticated understanding of the mechanisms of splitting and denial. For many people, it seems incredible that a person could not know that which seems so obvious and was talked about so recently. Such psychotherapeutic work may seem mundane to the therapist, especially as it lacks the glamour of bringing to consciousness that which is unconscious.

Stereotyped Openings of Sessions

It is not unusual for patients to begin sessions in a stereotyped fashion. It may be complaints about medication, comments about the past, or simply social pleasantries. How should a therapist understand such behavior? Obviously there can be no formula for all patients. However, in light of the common dynamic problems shared by the patients, it is often safe to presume that the functional basis for such a stereotype lies in (1) the need for the patient to test the trustworthiness of the therapist, since the patient cannot be certain the therapist will be as accepting of him today as he was the day before; (2) the simple wish to say "hello"; (3) the need for an opportunity to reorganize and reorient oneself in the presence of the other.

Principle of Hierarchical Interventions

More so than with outpatients, psychotherapists of inpatients must regularly adjust the level of intervention to the current state of the patient; at certain times different types of intervention are necessary and appropriate. For severely regressed patients at the beginning of hospitalization, behavioral interventions may be of highest priority. As the patient progresses in treatment and is more able to use verbal means of communication, traditional psychotherapy can play a greater role. In emergency situations, where verbal means of intervention have been tried and failed, other means such as seclusion (behavioral) or the use of medications (psychopharmacological) may be employed. It is an error, however, to presume that verbal means alone can never be used in emergencies. For example, a patient with severe character pathology including dyscontrol of her temper was admitted to the hospital in an agitated state following the break up of a two-month relationship with a boyfriend. At the least provocation, the patient exploded in rage at staff members for their incompetence, inconsiderateness, and insincerity. As nursing staff members attempted to talk with her about her troubles and complaints, she escalated in her degree of dyscontrol. She began to throw things about the unit. One of the staff members suggested that the patient be taken to the seclusion room, recalling that patients frequently damage objects and then assault people. The charge nurse thought they would have to be prepared for such an action, but she chose first to confront the patient with the threatening nature of her actions, and the inability of the staff to sit by while she mistreated the staff and patients as she herself felt mistreated by her former lover. The patient's behavior immediately ceased to escalate; she spent time talking to a staff nurse about how her relationships with men often failed, with her feeling used and hurt.

Chapter 5

Group Psychotherapy

Although group psychotherapy is common on inpatient units, the reasons for its use are seldom articulated. The most obvious and specific indications center on the multi-person aspect of groups; the social-interpersonal focus is natural to groups, even when the approach in group is individually focused. Thus, group psychotherapy is frequently used to supplement biological (psychopharmacological or other somatic) and intrapsychic (individual psychotherapeutic) approaches. Although one can address social-interpersonal factors in other formats—for example, in individual psychotherapy—these factors are the natural focus for a group. Additionally, the therapist can focus on "here-and-now" social actions; the group functions as a social laboratory with data for all to see. While all this occurs, the group psychotherapy situation affords the patients an opportunity to improve their social skills, and the therapists an opportunity to assess the patients' social skills. The loss of self-esteem common in patients on admission (see Chapter 4) not only leads to a decrement in social functioning, but also may leave the patients more amenable to changing behavior that group members can show to be maladaptive.

Group psychotherapy shares many features with other modalities of psychotherapy. Two features specific to group psychotherapy, however, are the sense of universality and the opportunity to be able to act altruistically toward others. Patients frequently hear in group about the shared aspects of the problems they are currently experiencing, that others have "been there" and that they "are not alone" in their experiences. They also see that others have received help, have helped themselves, and that the despair they experience will give way to better days. These experiences cannot be provided in short-term individual psychotherapy. The group psychotherapy experience also provides patients with the opportunity to help other patients. For some patients this behavior can interfere with their own treatment; for others it often makes it easier for the patients to accept help themselves. The ease with which patients can see the problems of other patients, and their need to change certain attitudes and behaviors, gradually leads to the willingness to accept the observations and conclusions proffered by others. All this can occur in a situation where the asymmetry of relationships is less extreme (individual psychotherapist to patient versus patient to patient in group).

Even the best designed and functioning milieus will contain countertherapeutic forces. Many of the meetings of an inpatient unit are used, in part, for the assessment and diagnosis of such forces. Community meetings, staff meetings, and group psychotherapies can provide important clues to such forces (see Chapter 2). With proper diagnosis, interventions can be effected within the group psychotherapy or elsewhere.

Is any of this *unique* to group psychotherapy? We believe that this question is misleading: we make no claim for its uniqueness, nor do we see any need for such a justification. At times, there is no doubt that seeing patients in groups is the most effective way to deal with certain interpersonal issues. Also, patients who require hospitalization often have common problems. Even so, there are times in which group psychotherapy is not useful for a given patient. For example, acutely and severely manic patients can rarely tolerate group experiences. Conversely, some patients are rarely accepted by other group members, such as those who are hospitalized for forensic evaluations of sexual abuse of children.

TYPES OF INPATIENT GROUP PSYCHOTHERAPIES

Group psychotherapies can be classified as being either task oriented or expressive. Three types of task-oriented groups commonly employed are problem-solving groups, educative groups, and socialization groups. In problem-solving groups, a concrete focus is selected and worked on by the group members. These groups tend to be useful with patients who have a tendency to think in a global, undifferentiated fashion. Here, the emphasis on breaking a problem, or problems, into components that can then be individually addressed is helpful. Such groups tend to be individually centered as opposed to group centered in their approach. These groups often focus on minor problems that are likely to be profitably discussed in such a format, but problem-solving groups avoid more difficult and often more important, but not clearly resolvable, problems. Additionally, problem-solving group approaches ignore group dynamics, treating them as an interference or annoyance.

Socialization groups focus on the experience of "being together." These groups are often used with chronic, severely socially impaired patients. Sometimes socialization groups are referred to as "coffee and. . ." groups. These groups are predicated on the assumption that participation in reasonable social interaction is beneficial in and of itself. There is essentially no effort at examination of the process, or working on particular problems. Thus the model is experiential, not reflective.

The educative group model was designed by Maxmen (1978). This approach fuses elements of the problem-solving and socialization models. A problem or event is chosen early in the group session, and an attempt is made to look at it in the here and now. Social problems likely to be common to most group members are preferentially chosen, and the groups, whose approach resembles being didactic, is led by either other patients or the therapist. This model is seductive in its rationality as well as its simplicity. It presumes that patients will choose the "right" actions through rational analysis in the group. However, since group dynamics are not considered, irrational forces are either ignored or denied, which may significantly limit the goals of such groups.

Expressive groups may be subdivided into three classes: process-centered groups; classical psychoanalytic groups; and psychoanalytically informed groups. Groups with a heavy emphasis on process interpretation require participation of high functioning patients. These patients must be able to tolerate substantial increases in their anxiety. The focus for the groups is on the irrational processes that occur. Transference issues are commonly focused upon. Interventions are primarily group centered and require the patients to be able to see issues on an abstract level. It is rare that hospitalized patients meet these entry and participation standards.

Classical psychoanalytic groups have been used with inpatients, but the match of this type of therapy with inpatients is questionable. As with process groups, these groups require high-functioning patients. The goal is generally one of rendering conscious that which is repressed; the time frame for such work is long-term, and the therapist usually adopts a passive approach. Interventions are group and individually centered and require a fair degree of abstraction.

A short-term or acute unit poses special problems. The rapid turnover of the patient population and the higher percentages of acutely disturbed patients on such a unit make specialized group approaches necessary. When, in addition, a short-term inpatient psychiatric unit serves as a training experience for residents, students, and trainees of multiple disciplines, the group therapy structure should serve as both a therapeutic tool and an important ingredient of the educational program.

We have developed a "psychoanalytically informed" group-therapy model on our unit. This model takes into account individual as well as group dynamics, and the techniques used respect the need of inpatients to remain fairly reality based, as opposed to exploring fantasy. Milieu effects are addressed as they affect both the group as a whole and individual members. A key element we have added is the use of multiple silent observers with each group (Oldham 1982); we think that this model meets many clinical and educational needs.

We will provide a brief review of the relevant literature in the areas of short-term inpatient group work and the use of observers with groups, followed by a description of the model. The usefulness of such a model is then discussed, with some comments regarding its technical problems. Several clinical examples are provided.

REVIEW OF LITERATURE

Klein (1977) pointed out that, in hospital work, if group therapy is assigned a peripheral role, risks arise of staff splitting and inefficient communication among staff members. Borriello (1976) made similar points. Many authors have emphasized, however, the central importance and usefulness of group therapy as one of several concomitant therapeutic agents in short-term inpatient psychiatric work (Battegay 1974, Beutler et al. 1984, Brabender et al. 1983, Parloff and Dies 1977, Standish and Semrad 1975, Stein 1975, Stein et al. 1955, Yalom 1983). In order to meet the needs of a heterogeneous patient population, some workers have devised a system of multiple groups, varying the group techniques to meet the different needs of each group—for example, the acutely psychotic group versus the predischarge group (Horowitz and Weisberg 1966, Kanas and Barr 1983, Leopold 1976, Yalom 1983, Youcha 1976). In some of those arrangements, all newly admitted patients are placed together in a group for a limited time, as a way to facilitate evaluation and diagnosis (Arriaga et al. 1978).

Maxmen (1978, 1984), addressing the problems posed by rapid patient turnover, proposed a here-and-now educational, problem-solving technique as a method applicable on short-term units. Here, although different types or levels of groups are not suggested, it is clearly advocated that only carefully selected patients be placed in group therapy. Maxmen (1978, 1984) emphasized the need for the group therapists to encourage patients to take responsibility for their own problem solving, rather than relying too heavily on staff members. Others, such as Waxer (1977) and Erickson (1981), advocated a similar educational approach as a method especially useful for short-term inpatient work. Some authors suggested a tactic of planned group activities or didactic exercises for the acutely disturbed patients (Cory and Page 1978, Farrell 1976). Two group approaches, therefore, to the problems posed by acutely disturbed patients on rapid-turnover services are to subdivide patients according to level of functioning and to adopt supportive group techniques.

In such short-term inpatient settings, it is especially important to maximize the efficiency of staff communication and use of time, which we feel can be facilitated by the use of observers. Most reports do not specify the number of therapists per group or whether or not observers or recorders are present.

Bailine and colleagues (1977) recommended a high staff–patient ratio in groups on their acute unit; they argued that large numbers of staff stabilize the group to offset the effects of rapid patient turnover. Gruber (1978) made a similar recommendation, encouraging all available staff and students to participate. He and his co-workers discouraged silent observers and urged a high degree of staff participation, which, they felt, minimized and controlled psychotic interactions. Most authors, however, imply or explicitly recommend a more traditional model of one or two therapists, often specified as senior, experienced staff members (Klein 1977, Stein 1975). Such groups are then highly staff restricted unless open to observation.

The presence or absence of staff members as silent observers at inpatient group therapy is infrequently addressed in the literature. Stein (1975) described the usefulness of such an arrangement with inpatient groups for resident training purposes. Klein (1977) reported the use of silent observers but found them less disruptive if behind a one-way screen, an arrangement alluded to by Yalom (1983) with higher-level inpatient groups. Maxmen (1978) pointed out that primary therapists can make better judgments about the advisability of follow-up group therapy if they observe the inpatient groups.

More often, reports on the usefulness of observers refer to outpatient groups, which frequently use a one-way mirror. Even in those reports, as pointed out by Bloom and Dobie (1969), the role of the observers, their location, and their degree of participation are not clear. Krasner and associates (1964), for example, reported the presence of observers, but some observers remained silent, and some functioned as modified co-therapists in a poorly defined way.

The use of observers with inpatient and outpatient groups is reported to have various values or purposes. Some workers cite the value of observers as independent or objective recorders of the group process, thus serving as an aid for the supervision of the group co-therapists (Kritzer and Phillips 1966). Bernardez (1969), however, questioned the ability of the observer to be objective. A second reason to use observers with groups is that many students and trainees at once can directly witness the group for their own education (Imber et al. 1979, Martin et al. 1977, Pinney et al. 1978, Stein 1975). A third reported function of observers is as a direct aid in the clinical care of the patients—for example, in time-limited groups, as a method of triage for placement in subsequent long-term therapy (Imber et al. 1979, Maxmen 1978).

As described by Lothstein (1978) and Stone (1975), special transference relationships are often stimulated by the presence of observers.

Some workers find such developments to be facilitating to therapy (Bloom and Dobie 1969), although others imply that they find them disruptive (Goforth et al. 1978, Krasner et al. 1964).

DESCRIPTION OF MODEL

As we instituted the modified therapeutic community model on our unit, we created three multidisciplinary teams and revised our small group therapy system.

Site

Group psychotherapy must take place in a space where the group can be a group. Busy corridors on the unit or areas in which staff or visitors can be expected to pass through are unsuitable and send a conflicting message to both staff and patients. There must be some assurances for privacy and confidentiality. The space must also be adequate for the numbers of patients and therapists. The same place – available on a regular and reliable basis – should be used. We have created three separate, private spaces on our unit, where our groups meet simultaneously.

Temporal Factors

The duration of group sessions should balance the ability of the patients to tolerate group with the need for an adequate amount of time to permit an issue to be developed and discussed. Ideally, durations are between 45 and 90 minutes. Many acute inpatients cannot tolerate 90 minutes in any meeting; we have found that 45 minutes is a reasonable time.

Session frequency has been reported from twice weekly to daily. Staff availability will determine some of these parameters. The group frequency must match the rapid patient turnover. Groups meeting infrequently will not have a chance to develop the cohesive forces that assist in the work of the therapy. The group will constantly be attempting to form; no group culture will develop or be transmissible. As described in Chapter 2, our groups meet three times per week, from 8:30 A.M. until 9:15 A.M.

Membership Factors

Two common approaches regarding the participation of inpatients in group psychotherapy are screening of patients and universal inclusion of patients. When patients are screened for admission to the group, group is usually viewed by the staff as a privilege that has been offered to the patient. When groups are constituted in this fashion, one result may be that two classes of patients seem to be created: those well enough to be selected and those who are "ill." This separation within the patient community can foster the maladaptive use of projective mechanisms. Furthermore, the group psychotherapy no longer provides an accurate biopsy of the milieu. On the positive side, the groups are easier to conduct and can function at a higher level.

When all patients are included in groups – without differentiation as to level of function – the group can serve as a biopsy of the milieu (Levine 1980). If there are conflicts within the unit, the group is likely to reflect them. In this sense, the groups are not sanitized for the therapists; the therapists may then see just what living on the unit has been like. The universality issue is pressed when all patients are accepted into group.

In our model, all patients are expected to participate in groups. The team patients (two teams with eight patients, one team with nine patients) constitute the three groups.

Staff Factors

Inpatient groups are often run by co-therapists. In training units, co-therapy offers more trainees the opportunity to conduct group and for longer periods of time. In our own model, since we do not screen out patients (with rare exceptions), the therapists often feel that they find the presence of the co-therapist comforting. On training units, it is useful to have experienced therapists rotate through, not only to serve as role models, but also as an indicator to both patients and staff of the value of group psychotherapy in the eyes of the senior staff. In situations in which the therapists may come from off the unit, it is best if at least one of the therapists is unit based. This unit-based therapist will be aware of issues within the milieu that might arise in a muted or distorted way in the group, issues not easily comprehended by an outsider.

In our model, two co-therapists sit in each group therapy circle, and they rotate every two to four months, pairing one experienced co-therapist with one less experienced co-therapist. All staff members, including students, are assigned to teams, and all team members on duty are expected to attend group meetings in the role of silent observers. Thus, each patient's primary therapist, social worker, one-to-one nursing staff member, medical student, and other team staff members are present at all group meetings in the capacity of co-therapist or silent observer. The observers sit together adjacent to the group and in full view of the patients. They are instructed to remain silent, even if addressed by a patient. The group co-therapists routinely explain to new patients that the observers do not participate. If a patient addresses an observer directly, the co-therapists direct the patient's attention to the group members. At times, such an intervention may take the form of encouraging group members to discuss their concerns about the observers; at other times, an interpretation of the wish of certain group members to avoid dealing with each other may be rendered. One observer is designated to record process notes of the group. After a group meeting, each team (staff only) meets for a team meeting. A brief discussion of the group (a five- to ten-minute rehash) is held, focusing on each patient's pathology and progress more than on group process per se. At a later time, once a week, the co-therapists and the recorder meet with a senior faculty member for formal group therapy supervision, reviewing the process notes.

Content Factors

The classical instruction in psychoanalysis, involving "talking about everything that is on your mind," is *not* an appropriate instruction for brief inpatient group psychotherapy. We suggest that a modified agenda with a prescribed focus be used with the groups. Patients are advised that appropriate tasks for such groups to focus on are: problems that brought them into the hospital, problems that develop during the hospitalization, and problems that they will have or anticipate having upon leaving the hospital. Technically, this is not a simple here-and-now approach. It includes events that have happened recently (e.g., weekend incidents on the unit) and future events (e.g., what it will be like to talk to co-workers after having been out ill). Specifically excluded are discussions of events from the distant past or projections far into the future; pursuit of such topics is considered to be an avoidance of an issue. Fantasies are appropriate if they seem to illuminate an area delineated above. On the other hand, dreams rarely would be explored.

Procedure Factors

We have found that, for a group psychotherapy session, the following agenda works well: attendance, new members, imminent discharges, and critical incidents since the last group. Group therapy sessions should begin with an accounting of the members. The absence of a group member can be a centrally important issue; if avoided, especially if the group member's psychiatric state is deteriorating, patients' fears about what is causing the deterioration, whether the doctors know what they are doing, and so forth, can be fueled. The absence of a co-therapist can also be traumatic; unless the issue is raised, it may not be discussed. New members are oriented to the group, including the site, time, duration, and proper content of group sessions. The new member is then inducted into the group with the request to briefly tell the group what led to his hospitalization. One would expect a partial, but comprehensible explanation from a patient at this point. Here, the group learns to put psychiatric stories together; they learn about patients' problems and how they develop. Patients who reveal every detail about themselves without demonstrating any discretion usually have a guarded prognosis, as do patients who refuse to talk at all. Patients who are soon to be discharged are asked to speak next. The invitation is, "Say something about what your hospitalization has been like and what your future plans are." If feelings about leaving the hospital do not arise spontaneously in the discussion, they are specifically explored. As a third agenda item, if there have been any special incidents—fights, suicide attempts, elopements—since the last group, these are brought up for discussion by the therapists or by the patients. Sometimes patients seem too frightened to raise an issue for discussion; the therapists must be the ones to raise it. Regardless of who raises the issue, the discussion should begin with a recitation of the facts as they are known to the patients and then the staff. Distortions that characteristically occur can be delineated and corrected. The feelings and concerns of the patients can then be fruitfully explored.

Process Factors

As in many forms of group psychotherapy, it will be appropriate at times to focus on the group itself and on group issues. A typical first-level intervention might be to the group as a whole. If the therapist is regularly going to address interventions to individuals, why do this in a group? When possible, issues and questions should be reflected back to the group members for their consideration and exploration. Nevertheless, the group therapists are responsible for insuring the decorum of the group members. Sometimes the therapists must act like control rods in a nuclear reactor, titrating the amount of affect that the group can deal with. Group therapists cannot permit members to threaten one another or to do violence. Since the groups are short-term, the therapists must help provide the continuity of the culture of the group and insure the safety of the members. Not infrequently, groups can collectively lose their grasp of reality and their common sense. Often this will appear in the form of group members not seeing the incoherence of a patient's statement, or their suspension of common sense upon hearing an implausible story. Here, the therapists must maintain the group's allegiance to reality and confront the defensive avoidance of the craziness of the story. Sometimes it merely means that the therapist will have to state that he has found it impossible to follow the new patient's story. At other times, the therapist may have to define certain behaviors as threatening or frightening. Having received permission to identify an external event as frightening, patients often feel unburdened, having previously been unable to distinguish between their own irrational fears and a rational one. The dynamic focus regarding process issues is typically on a single session as opposed to sequences of sessions. The continuity between group sessions may be weak; too much goes on during the day among patients to expect the group to be central. The admission of an acutely agitated patient who attends the next group may have a more profound effect on the group process than any intervention within the group.

Interpretation

Interpretation is widely regarded as the essential tool of the psychoanalytically oriented psychotherapist. There is a certain glamour and excitement about embarking on the task of releasing repressed material and bringing to consciousness that which is unconscious. However, with many inpatients the problematic material is already in consciousness, only it is split off and is intermittently denied. We agree with Katz (1983), who advises against techniques such as interpretation of metaphors in psychiatric hospital groups. Rather than focusing on unconscious fears and wishes, the group therapist will need to utilize clarification and confrontation, a type of work that often has less appeal to beginning therapists. Clarifications and confrontations will need to be made repeatedly and from many different vantage points, sometimes to the group as a whole and sometimes to the group regarding one of its members. Often, following repeated clarifications and confrontations, group members will develop more realistic views of themselves and of each other, a product of bringing together split-off fragments of senses of self and others (see Chapter 3).

PATIENT–STAFF INTERACTIONS

We view the primary tasks of an acute unit as rapid diagnostic evaluation and rapid symptom reduction for acutely disturbed patients, looking toward early reintegration into the community with after-care support or appropriate placement in extended care facilities, as indicated. A secondary task of such a teaching unit is to maximize the opportunities for residents and students to learn. Since group therapy is a central experience for all patients and staff members, the goal of the group is to help accomplish the unit's goals of patient diagnosis and treatment, and staff training.

Before instituting the present structure, we found that group therapy was experienced by the staff and the patients as a peripheral event, a situation comparable to that reviewed by Johnson and Howenstine (1982). Staff-splitting issues described by Klein (1977) were frequent, so that the group therapists were often disagreeing with other staff members about treatment decisions. In addition, time pressures led to poor communication from the group therapists to the primary therapists regarding the occurrences in group meetings. We have found that, by having all staff members present for all group meetings, communication is effective, and group therapy takes on central importance. In addition, the efficiency of team rounds themselves is greatly enhanced, since team meetings occur just after all staff members have collectively observed the patients whose treatment is being discussed. Patient evaluation and diagnosis are facilitated as well. We urge co-therapists to adopt an educational, psychoanalytically informed, structured approach, sometimes utilizing an object-relations framework, as described in Chapter 3. Encouraging patients to focus on solving the problems—often interpersonal ones—that led to hospitalization seems to minimize transference rivalries and distortions that might occur in longer-term groups or in groups lacking structure or objective tasks (Kernberg 1975a). As a result, we have not encountered significant difficulties when a group co-therapist is also the primary therapist for some of the patients.

Our experience and views correspond with those of Maxmen (1978) in one sense: we think that patients reintegrate more quickly if they are encouraged to participate actively and responsibly in their own treatment. We prefer to attempt to include all patients in our group work, rather than only selected ones; the group functions as a strong organizing and reintegrating influence on the more disturbed patients while they receive concomitant psychopharmacological treatment and other therapies.

Occasionally, an acutely agitated patient is excluded from group meetings by the staff or is allowed to leave the group. Gruber (1978) suggested that large numbers of staff members present at group meetings minimize psychotic dyscontrol. We have experienced a similar effect by having all team members present, yet we think that a high staff-patient ratio, with all staff members actively participating, discourages responsible patient participation. Thus, dividing the staff into co-therapists and silent observers accomplishes both goals. Certain patients, particularly paranoid ones, do indeed demonstrate intense transference reactions to the presence of observers. Such reactions, however, mirror similar mistrustful reactions in other settings, and we find that the presence of all staff members underlines the reality of open communication on all issues. In the long run, we find that such reactions, properly dealt with, facilitate treatment, as described by Bloom and Dobie (1969). In connection with the presence of observers, our overall experience corresponds with that of Burgoyne and colleagues (1978), who pointed out that therapists and observers are more concerned with the potential negative effects of observation than are the patients; we find that new staff members frequently express such concern initially, but they soon feel their concern to be unwarranted.

Although Bailine and co-authors (1977) suggested that a high staff–patient ratio in a group stabilizes the group due to the rapid patient turnover, they did not comment on the disruptiveness of constantly changing staff members. We think that, by having two regular continuous co-therapists over a period of several months, we provide greater stability. Such an arrangement would be even more important for those services with an even shorter length of stay. (Each of our teams has occasional periods with much more rapid turnover, at which times we experience the model to be stabilizing and effective.)

Our structure also allows students on time-limited assignments to this unit, as well as nursing staff members on varying shifts, part-time students and staff members, researchers, and volunteers to attend group meetings when on duty, as silent observers, without disrupting the group by their discontinuity. The educational needs of trainees and interdisciplinary staff members are addressed, since they can learn about group therapy as well as directly witness interpersonal interactions among patients (Pinney et al. 1978, Spensley and Langsley 1977).

We find it advantageous to dissociate formal group process supervision from a more immediate post- or rehash meeting, since we think that different purposes are accomplished by each. The brief rehash focuses on further understanding the interpersonal functioning and pathology of individual patients in a group setting, with a view toward creating, monitoring, and revising each patient's treatment plan. Although some attention to group process occurs in that brief discussion, a later, more detailed supervision of group process allows the co-therapists to concentrate on learning group therapy, theory, and techniques – separate from the immediate pressures of team decisions regarding treatment plans. That supervision is facilitated by the use of group process notes, recorded by one of the silent observers.

Certain technical problems exist in the group therapy structure suggested. Regular challenges confront the co-therapists in working with a rapidly changing group of patients having a wide spectrum of diagnoses. Certain problems are posed by the specific addition of silent observers to the group periphery. Two main difficulties have been encountered, the first being the inhibiting effect of the observers on the co-therapists. Since the group serves as a training experience by design, some of the co-therapists are inexperienced. At times, they have felt considerable inhibition due to a feeling that their early attempts at group therapeutic work are on display. At times, too, they have felt confused by differing views of the group offered by different observers.

A further complexity is posed by the variety of ways the presence of observers affects the group therapy process itself. For example, the patients become acutely aware of the presence or absence – among the observers – of staff members important to them, which may preoccupy patients, without such concerns being clear to the group. In addition, when an acutely disturbed patient on constant observation becomes agitated and leaves in the middle of a group meeting, the nursing staff member among the observers who is assigned to watch that patient also leaves. At such a time, then, that one observer is behaviorally not silent but is an active influence introduced into the group process. Similarly, observers may form a sort of barricade, dissuading patients from acting on impulses to leave. Such an effect is, we think, an asset to the group work, but it introduces complicated hidden influences on the group. Another such example occurs when the rare emergency arises, at which time the observers join in to assist, again with a decided effect on the group. In all those matters, it becomes part of the task of the co-therapists to focus the group's attention on significant effects that the presence, absence, or activity of the observers may be having on the group.

CLINICAL EXAMPLES

A severely character-disordered journalist, hospitalized for alcoholism and depression, soon divided the staff members so that some felt convinced by his articulate pleas that he was better and ready to leave the hospital, and others were concerned that he was a serious suicide risk. The patient dominated the group with angry complaints that he was being unreasonably kept in the hospital, which he felt jeopardized his career. He was confronted by the co-therapists with his denial of his recent job loss, his depression, and his alcoholic dyscontrol. Then the group members, relieved to be less swayed by the intimidating patient, actively discussed his denial and expressed their concern. Between group meetings, the patient continued individually to convince selected staff members and patients that he was being unjustly retained, but only by steady group confrontation did his profound psychotic depression eventually become clear to others, including many team staff members among the observers who had secretly sided with the patient.

A group was saying good-bye to one of its favorite members when a newly admitted psychotic patient commandeered the group time to call out to his individual therapist among the observers. The group co-therapists explained the silence of the observers, encouraging the patient to try to attend to the group focus. Another patient later complained that she did not like being observed, nor did she feel that anything useful could happen in the group, due to the new patient's irrational interruptions. The departing patient then described how helpful the group had been to her when, on admission, she had felt terrified and had been psychotic herself. She added that it was calming and reassuring to her to know that team staff members, including her therapist, were present among the observers.

In the middle of one group a patient who had made a recent suicide attempt suddenly began to exsanguinate, arterial sutures having burst. Observers rushed the patient out, some of them returning soon to report that the patient was safe. The co-therapists, by their uninterrupted presence, helped the group deal with the frightening situation, and the observers became the rescuers. For several weeks thereafter, the observers were silent in word only, due to the impact of their reassuring presence. In fact, the co-therapists became devalued for having "allowed" life-threatening danger to come so close, and the observers were idealized—group processes that the co-therapists helped the group understand and that the observers learned in a vivid, powerful way.

Chapter 6
The Community Meeting

Although serious questions have been raised about the applicability of the therapeutic community approach to modern short-term hospital treatment of acutely disturbed patients, as described in Chapter 1, such inpatient services continue to use and value community meetings. Several studies have been concerned with the most effective techniques for structuring and conducting these meetings. Klein (1977) noted the dearth of literature on the proper technique for running community meetings, and he subsequently addressed some of the issues involved (Klein 1981). Edelson (1970a,b) attempted to provide a model, but his narrow emphasis on the sociotherapeutic aspects restricts its usefulness. Whitely (1975) noted that, in Edelson's model, the introduction of psychotherapeutic materials would be viewed as "detrimental" to the sociotherapeutic process.

Our interest in community meetings was spurred by the difficulties we encountered with them. As others on similar units have observed, we found that a common approach was followed by the leaders running the meetings—a fusion of small-group psychotherapeutic techniques with Tavistock study group methods (Bion 1961). All patients and staff gathered in the same area for a fixed period of time, sitting in a large circle, and issues were discussed as they arose from the group. Except for the fixed duration, location, and designated leader, there was no explicit structure. The leader often intervened in an oracular manner, sharing with the group his understanding of what was going on. These interventions were typically interpretations of the community's resistance to dealing with some issue. Predictable community responses to such interventions were prolonged periods of either silence or chaotic interaction. Either response would be interpreted as proof of the correctness of the interpretation. "Rehashes" or "posts" were similar to the discussions one might hear after open-ended, expressive, small-group therapies, as if the obvious differences in size, composition, and duration would have little or no effect on the way the group phenomena should be understood (Kreeger 1975). Especially with severely regressed patients, an attitude of permissiveness in large groups, combined with heavy reliance on psychodynamic interpretation without concomitant reinforcement of reality testing (Main 1975) frequently leads to "failures" (Pardes et al. 1972, Van Putten 1973). In this respect, we differ with Winer and Lewis (1984) regarding the therapeutic effects of interpretations in community meetings; while we agree that many transference influences are at work in large groups, we view such an interpretive approach as inapplicable to brief hospital work.

In spite of the absence of instructions or training, both patients and staff were expected to know how to participate in the community meetings. Although it is not considered reasonable for a therapist in training to conduct therapy without supervision, we had not heard of supervision being offered for the techniques of running a community meeting; we started to develop our own. A line-by-line, process interpretation of what was said and what might have been said was performed. This procedure helped clarify our understanding of the structure and techniques for running community meetings.

Whereas Van Putten (1973) argues that the difficulty encountered by some patients in community meetings is a result of biological vulnerability, and others ascribe it solely to large-group process (Turquet 1975), we believe that feelings of confusion and distress with resulting dysfunctional behavior can be understood as a product of organizational (systems) forces that affect healthy persons as well as sick ones and are not necessarily solely by-products of large groups. Staff members often reported sharing the feelings of confusion and distress experienced by the patients who were referred to as "failures," although typically staff would "act out" by becoming passive and withdrawn rather than overtly disruptive. We began to realize that the sources of failure might not be the patients but the procedures of the staff. Levinson's concept of role (1959) helped us bridge the gap between our initial observations and a remedy for the situation. The role of the patient in a therapeutic community is complex (Herz et al. 1966). The lack of training and instruction for the leaders and other participants in the community meeting leads to role ambiguity (Kahn et al. 1964), which creates difficulties for the participants. Thus, we revised our approach to the community meeting and developed a different mode of interpersonal interaction for it.

The community meeting can serve as a mechanism for the enculturation of patients, encouraging them to act responsibly and to demonstrate their capacity for effective functioning with fellow patients and staff. Our revised procedures focus on issues of concern to the entire community, providing an opportunity for information transfer between patients and staff. Roles and role relationships are repeatedly clarified. When participating as equals, patients report an increase in self-esteem, and there is a concomitant decrease in regression and antisocial behavior. Behavior implicitly associated with chronic patienthood is discouraged, and reality testing is demonstrated and encouraged.

The results of our revision were greater patient and staff participation, improved quality of communication, and better morale; there were fewer "failures," which is in accordance with the previously cited experimental studies. However, the initial reactions of staff members were complex and included some feelings that the leader was unfeeling or authoritarian. We believe this reaction was a product of organizational regression in which disruption of the usual meeting format results in distorted perceptions of the leader (Kernberg 1978). These distortions were corrected as further supervision provided an opportunity for clarification of the benefits of the structural and technical changes.

STRUCTURAL ASPECTS

The first structural concern is the duration of the meeting. It must be of sufficient length to permit adequate and meaningful discussion of issues, but it cannot last beyond the tolerance of substantially disturbed patients. We have found that approximately 45 minutes provides a reasonable balance. The seating arrangement is the second structural parameter. Seating arrangements can have a powerful impact on the control of antisocial impulses. Since our patient population includes voluntary and involuntary patients, we have found it helpful to organize two-thirds of the seats in auditorium fashion (sociofugal) and the remainder in a semicircle facing these rows (sociopetal) (Lothstein 1978). We expect some patients to harbor vehement antisocial attitudes and to be in poor control of their violent impulses. Therefore, although seats are not assigned, staff members arrange to sit next to disruptive patients. The leader of the meeting sits so that he can be seen by all. With this seating arrangement, we have never had an altercation during or immediately following a meeting.

A third structural parameter is the organization of the meeting. All nurses, therapists, relevant activity–therapy staff, students, and ward administrators are expected to attend the meeting. Other personnel, such as dieticians, may be invited when special issues emerge. The task of the leader, who is responsible for implementing these procedures, is an extremely complex and difficult one; he or she must deal with multiple nonconcentric systems—the patients, the staff, the unit as a whole, the short-term treatment section within which the unit operates, and the hospital at large (Kernberg 1975a).

TECHNICAL ASPECTS

Six techniques in running a community meeting are of special importance. First, at the beginning of the meeting a roll call or attendance is taken, including both patients and staff. The absence of a therapist may have a profound effect on his or her patients. For example, in inclement weather, fantasies that an absent therapist was in an accident are common. These concerns may be alleviated by sharing information about the delay in a staff member's arrival. Staff members take special care to telephone in to notify the community about tardiness. Similarly, the unexplained absence of a patient fuels fantasies of danger and causes fear within the community. After roll call is completed and all patients and staff are accounted for, new members of the community—staff, patients, and visitors—are introduced. New patients are not asked to describe why they are in the hospital; such a request can be humiliating in the presence of a large group.

The second technique is the use of an agenda. It is important that an agenda be created openly so that all members of the community will know what items are to be discussed. Failure to create an open agenda leads to the development of a secret agenda, which has a disorganizing effect on both staff and patients. Too many or too few items on the agenda may give important clues about undercurrents within the community. In this respect, there is often a similarity between interaction of meeting members and the group leader and that of individual patients and their therapists. In individual psychotherapy, flooding the therapist with verbalizations or resorting to prolonged silences may reflect transference issues or may serve as a means of resistance. The agenda can at times provide a clue to similar processes. The leader may recognize the presence of transference phenomena, but he does not interpret them as such. Instead, he may enter as an item on the agenda the fact of too many or too few items. When this topic is later addressed, he may occasionally open the floor for discussion but more often will suggest a possible meaning—excessive silence might be related to a reluctance to discuss an upsetting event that happened the previous night, or a flood of agenda items might reflect a recent influx of new patients who need further orientation to the community. A simple, concrete, plausible, "cause and effect" suggestion helps to focus the discussion and organize the psychotic patients, even if the suggestion is incomplete. In this way, the leader's technique corresponds to an "inexact interpretation" (Glover 1931) in therapy. Outside the meeting, patients may get together with or without staff to select items for the agenda or suggest a preferred sequence of discussion. However, these items are officially placed on the agenda during the open meeting. The leader makes an order of priorities, permitting the inclusion of emergency issues.

A third technical aspect involves the process of information gathering. It is important that there be no reliance on secret information not open to all members of the community. Since the focus of the meeting is on those issues of concern to the entire community, all relevant information should be presented publicly. A grievous and disorganizing error frequently committed by inexperienced community leaders is to begin interpreting a process before collecting sufficient information. Too early an interpretation has many damaging effects, including denigration of the issue at hand (the message is that only underlying and not manifest issues count), the risk of missing the actual underlying issue, an increase in resistance rather than improved insight and understanding, and the inhibition of active, responsible participation by the patients in the discussion. Because the patients may be psychotic or have severe character disorders, it is usually helpful to maintain a concrete focus in discussion, remembering that reality issues must be clarified before proceeding to fantasy. It is surprising that although in psychotherapy therapists are usually careful to clarify before they interpret, in community meetings they often are too quick to interpret. The sociotherapeutic task (Edelson 1970b) is also facilitated by soliciting information from the entire community rather than from specific patients. This task is accomplished by asking what do members of the community see, understand, and feel, rather than asking a specific patient what he thinks. In this way, the meeting maintains its proper focus, and regressive, pathological forces are not augmented.

A fourth technique is to bring an issue to closure before moving on to another topic. If closure is not reached, the more disorganized patients have great difficulty in following the proceedings.

A fifth technique is to focus on separation experiences. Careful attention is paid to patients who are being admitted or discharged. The rationale for this procedure is that the dynamics of separation are especially important for psychotic inpatients and are of primary and central concern.

Sixth, whenever possible, it is important to maintain a supportive beginning and ending to the meeting. To begin sessions with disruptive items does not permit the sicker patients to maintain the cohesive prosocial attitude which they must struggle to rediscover each day. Similarly, if meetings end with a disruptive item, it typically affects the patients' ward behavior immediately following the meeting. Ending with more benign issues permits patients to better understand the process of the meeting and subsequently to maintain prosocial attitudes.

A TYPICAL MEETING

The meeting begins with seats arranged for both patients and staff. The staff usually handles this task, depending on the status of the patients on the ward. The leader of the meeting introduces himself, reviews the structure and function of the meeting, indicates when it will begin and end, and whether smoking is allowed. He explains that an agenda is used and asks community members to raise their hands and wait to be recognized in order to allow business to be conducted in an orderly fashion. After attendance is called and all patients and staff are accounted for, new community members—patients, staff, and visitors—are introduced. An agenda is then prepared. First the leader calls on the patient who is elected president of the patient committee, to report agenda items that have been suggested by other patients or that he wishes to propose. These items are entered on the agenda. The agenda is then opened to the floor for any community member to enter an item.

The first item to be discussed is the patients who are about to be discharged, usually about four or five patients per meeting. Each patient about to be discharged is asked to say something about his or her experience in the hospital and plans for the future. The leader then asks for comments and reactions, soliciting responses from other patients before calling on staff members. The patient's therapist typically makes a summary comment with his good-bye, briefly reviewing the patient's progress during hospitalization, which provides some concrete evidence of improvement. It is useful to select for the first and last patients those who have had positive experiences, in order to maintain a hopeful attitude. Occasionally a patient requesting discharge against medical advice will be discussed and group response solicited. Frequently, other patients who had previously considered leaving against medical advice encourage the patient to stay, discussing their previous ambivalence, its resolution, and their satisfaction with their decision to stay. After the discussion of patients being discharged, the leader moves on to the rest of the agenda, which may include items such as lack of availability of towels, dissatisfaction with snacks, the need for repairs to the stereo, and so forth. Complaints and suggestions are discussed and referred to appropriate agencies within the hospital, and ward policy is clarified. Several issues regularly recur—the use of illicit drugs on the unit, sexual activity between patients, and the behavior of especially disruptive patients. These items are typically raised by either patients or staff in the context of hall tension. The issue of illicit drug usage is usually raised by a staff member; only on the rare occasion when a patient has become flagrantly psychotic and assaultive do patients bring up the subject. The usual process of placing the item on the agenda, collecting information from the community, and achieving closure is followed. Closure includes a reiteration of the hospital policy that forbids the use of illicit drugs and a brief statement about the medical risks of such usage. When it occurs, the impaired functioning of a patient who abuses drugs is noted. However, if there are no obvious rallying points for educating patients about the risks, the issue is handled routinely with minimal attempts to develop it. We have found that without fresh clinical material, a detailed discussion of the subject is not productive.

Our unit does not permit sexual activity between patients – as some hospital units do (Rapoport 1960) – for we have found such activity to be countertherapeutic. The formation of couples on a unit is a concrete example of "pairing" phenomena (Bion 1961); the members of the couple usually are either comfortable on the unit and unengaged in treatment or in the midst of protest. In either situation, their treatment begins to suffer. Also for the many regressed patients who are frightened by sexual urges, frank sexual acting out can be terrifying and further disorganizing.

If a specific patient's behavior is the source of tension or causes concern about safety, it is discussed. If patients do not bring up the problem, and the staff feels that the impact of this behavior has become a community issue, a staff member will enter it on the agenda. The detail in which the staff may describe such a patient depends on their assessment of the amount of information the community needs to know to make sense of the situation. Staff members who have not yet heard about the recent disruptions can act as monitors, judging whether enough information has been shared or if there is significant ambiguity and confusion, requiring a more focused and detailed discussion. Staff also can acknowledge the reasonableness of the patients' fearful responses to threatening behavior. The explicit naming and labeling of issues in itself has a helpful effect on the patient community.

Often the final item on the agenda is the election of members to the patient committee. The patients in consultation with the staff have created a three-person patient committee that serves as an advisory committee to the staff and community. Each patient serves up to three weeks, and one member is elected chairperson. It is important that both staff and patients vote openly for the members of the committee. In addition to its advisory role, the committee supervises the organization of various ad hoc committees for parties, for clean up, and for trips discussed at the community meeting.

CONCLUSION

Although there have been many critiques of community meetings, the literature provides few details on how to run them. The experimental literature has documented the need for structure, but little attention has been paid to what constitutes structure. We have identified specific structural and technical aspects of community meetings, provided full descriptions of them, and presented our rationale for emphasizing them. Rubin (1979) speculated that the critical intervening variable that determined the effect of the community meeting on the patient was the patient's ability to follow the proceedings. Our model can easily be followed by all but the most disturbed patients. Only rarely are patients unable to participate at least passively, and then usually only for one or two days.

We have found that these structural modifications and reliance on the flexible use of the specified techniques permit both patients and staff to feel more comfortable with large-group community meetings and to perform more effectively. These parameters may be tailored to the needs of specific communities and to units with different patient populations. Even our own unit, which receives acutely psychotic and involuntary patients, can loosen the structure if there is a significant shift to healthier patients. We believe that formal training of the staff who run such meetings is an important component in assuring their effectiveness and success, and we disagree with authors, such as Rubin (1979), who deemphasize the need for such training. Orientation of the patients also aids in their participation in the community meeting.

Part III

Specific
Clinical Problems

Chapter 7
Dealing with an Acutely Psychotic Patient

The patient was a 22-year-old single male, hospitalized with the chief complaint, "I need help for an eating disorder." The patient had begun to have difficulties in his teens, characterized at first by social isolation, poor school performance, self-induced vomiting, and significant weight loss. He demonstrated psychosexual confusion, generalized anxiety, and during his last two years of high school he was tutored privately because of persistent refusal to attend school. He was hospitalized on numerous occasions, and during the year prior to his admission to our hospital, he spent several months at a residential rehabilitation facility. He was asked to leave that program because of persistent symptomatic behavior and weight loss. His weight fluctuated between 90 and 100 pounds, and after each of several medical hospitalizations, he immediately lost any weight he had gained. Antipsychotic medications were tried because of the development of paranoid delusional thought content, including thought insertion and thought broadcasting. However, because of noncompliance with medications as an outpatient, he was referred to us for hospitalization. Neither his parents nor his one sibling, a sister, had any history of psychiatric illness, although there was history of depression in the extended family.

On the mental status examination administered on admission, the patient demonstrated inappropriate affect, a thought disorder charac-

terized by tangentiality and circumstantiality, paranoid delusions centering around his father, grandiosity, and auditory hallucinations. He
quickly became mute, withdrawn, disheveled, had postprandial vomiting, and had continued weight loss. Antipsychotic medication was
begun, with dramatic, rapid improvement. His steady improvement included involvement in on- or off-unit activities, involvement in psycho-
and sociotherapy, and weight gain to 110 pounds. As he began to leave
the hospital on passes, however, he demonstrated some regressive return of symptomatology. It was felt that he should be placed on alternate level of care status to await placement at a halfway house, and although this plan somewhat lengthened his hospital stay, it effected a
successful transition to a halfway house and day treatment program.

Therapy Session (early in hospitalization):

T: How are you doing?
P: I'm trying, I'm doing all right. I'm helping others and helping my-
     self.
T: How are you helping others?
P: Do unto others. I'm trying to find myself. Nice guys finish last.
T: Trying to find yourself?
P: What do you think I'm good at doing?
T: We're here to learn more about that. Can you tell me about the
     problems that brought you to the hosptial?
P: [silent, fidgeting, gaze averted]
T: You're having trouble communicating with me?
P: I have two role models, my mother and father. I don't know which
     one to follow.
T: Was that one of the problems that brought you to the hospital?
P: No. It was psychic experiences. Or my eating disorder. You know
     about it? I was uncomfortable at home.
T: Tell me about it.
P: I want to be strong like my father and delicate like my mother.
T: Is that how you see yourself?
P: Yea. Is that funny or what is it?
T: Can you tell me more?
P: I don't know. I experience myself in different ways. I was angry to-
     day. I wanted to go on the trip with the other patients. But it's
     okay. I can cope [sigh].

T: You seem exasperated, bothered, or upset. Like yesterday in group, when you were upset about someone smoking.

P: I'm helping others. It's hard for people.

T: Tell me about your eating disorder.

P: I've always been a picky eater. I feel scared and afraid. I'm worried you won't be content with my eating small amounts.

T: In group, you said your eating was okay. Were you just feeding a line to everybody?

P: No; I'm here to help others. Does that make sense?

T: I'm not clear why you are so concerned whether that makes sense. Can you tell me more about your eating disorder?

P: By not eating, I help others. They need encouragement to eat. I feel in here they're crying to me for help.

T: Could I hear them crying to you for help? Could I hear their voices if they cried to you for help?

P: Sometimes. Not now [sigh].

T: You seem angry.

P: No. You're a nice guy.

T: Why is it hard to keep your thoughts going?

P: It'll help to mature together and grow together.

T: Do you feel you have special powers?

P: No. It's hard, though.

T: How do you influence others?

P: By giving myself.

T: [asked patient some proverbs and serial sevens] Okay, let's stop today.

P: Is it okay to express anger?

T: What did you have in mind? There are good ways and bad ways.

P: Like yelling.

T: We can talk about that some more later; we'll have to stop today.

Comment:

The supervisor pointed out that the therapist seemed to be having trouble listening to some of the patient's efforts to communicate. The patient repeatedly asks if he made sense; it might have been helpful for the therapist to explore the patient's concern about making sense, and his degree of awareness about his psychotic condition and its effect on others. The therapist does attempt to clarify some of the patient's concerns, and when he is confused by the patient, he does not shirk from asking the patient directly about the extent of his psychotic process. This information is extremely important to know, but in this session, the therapist seems to fall back on a thorough mental status examination as a way of introducing his own organizing principle to the confusion. Such a maneuver is usually benign, and if it helps reduce the therapist's anxiety and provides new information, it is an acceptable enough technique. The patient seems to show concern about the therapist's appraisal of him or feelings about him, an aspect of this session not appreciated by the therapist.

Therapy Session

P: How've you been doing? They cancelled my group. How was your weekend?

T: We're here to talk about you!

P: I feel great.

T: People seem pleased with your increased participation in group.

P: I'm glad. My parents will be here tonight. Larry and I had sex in my house. I wonder if his mom found out or not. I won't press him about sex. The pills are better. What's Acutane?

T: Has acne troubled you? Have you seen a dermatologist?

P: Yes. It's uncomfortable. The pores open on the pillow at night. I'd feel better about myself if it cleared up. The meeting with my parents was good. I did feel less angry. I ate with my mother. I used to get sick at the table at home. That sounds gross. I'd want to get rid of it. When I don't eat I think weird thoughts.

T: What causes it?

P: Insufficient nutrition.

T: Then why are you on Prolixin?

P: To control it.

T: What do you think of having an illness?

P: It's scary. And depressing. At age 10 my sister choked. I don't want to be hurt.

T: It's scary?

P: Yes. About not breathing. I don't like big things in my mouth. I'll try anything once. Things are better. If I get bigger than my dad, he might not be my dad any longer.

T: What do you mean?

P: Losing control. It's okay though. He's funny. If my father's okay he won't strike back with his mouth. If I get lost in town, he gets mad.

T: Is there tension between the two of you?

P: [silent]

T: What are you feeling?

P: It's secret. [silent] At least I'm showing him I can be independent. For example, at Franklin Farm. He wants me to be young. I feel happy and scared. It's like he's my mom. If I need something, he'd get it. When I was 16, this sex thing, I was attracted to men. Dad steered me to women.

T: How do you feel about that?

P: My dad hates the homosexual idea. I met a girl in the hospital.

T: How do you like her?

P: She's nice.

T: Are you interested in her sexually?

P: I don't know. I need more self-confidence. I feel closer to guys. I never perform sexually very well. Maybe it's the medications.

T: Are you worried about that?

P: Wouldn't you be worried?

T: Most men would be worried.

P: I am. But I can be close to people, too. I need to be in love. Don't get me wrong. I don't want to rape anybody.

T: Have you had thoughts about that?

P: No. My sister wouldn't bring home dates. My dad would give them dirty looks. She brought a girl home once. Dad said she was too fat. Did you see *Zelig*?

T: Yes.

P: I liked it. I was thinking of you, as the psychiatrist. No, that's crazy . . . you'd have to be Mia Farrow!

T: We'll have to stop now.

Comment:

Several weeks have elapsed since the previous session presented above, and antipsychotic medications have been begun. Yet in this session, the patient's active psychotic process continues to be obvious, particularly shown by thought derailment (loose associations). Still, from several implied subthemes, there seems to be a dominant theme – the patient's preoccupation about his homosexual feelings and experiences, and his fear of reprisal. The patient's homosexual feelings toward his therapist are revealed by his question about a motion picture which portrays a patient falling in love with his psychiatrist. The supervisor pointed out the therapist's obliviousness to these concerns, as well as his countertransference-induced response, which mirrored that of the patient's father, i.e., showing interest in the patient's heterosexuality and sidestepping his homosexual impulses. This session demonstrates how, in spite of an active psychotic process, there can be coherent themes in the material, as well as transference-countertransference issues of importance to both appreciate and address. Since the patient might have begun to respond to the antipsychotic medication, he might have had the capacity to experience relief and to become less disorganized had his therapist been more comfortable with the patient's impulses.

Therapy Session

P: I'm feeling better. The medications are adjusting better. I feel less depressed. A lot of people get sick from their medications. Together, we do well.

T: What do you mean together?

P: You and I – we adjust them well. Do you have a discharge date for me yet?

T: I was thinking about the same thing. What plans are you making?

P: To get a job, live at home.

T: How do you feel about living at home?

P: Pretty good. Oh! Are you writing down everything I say?

T: Does that bother you?

P: It makes me anxious. It's like a test.

T: It is not a test.

P: [visibly more relaxed]

T: Last week, your father was angry when you went home for lunch?

P: You want to hear more? He doesn't want me home until I'm ready. It's between you and me. Things are very structured lately. I've been trying to keep things together, doing a good job.

T: What's it like at home?

P: Things are better. I'm able to eat. Is not eating associated with my illness?

T: Yes. Did you have a question about that?

P: Growing up, I had to listen to my father at meals. I lost my appetite. I danced before meals. I don't want to gain weight and be bigger than my father.

T: You're afraid you would lose his love?

P: It's difficult. I've begun feeling more independent. I got a letter from Janet. Oh, I'm changing the subject.

T: What were you referring to?

P: It's related. My father introduced me to Janet. He was trying to help me make friends. Plus keeping friends. Larry and I get along well. He's cheap.

T: Do you have problems talking about your father?

P: We used to fight a lot. He's mellowed.

T: How do you mean?

P: He used to shake. But it was natural then. Things are better now. Both of my parents have bad backs.

T: Have you thought about leaving home?

P: Yes. My dad would support me. I'd need a roommate. But people are all talk. My cousin, Larry, one of the patients on the unit. My sister doesn't want to room with me. She said I'm not independent enough. Do you think I can work?

T: Yes. But I'm not sure what you could do.

P: They put me right in vocational activities, without any testing. Do you know my discharge date?

T: Your parents will need to be involved in that decision.

P: Why?

T: If you go home, they'll be involved.

P: Oh.

T: How do you feel about Franklin Farm?

P: Bad. I lost weight there. Maybe Crescent Lake. How long have I been here?

T: It's hard to say the exact time. The social worker asked me to get papers to refer you to several places when you leave. We'll have to stop now.

Comment:

After several more weeks of hospitalization, the patient is clearly less psychotic and less anxious. Equally clear is the therapist's decreased anxiety, reflected by his greater responsiveness to the patient. The therapist perceives the importance of the patient's relationship with his father, and he focuses the patient back on it when the patient changes the subject. The supervisor commented on the therapist's greater ease in the session, but noted still the omission of any discussion of the therapist-patient relationship. The patient's opening comment ("together, we do well") was followed quickly by another ("do you have a discharge date for me yet"), which revealed the same continuing dynamic shown more explicitly in the previous session.

Therapy Session

P: I wanted to go home.

T: Have you thought about a halfway house?

P: If it's close by, I'd consider it, but I want to leave. Could I go home on the 1st?

T: There seems to be a lot of turmoil at home between your mother and father and between your father and you; you seem not aware of it.

P: Well, yesterday at dinner, my mother . . . she mentioned that they were considering divorce. Perfect timing! I'm a restraint! I never said it before. I wish they'd stay together. One time I wished my dad would leave and I'd be with my mother. Maybe I'm growing up.

T: What do you mean?

P: They have a lot going for them. At times I wish they would make up – I wouldn't have my dad hogging down on me. It's better though. [silent] I'm mixed up. Sometimes they have fights. My father threw food at my sister.

T: It can be scary at home?

P: No. They show a lot of love and concern.

T: It's scary to be away from home?

P: Yea. There are no activities here. At home I can walk out the door whenever I want. I don't want a halfway house that's locked.

T: They don't lock halfway houses.

P: [looks relieved]

T: I have a sense that you want to go home.
P: It's more comfortable there.
T: You feel you'd be taken care of?
P: Yea. How long do I have to stay here?
T: Probably three or four weeks or more.
P: Why!
T: Well, you had some setbacks last week, and it's necessary to stay long enough to feel steady.
P: It was probably because of the medications.
T: It's not the best idea to leave prematurely. We'll have to stop now.

Comment:

In this session the therapist, responding to the supervisor's ongoing suggestions that he help the patient focus on difficult issues due to the patient's greater anxiety tolerance, confronts the patient with his avoidance of the recent talk of divorce by his parents. The patient is able to discuss it, although he becomes somewhat confused and resorts to denial and a wish to return to an idealized home. The therapist brings him back to reality by pointing out that discharge could not be imminent until further disposition planning has occurred.

Therapy Session
P: I went bowling. I got 105 and 65.
T: Have you had problems with stiffness?
P: No, no problems. I'm glad I took my medicine in the morning. The Cogentin helps. Things are going very well with the meds. I'm happy with the way things are.
T: Your mother seemed concerned. She thinks the medications are causing you to shake.
P: Well, that's true to an extent. There's only so much Cogentin I can take. I'm happy with the way things are. At first, with the meds, I'd shake; I couldn't cut my meat; other patients had to do it for me. That was aggravating. But now it's no problem. Is it too soon to request discharge group?
T: No.
P: I asked for vocational testing. My parents are interested, and so am I. But *I* did it! Is that okay?

T: Sure.

P: I was hoping they would answer some questions about myself.

T: Such as?

P: What I am talented in. What jobs I should do. I dropped woodshop. They had me doing sanding, cutting. It's not like stained glass.

T: In what way?

P: Those activities . . . . there's a lot of pressure.

T: Are you feeling anxious now with me?

P: A little bit. Not really.

T: I can see that your leg is shaking.

P: Yea. Everyone has his *shtick*. I call it my Prolixin kick.

T: Are you nervous around others?

P: Only when I can't feel I can speak my mind.

T: What do you mean?

P: I don't want to feel angry. I guess you know my mom was in a car accident and had a minor concussion. She was unable to visit Wednesday night. I phoned last night. I was upset that they didn't visit. She said I was not considerate enough. I said my sister could take the bike to work, and dad could come here in the car.

T: Maybe you *do* deserve special treatment.

P: There were some times I felt that way in the hospital. My parents give me money. I have to be careful not to run out. I need money for food. They know I eat like a bird.

T: Do you feel you weigh too much?

P: No. I'm happy with my weight. I bought an anorexia book. Or rather my mother did. I haven't read it yet. I'm afraid.

T: What concerns you?

P: I'm thinking my symptoms may return.

T: What do you think?

P: I don't really know if I had anorexia.

T: What do you think your eating disorder refers to?

P: Depression. Or anxiety. I'd drink Pepto Bismol to lose weight. They asked me to leave Franklin Farm. The doctor there gave me Xanax. I was only supposed to have 3 mg. He gave me whatever I wanted up to 6 mg.

T: Why?

P: I don't know. At home I'd be hungry and not eat. I'd drink Pepto Bismol.

T: What did you think would happen if you didn't eat?

P: I came in the hospital. I always had a good time in the hospital. I'd meet nurses, friends.

T: All your friends are associated with sickness. What about that?

P: Yea! What about that! Larry. Two friends. All my friends! Franklin Farm was a good experience. I'd like to visit. It was too religious. I broke tradition there and went to the movies on Sunday. I was the first one. Then I left and went home and got sick. Maybe you're right. Maybe I shouldn't go home. Maybe I should go to a halfway house.

T: I think you're too comfortable at home. You don't have to do anything for yourself.

P: No. Since my mother works I do more.

T: Maybe I'm wrong.

P: Actually I'm in here because I'm *not* comfortable at home.

T: Perhaps you're scared of the halfway house.

P: A little. But I have to try. Don't you think so?

T: That's logical. We'll have to stop today.

Comment:

Here, the therapist seems to show some trouble implementing the suggestions received in supervision, possibly reflecting a misunderstanding in the supervisory process. In his efforts to encourage the therapist to help the patient confront difficult issues, including that of the patient's relationship with the therapist, the supervisor may have given insufficient attention to the need to provide positive support and ego-strengthening feedback, particularly to a schizophrenic patient in the reconstituting process. Hence, the patient's repeated attempts to emphasize his accomplishments are undermined by the therapist's insistence on focusing on the patient's anxieties and medication side effects. Somewhat abruptly, at one point, the therapist asks about anxiety "now with me," but leaves the topic equally quickly. Although the patient seems to try to comply with the apparent wish of the therapist to focus on pathology (e.g., "I'm thinking my symptoms may return"), as so often happens, he persists in setting the therapist straight! Hence the patient's insistence on the good aspects of hospital—friends, Franklin Farm—and his almost gentle concluding point that, yes, he was "a little" scared of the halfway house, but "I have to try. Don't you think so?"

Therapy Session

P: I had two appointments on Wednesday and Thursday. I finished vocational testing.

T: How did it go?

P: Interesting. Though I have difficulties with mechanical and spatial skills. Will I be out of here soon?

T: Things are going that way. A lot depends on the interviews. Tell me about the vocational testing.

P: I couldn't wait to finish.

T: I'm surprised.

P: No, I just wanted the results. It's not graded yet.

T: How did you feel about them?

P: Some things were difficult. Especially the mechanical things. I guess I'm not as smart as I thought.

T: How does it feel to realize that?

P: [no response]

T: You seem tired.

P: It was a busy weekend. I had lunch with my parents. Did you say I can request discharge group?

T: Yes.

P: What if I go home, and then go to these places later?

T: We can talk about that later. Have you thought about leaving the hospital, what it will be like?

P: It will be productive.

T: Have you thought about not having any more sessions with me?

P: [silent]

T: It doesn't seem you've thought about that yet. What about other things?

P: Well, I want to stay busy. Get a job. I'd buy clothes. No, a car. I tried to get my license five times and was turned down. I was on medications.

T: That must have been frustrating.

P: It's better now. I feel more like myself.

T: Good.

P: I'm not hallucinating. I'm thinking clearly. Though I seem to have less of a sense of humor. Is that related to the medicines?

T: How do you feel?

P: I'm not sure. Will I have to wait long for a halfway house?

T: I'm not sure. You'll have to ask them.

P: I feel better now. It took long enough.

T: Has it been difficult?

P: Yes. People tell me I'm still stiff. I don't know.

T: It's your body, you know best, and it sounds like you feel comfortable the way you are.

P: Except for the sexual frustration. I have no desire.

T: Tell me about that.

P: It's related to the medications. They could be lowered.

T: Do you get erections?

P: Yes.

T: Do you masturbate?

P: Yes. But not a lot.

T: You know not all men masturbate.

P: I want an active sex life. I'm not able to come. I feel like I have to urinate. I want it to get pleasurable. Do you think vitamins will help?

T: I still don't understand the problem. Do you get erections in the morning?

P: Sometimes, yes.

T: That's normal.

P: But it's not pleasurable. I need advice. I have fantasies.

T: Can you tell me about them?

P: They're private.

T: Perhaps they're tough to talk about. I want you to know that you can talk about them here. You can when we have more time, at greater length. We have to stop for today.

Comment:

In this session, the therapist is clearly attempting to respond to the supervisor's emphasis on trying to strike the right balance—not to overlook the patient's need for reassurance and support, yet not to sidestep anxiety-laden areas if they arise in the material of the session. Still, the therapist's success in this task is uneven. He responds sensitively to the patient's needs for support about his vocational potential, yet instead of asking what made the patient conclude from the tests that he was "not as smart" as he thought, the therapist, attempting to elicit the patient's affect, assumes that the patient's conclusion is correct. Later, when the patient introduces his concern about his sexual functioning, the therapist encourages him to discuss the problem but, attempting to reassure the patient by saying that "not all men masturbate," the therapist overlooks the patient's wish for active, potent sexuality. The therapist, responsively, later invites the patient to discuss his "private" sexual fantasies; however, the session was completed at the time. The supervisor agreed that, whereas under other circumstances one might extend the session a bit to allow time for a difficult area, the therapist rightly postponed this discussion since the patient had not brought it up at all until the very end of the session.

Therapy Session
P: [ten minutes late] Oh, you have a cake! [brief friendly discussion about it] Do you know when I will have an interview at the other halfway house?
T: I don't know.
P: How long will it be until I leave?
T: I don't know; have you thought about leaving?
P: No. What do you recommend?
T: Have you thought about not meeting with me any more?
P: Well, I could see Dr. Richards, my doctor before I came in.
T: How would you feel about that?
P: He's been calling, and writing to my family.
T: He seems concerned. I've tried to call and let him know how you're doing. Do you mind?
P: No. I can't wait to leave.
T: Does not having a definite date bother you?
P: Yes it does.
T: You like things to be neat and organized.
P: Yea.
T: People in the group this morning said they were bored.

P: I'm bored. We should have more board games.

T: I wonder if you find our sessions boring. How do you feel about our time?

P: It's not boring; I have time to talk about things.

T: What do you see as the purpose?

P: A chance to see how things are developing.

T: Are there things we don't talk about that you feel we should? I'd like you to feel comfortable talking of private things.

P: I'm comfortable.

T: We missed a couple of sessions. I wonder if it's related to difficulties talking about things.

P: No! Another patient was discharged. Oh, I got a call from Rachel. She wanted to meet me to have lunch.

T: Do you think that's a good idea? Often we discourage people from meeting outside the hospital. Sometimes people get sick again. If you're close to people, it can have a big effect if they get sick again.

P: I don't like to think about getting sick again. I want to be out of here soon.

T: Did you set up a meeting with Rachel?

P: No. We get along well.

T: You get along well with most people?

P: Yea. I want to get out of here. How come others get discharge dates but not I?

T: People are different; you're doing some things. We'll have to stop now.

Comment:

This session demonstrates that the therapist had achieved a significant level of comfort with the patient and with the need to discuss the patient–therapist relationship. The warmth felt by both patient and therapist toward each other comes through, and the therapist's responsivity to the patient's leads is also clear. The supervisor felt no need to advise alternate strategies for this session.

Therapy Session

T: How did you feel about the other patient eloping?

P: The group members were concerned. I want a part-time job. Maybe at the shopping mall.

T: Tell me about that.

P: I don't know about now.

T: What do you mean?

P: There's a booth there – they're recruiting for Christmas.

T: What kind of job were you thinking of?

P: I don't know.

T: You know, it might be a lot to handle right after leaving the hospital.

P: It might.

T: In my experience, it can be a problem right after leaving the hospital.

P: Just because you apply, you're not necessarily going to do it. I want to get a driver's permit.

T: How do you feel about leaving?

P: I've got a lot of support. I'll miss people. I want to get my own apartment. I talked to my friend Donald. He wants to get an apartment in the Village. How long is the day hospital program?

T: About three to four months.

P: OK, I'd like a job after that.

T: That would be more reasonable than right after you leave here. Does it make you feel bad to wait?

P: A little. I won't have any money for Christmas! [laugh] I'd like to see *Cats* but it costs a lot of money. The only tickets available were on Christmas Eve. I tried to get tickets to *Dream Girls*. Oh . . . I want to get back to talking about a job.

T: You seem rarin' to go! Have you thought any more about not meeting with me?

P: Will I be able to see you?

T: No, it doesn't seem so.

P: You don't normally see people after they leave the unit. How long have you been working on this unit? Well, I'll have therapy at the day hospital, and I like Dr. Richards. I would like to see him. He is concerned. But I'll have to take a bus.

T: How do you feel about not seeing me any more?

P: I'll have to adjust.

T: Do you fear what it'll be like?

P: I'll have to adjust. How long will I have to be on the medicine?

T: At least a year.
P: They gave us a sheet, in medication group.
T: It'd be good to bring it in. Not to get off the track, though. I have strong feelings about not seeing you any more. We've had a relationship now for more than three months.
P: Four months.
T: It will not be easy not seeing you any more.
P: [laugh] You're a nice guy and a good doc! I have those feelings, too. It'll take time. It's been a productive four months. I don't have any hallucinations any more. Nor those eating problems any more. I guess the eating problems were related to the hallucinations.
T: Probably both were related to the schizophrenia.
P: Is that right? Karen is going soon. I miss Rachel.
T: How is it, missing people?
P: Tough . . . What else? . . . Well, I guess I've told you my life's story! (laugh)
T: Right on schedule — we're out of time, and you finished your life's story! [laugh]

Comment:

In this final session of this series, the warmth and friendliness mutually felt between patient and therapist continue to be apparent. The therapist presses the patient to talk about their separation. The supervisor felt that, although perhaps the therapist put it a little strongly, the therapist's expression of his own sadness at the prospective loss of the patient was appropriate in this type of therapy with this type of patient.

Chapter 8

Issues in the Treatment of Schizophrenic Patients

CONFRONTING THE PATIENT ABOUT HER ILLNESS

The patient was a 31-year-old single unemployed woman, admitted voluntarily, although her chief complaint was "My doctor thought I had to be here." She had a history of poor functioning for nine years, characterized by frequent fights with her parents, sporadic and poor occupational functioning, bulimia, and alcoholic binges. Her earlier experimentation with amphetamines had given way to only alcohol abuse, but she developed an obsession with her weight, leading to wide fluctuations in her weight (e.g., a 30-pound weight loss). She denied a history of prolonged major depression or mania but periodically did report auditory hallucinations. Her family, particularly her locally well-known father, had colluded with her to deny the presence of a worsening psychotic illness, contributing to repeated noncompliance with treatment.

On admission she was inappropriate in appearance, seductive, and emotionally labile, shifting rapidly between cooperativeness and hostility. She was circumstantial and fluctuatingly incoherent, and she had delusional thought content. Soon after admission, she admitted to having auditory hallucinations of male voices telling her to feed them with her breasts. She was begun on antipsychotic medication, with rapid improvement characterized by disappearance of the hallucinations and by consistently increased participation in activities and therapy. Her bulimic symptoms and weight loss persisted longer, but they too abated with further treatment. Psychotherapy was linked closely to family therapy, with a concerted effort to help the entire family deal with the reality of the patient's illness. By the time of her discharge to a day hospital treatment program, she had maintained gains in being able to acknowledge her illness to herself, and the family seemed more realistic about helping her aim for more modest life goals consistent with both her abilities and her illness.

Therapy Session

P: I never liked you!

T: I wonder if what is upsetting you is my telling you that you have a psychiatric illness?

P: Yes! Don't you have problems? Don't you need medications?

T: We're not here to discuss me. You have an illness we call schizophrenia. We have a treatment for it which we can offer, consisting of drugs and supportive therapy.

P: It's not nice to tell someone that!

T: I'm trying to be honest and respect you.

P: Thanks! I don't want to talk!

T: That's up to you.

P: I'm returning to the unit. [left]

Comment:

In a prior family session, the therapist had confronted the patient in the presence of the entire family about the reality of and the nature of the patient's schizophrenic illness. In the brief session above, the therapist immediately assumes that the patient's anger relates to the therapist's head-on confrontation of a long-cherished collusive denial in the family about the patient's illness. The patient's response seems to demonstrate the correctness of the therapist's assumption, and the therapist attempts to calmly persist in facing the reality of the patient's illness and the treatment recommendations which follow.

Therapy Session

T: How was your weekend?

P: I had a nightmare. There was a psychiatrist in it, Dr. Korngold. He was telling me his problems. His mother was standing behind him. It was upsetting. I talked to my father. He interpreted it as my own fear of dependence.

T: What was it about it that was scary?

P: I don't know. I'm just going crazy. I've been worried ever since you told me I was schizophrenic.

T: What does schizophrenia mean to you?

P: It means off the deep end.

T: Do you think that applies to you?

P: I'm not out of touch with reality.

T: Psychiatrists don't use the word "crazy." Do you have any other ideas about what schizophrenia means?

P: Having hallucinations and being scared of things that aren't there.

T: Does that therefore mean crazy?

P: No. What caused the voices?

T: We don't exactly know the cause. There is a biological, biochemical component, but I wouldn't use the term "crazy." Also, schizophrenia is associated with difficulties in social and occupational functioning.

P: I feel uptight every time you mention it. I just lack goals. I have changed jobs a lot. If I talk about it, it just makes it worse.

T: It'll be important for you to work on these things at the day hospital.

P: I'm glad to be going to the day hospital. It'll help me avoid some of the problems I have at home.

T: How did the visit with your parents go?

P: No problem. I feel uptight, though. I fear what my mother and father and brothers and sisters think. I don't want to look too anxious. I took a couple of drinks. My father yelled at me.

T: There are reasons not to drink. There are sometimes problems of interactions with drugs, and of course the problem of addiction.

Comment:

By this time, several weeks later, the patient is nearing discharge, to be in day hospital treatment. Whereas previously the patient's defense of projection, in her psychotic state, had led to accusing her psychiatrist of needing medication, by this time these feelings appear in

dream material. Again the patient reprimands her therapist for in-
sisting that she face the truth, but this time she does not deny it so much
as protest discussing it. Again, the therapist calmly indicates his view of
the importance of talking directly about the illness and its origins and
manifestations.

Therapy Session
T: You said earlier you had good and bad feelings about the hospital?
P: I've learned to talk about feelings. About anger. Sometimes I can't
     talk to people. When they don't show affection.
T: What are your feelings about seeing a new therapist?
P: It'll be a new adventure. I've learned things. Also, sometimes I
     couldn't talk to you. You didn't show affection.
T: Do you expect that from your psychiatrist?
P: Yes. Or I don't want to talk.
T: Do you think it's more appropriate to get affection from profession-
     als or from friends?
P: My friend left the unit. I'm lonely. I fear people might hurt me.

Comment:
     In this excerpt from a session close to the patient's discharge, the
patient demonstrates her ability to benefit from talking about feelings.
She shows an infantile need for unqualified love and affection from
others, along with continuing primitive defenses and fears. Yet she
seems to have achieved a fairly good equilibrium, and she admits that
she has learned things from her therapist, this time without the protest
about being educated, but instead objecting that her therapist is not af-
fectionate enough. Although such a wish reflects her continuing illness,
it occurs at a time when she is about to lose her therapist and hence is
not entirely inappropriate.

DEALING WITH SEPARATION ISSUES

The patient was a 23-year-old single man admitted involuntarily for his
first psychiatric hospitalization, after a long history of social isolation,
deteriorating functioning, and recent bizarre and threatening behavior.

Although his chief complaint was "My mother keeps me awake," the patient had been becoming increasingly agitated, sleeping and eating little, and pacing his parents' bedroom at night, frequently opening his mother's eyes while she slept. The admission followed an episode of behavior during which the patient chased his mother around the house and threw heavy objects at her. The family history was positive for depression, alcoholism, and suicide, but the patient had no history of alcohol or substance abuse or of previous major depression. Noteworthy on admission mental status were the patient's inappropriate affect, guardedness and suspiciousness, and questionably delusional thought content. After admission, the patient became increasingly anxious and withdrawn, refusing to eat, and he revealed frankly delusional thinking. Treatment with neuroleptics led to marked improvement, along with an ability to enagage productively in psychotherapy.

Therapy Session
T: Let's talk about your relationship with your parents.
P: Okay.
T: Do you have trouble communicating? Difficulties with your mother?
P: She's too idealistic. We have poor communication. She's been bugging me. Comparing me with others. Wanting me to be successful.
T: Comparing you with whom?
P: Everybody.
T: Your brother and sister?
P: Yes.
T: Anyone else?
P: Well, no. Well, with friends. She says I should have a job. I should be a lawyer, doctor, dentist. Now she's starting to realize I'm too bad off.
T: What do you mean?
P: Not to bug me.
T: I'm confused.
P: It sounds crazy, but that's the way she is.
T: How do you deal with it?
P: I'd ignore it.

T: Did it make any change?

P: It was building up.

T: And your father?

P: He watches TV. He says education is everything. He has a one-track mind. We have no communication. My mother pesters me to get a job, leave the house, be happy.

T: How does that make you feel?

P: My father doesn't push me to leave.

T: Do you want to?

P: Yes. But I have no job. It's confusing. We're all like empty shells.

T: Do you communicate with anybody? Your brother or sister?

P: No. Yes. Maybe my brother. He went to California, and he didn't talk to my parents any more. I'm confused. Can we have family therapy?

T: Yes. What would their reaction be like?

P: Good. They disagree though. My father says this, my mother says that. There's no communication.

Comment:

The patient in this session demonstrates a thought disorder, yet he is able to follow the therapist's relatively structured, directive technique. The therapist focuses the patient at once on an area that he judges to be of central importance, but that does not threaten the patient inordinately. Although the patient's difficulties in communicating clearly soon become apparent in the confusing communication with the therapist in the session, the therapist chooses not to direct the patient's attention to that interaction. Instead, when the material gets hard to follow, he shifts the patient's focus from his mother to his father, and later to his siblings.

Therapy Session

T: How are you doing?

P: I have this drug problem.

T: That's important but may lead us to avoid other issues.

P: Yes, yes, but the drugs . . . .

T: Do you see what I mean?

P: Yes. Where shall we start?

T: Where would you like?

P: Communication problems with my parents!

T: I understand you learned that your mother had had a call from your brother.

P: I think I remember.

T: How do you feel about it?

P: What do you mean?

T: I wonder if you thought your mother wanted you to leave – if the conversation implied that to you.

P: Well, she didn't. Well, she wants me to leave when I'm a doctor.

T: Last week you said she was pushing you around at home.

P: Did I say that? Well, yes, she says once I'm a doctor. She gives signals.

T: Do you never discuss leaving home?

P: No. Communication is like telepathy.

T: How do you know it's right.

P: I don't. Communication is a problem.

T: Do you think people can read minds?

P: Yes. Telepathy. Some though, not others.

T: Perhaps that leads to a fear of me, yet to help I have to know what you're thinking.

P: Right. For example, my mom has lung cancer. She smokes. I know she has it.

T: Did you tell her?

P: Yes. She knows.

T: Were you specific?

P: Not really. I asked her about her cough. She knows what I mean.

T: You're concerned about your mother.

P: Yes.

T: Are there other thoughts you're scared to let her know?

P: I'm afraid to let you know them. I'm afraid you'll keep me here. They're about violence. When I was younger I used to be violent. My thoughts are not violent now.

T: How do you feel about leaving home?

P: When I have a girlfriend to replace my mom and dad.

T: You remember that I'll be leaving the unit at the end of the month. How do you feel about that?

P: It's upsetting. We get to know each other, working together and meeting together and talking together, then you have to leave.

T: It's understandable if you are angry.

P: I'm not angry.

T: It'd be okay if you were.

P: Well I'll be nervous to talk to a new doctor.

T: We'll be communicating a lot of information to the new doctor, so that it doesn't need to be starting from scratch.

P: Yea. I could have a new doctor every day!

T: We have to stop today.

P: These sessions are short.

Comment:

The patient wishes to focus on issues relating to medications, which the therapist does not allow. (The patient had previously told the therapist of this problem, and the therapist felt it had been sufficiently dealt with.) After the therapist's firm insistence, the patient resumes discussing the problem focused on in the previous session. The therapist then introduces a related piece of information, knowing that the patient had overheard a conversation between his mother and brother in which the brother was urging the mother to extrude the patient from the home. The patient becomes defensive, and he reveals psychotic thinking leading to delusional thought content about his mother, material demonstrating his profound ambivalence toward her. The therapist chooses not to confront the patient with or to interpret this material, but to continue to encourage him to talk about it. However, when the therapist's encouragement helps the patient reveal his thoughts of violence, the therapist, unaware, shifts the focus back to earlier material. He then asks the patient to discuss his feelings about the therapist's imminent departure from the unit, attempting to get the patient to reveal angry feelings, following which the therapist reassures the patient that he will certainly communicate effectively with the new doctor. Here is an example of the therapist's unconscious at work, as his supervisor pointed out. Whereas the patient *was* aware of violent fantasies toward others, which the therapist was unable to hear about, the patient was *not* aware of angry feelings about the therapist's departure. Since there can be a range of all kinds of feelings about separation, the therapist may have focused on anger alone due to the patient's previous reference to violence. The introduction of the separation issue toward the end of the session was awkward, perhaps contributing to the patient's perception that "these sessions are short."

Therapy Session

T: How are you doing?

P: My knee is killing me.

T: What is it?

P: Arthritis. I feel despair. I wish I were home.

T: You look sad.

P: I'm losing strength in my hands.

T: What's causing that?

P: I don't know. I'm scared I'll have arthritis in my knee for the rest of my life.

T: Anything else?

P: I'm angry at my parents for bringing me here. Things could have been solved at home.

T: It sounds like you don't like it here. Were you feeling happier earlier?

P: The lights bother me when they make their sleep checks. I don't know. My knee is hurting. What can we do about it?

T: I'll give you some aspirin, and we'll get a consultation about it. I wonder if your knee, like the medications before, serves to avoid talking about other things. Like the sad feelings. Maybe the feelings about my rotation to the other service.

P: I don't care. As long as I have somebody here.

T: The last session you said was too short.

P: No. I just wondered about it.

T: Are you aware of other feelings?

P: Yes. I'll have to tell my story all over to someone. But they'll know everything after a while.

T: Any other feelings? Angry ones?

P: No.

T: Are you scared to tell me?

P: No. Do you mean I want to kill you? Just kidding. I'll tell you what I
    feel. You should be able to know what I'm thinking. I guess this
    isn't the place to be at Christmas. I should be at home with friends
    and family. I felt sad before Carol [another patient] left. That was
    sad.
T: How did you feel about the pass?
P: I didn't want to have to come back. I wish they hadn't sent me. My
    knee hurts. I don't need to be here anyway.

Comment:

In this session the patient demonstrates less of a psychotic thought
process, uses somatization defenses, and is much more aware of depression. The therapist receptively listens to the patient's feelings, but again
suggests the defensive use of that material. Here, he raises the issue of
his leaving early enough in the session to allow time to discuss it, and the
patient this time stuck with it long enough to acknowledge its importance, admit fleetingly, by a joke, his anger, and make the link to other
sad feelings related to his family and the holiday season.

Therapy Session
T: How are you doing?
P: Scared of the new guy on the unit. He marked up the pool table. He
    could hurt me.
T: I understand your fear. We'll not allow you to get hurt. Let the
    staff know if you're frightened.
P: You do your job. But . . . .
T: Let the staff know.
P: Good.
T: How did your visit go with your parents?
P: Okay. Not much to say.
T: Any thoughts about a Christmas pass?
P: Pro – I'd be with my family. Con – it would feel bad to come back.
T: Do you have mixed feelings about going home?
P: Yes. After the holiday. You get the blues. Society tells you it's a
    family time, but there's a letdown.
T: Would you be more comfortable staying here?
P: I would. Would it affect my discharge plans?
T: No.

P: Maybe a pass at a different time from the holidays.
T: Yes. The holidays can be a difficult time.
P: Yea. It can be sad.
T: Plus being sad about my leaving.
P: I have fears about a new therapist. But it won't affect me that much.

Comment:

The therapist had kept in mind the patient's mixed feelings about the holidays, which he had mentioned in the previous session. In addition, between the two sessions, the patient had requested a higher status and a pass, both of which were not approved. The patient was initially quite angry at his therapist about his refusal, but later appeared happy, telling his therapist he was pleased about "how well we communicated." In this session, the therapist asks the patient about a pass for the holidays, and he supports the patient's wish to remain in the hospital. He then nicely links the patient's sadness about the holidays with his sadness about losing him, which, having been previously discussed, is now appropriate to introduce even at the end of the session.

DEALING WITH A POTENTIALLY DANGEROUS PATIENT

The patient was a 21-year-old single unemployed man who was admitted voluntarily after being given a choice by a judge of further hospitalization or of sentencing for having stabbed his stepfather. He had been apparently well until two years prior to admission, when he moved far away from his parents at a time when they were experiencing marital difficulties. He was fired from his menial job after becoming obsessed with one of the females at work, following which he developed delusions that the Mafia and FBI were trying to turn him into a homosexual prostitute. He became convinced that his biological father and his stepfather were gay and were trying to seduce him, and he began to experience hallucinations, thought broadcasting, and thought insertion. He decided to kill his stepfather and then himself; he stabbed but did not succeed in killing his stepfather while the stepfather, concerned about the patient's mental state, was driving him to a psychiatrist's office. Taken into custody, the patient cut his wrists several times and tried to hang himself while in legal retention. He had three months of psychiatric hospitalization in a chronic care facility, where he received pharmacotherapy, with considerable improvement in his condition. He was deemed capable to appear before the judge, who recommended the more intensive course of hospital treatment.

On admission the patient was anxious, with restricted affect, but he was entirely coherent and denied delusions, hallucinations, suicidal or homicidal ideation. His diagnosis was thought to be schizophrenia, paranoid type, in partial remission. His hospital course did not include any further suicidal or homicidal behavior, although he demonstrated anxiety and concern about the continuing difficulties between his mother and stepfather. After discharge, he was referred for day hospital treatment and for outpatient psychotherapy and continued pharmacotherapy.

Therapy Session

T: How are you doing?

P: Fine.

T: Tell me about your family.

P: I don't like how my stepfather treated my mother. He didn't respect her. He dominated her, told her to shut up, had to be right.

T: Did your mother complain?

P: No. But it was obvious.

T: Is this something new, or was this long-term?

P: It's worse the last few months. I couldn't stand it.

T: Do you feel he respects you?

P: I couldn't stand up to him.

T: What do you think is going on between them?

P: Divorce. My stepfather is building a studio to move away to.

T: Before or after Colorado?

P: Before. It'd be a mess. We'd have to move. My mother would have to get a job again.

T: Like the first divorce?

P: Yes. It was horrible.

T: What are some of the other problems?

P: My brother and sister don't respect my stepfather. I would get mad. He would get mad because he was treated so badly.

T: And your mother?

P: She defended the kids. I was in the middle.

T: How did you feel about your mother sticking up for the kids?

P: I was upset. It seemed the same to me. First my father left; therefore the others didn't like me. She should have been stronger. It does make me angry. There are good and bad things about my stepfather.

T: How would it be if you were home right now?

P: I understand they're getting along better.

Comment:

In this partial session, after the patient had stabilized for several weeks, the therapist chooses to investigate the patient's feelings about his family. He reveals his continued ambivalence and confusion, saying that, on the one hand, he didn't like the way his stepfather treated his mother, but, on the other hand, he didn't like the way his siblings treated his stepfather. (In fact, the patient was extremely close to the stepfather and was his stepfather's clear favorite.) The therapist reminds the patient that he had experienced a similar stress when his biological father and his mother had divorced. The patient reports having felt "in the middle," but adds that he sees good and bad in his stepfather, and he calls upon denial to contain his anxiety, claiming that "they're getting along better." The supervisor had previously felt that the patient had been ready for some time to tolerate a more focused, explicit discussion of the patient's feelings about his family, but the therapist had been uneasy about confronting the patient. In this session, the therapist did begin such a focus, but he stopped short of discussing the patient's prior psychotic state, his self-destructiveness, or his aggressive dyscontrol.

Therapy Session

T: How was your weekend with your parents?

P: Fine. It was kind of rough, though, sleeping with my parents.

T: How do you mean?

P: I'm used to doing it myself.

T: You felt pressured?

P: They were trying to be nice.

T: Why was it rough?

P: Maybe that's the wrong word. Maybe I'll move into a trailer with a friend.

T: You changed the subject.

P: Well, it was no big deal. They were nice. A strange thing happened this weekend – a patient grabbed me.

T: What do you mean?

P: She scared me. I waved at her, and she grabbed me.

T: Did you think you caused it?

P: No.

T: It was scary.

P: Yes.

T: Did it remind you of your problems?

P: No. It reminded me of being in a mental hospital. I'm leaving soon, and the newer people are sicker.

T: Do you have concerns about leaving?

P: Some. I wonder what people will think at my stepfather's work. But they'll accept me.

T: It's reasonable to be worried about that.

P: I'm pretty sure I can handle it.

T: Are you scared you'll lose control again?

P: A little. But it'll be no problem.

T: Well, the way to minimize the problem will be to see a psychiatrist and to take your medication.

Comment:

In this session, after the patient's first pass with his family, the therapist more actively persists in exploring the patient's affects and his sense of control. He picks up on the patient's report of "rough" aspects of the visit, and he urges the patient not to change the subject. Interestingly, the patient's associations bring to mind another patient's loss of control toward him. The supervisor felt that a more active, explicit approach would have been more helpful at this point, helping the patient see more clearly his anxiety about further violence toward his family. However, the therapist did ask, if too vaguely, if the experience with the other patient reminded him of his problems. Later, the therapist became a bit more direct by asking the patient if he feared he'd "lose control again."

Therapy Session
T: How did your visit go?
P: Good. It was uncomfortable. There's not much to do at home. Just watch TV. I felt anxious.
T: Can you tell me about that?
P: I don't know. I felt one time that I wanted to come back to the hospital. I remembered you'd said I'd feel that, but I hadn't believed it.
T: Was there anything particular about being home that made you anxious?
P: I expected more. I thought it would be less boring. My mom and dad talked to each other. I think they're fighting again.
T: Did you discuss that?
P: No. They said it was just natural.
T: Do you have doubts about living at home?
P: Yes. I fear they'd fight. Maybe I should move out.
T: Did you tell your parents about these feelings?
P: No. They'd feel hurt.
T: Can you talk to them?
P: No. Wouldn't you think they'd be hurt?
T: I don't know. Maybe. But there seem to be some communication problems.

Comment:
    After the patient's further visits with his family, the therapist backs off from a direct discussion of the family tension, as shown in this excerpt from a session. The therapist's focus on the communication problems is clarifying, but the patient's hints that his parents' fighting so frightened him that he contemplated moving out are not picked up. The supervisor reminded the therapist that just such parental fighting had precipitated the patient's previous move away from home, followed by

his becoming ill, and that the patient might have felt relieved by being able to discuss his fears more openly while still in the supportive environment of the hospital and the therapist's office.

Therapy Session

T: How'd your weekend go?

P: Good. Better. I felt anxious Friday night. I was with the band, but I wanted to go home. I was bored, nervous. There was nothing to do. It was enough.

T: Enough?

P: I was bored. I'm rusty on my guitar. But it went well. Saturday went well. I saw Dr. Levy. I felt comfortable. It can be a problem if there's nothing to do.

T: Did you feel scared?

P: I felt paranoid. I kept thinking about how anxious I'd get.

T: Were you scared you would get out of control?

P: Not really. It isn't so easy to leave the hospital, as you told me. It surprises me.

T: Were you anxious that you might hurt yourself?

P: Not really. But I was scared. I've acted on those thoughts before.

T: Were you scared to tell me about that?

P: Yea. The thought did cross my mind.

T: It's good you told me. Did you make a plan?

P: No. I feared I would act on the thoughts as before. I was not planning suicide. But what if I'm upset. I'm scared I'd act on the thoughts.

T: Did you want to die?

P: No.

T: What if you're upset—who would you talk to?

P: I'd call Levy. I learned here to do that.

T: You've also learned that thoughts aren't the same things as actions.

P: It would be no problem.

T: Do you think you feel suicidal?

P: No.

T: Do you think you would be able to tell me if you did feel that way?

P: Yes. If I need to come back in would that be bad?

T: We'd have to see how things went. If you need to come back, we can work that out.

Comment:

After the patient's second weekend pass, and after further supervisory discussions, the therapist is clearly more alert and comfortable in picking up the patient's cues. Picking out the patient's report of feeling "anxious" from a lot of defensive denial, the therapist asks the patient if he feared getting "out of control." He persists by spelling out his question, asking if the patient felt suicidal, and the patient admits being frightened of such impulsive behavior. The therapist still, however, avoids questioning the patient about his fears of homicidal behavior. Although the therapist consistently felt personally safe with the patient, he seemed to almost believe that discussions of homicidal impulses were either taboo or would increase the likelihood of such behavior. The countertransference sources of these anxieties in the therapist were discussed in supervision, and the therapist was able to explore these feelings with the patient before the patient's discharge.

Chapter 9
An Object Relations Approach to the Treatment of a Disturbed Adolescent

The patient was a 16-year-old girl admitted voluntarily with the chief complaint "My parents think I need help but I don't." This was her first psychiatric hospitalization, following two years of increasing suspiciousness, anxiety, and withdrawal. She had experienced insomnia, fatigue, and nervousness at school, leading to refusal to attend more than one or two classes per week. She was convinced that classmates were staring at her in a hostile fashion, and she eventually refused to attend all classes and was tutored at home. A consultation was obtained, but the patient refused the recommendation of either outpatient treatment or antipsychotic medications. She began to wear sunglasses at all times, developed bizarre behaviors such as covering the telephone with a handkerchief when using it, and insisted that all curtains be drawn at home because of her conviction that the house was "bugged" and that people were watching the house. In this period of time, her parents had had increasing difficulties, leading to a consideration of separation, and at that time the patient was hospitalized. The father had no psychiatric history, but the mother was in therapy for depressive episodes. Family history was positive for schizophrenia and depression in other family members. The patient's only sibling, a brother two years older, was asymptomatic.

On admission, the patient's appearance was unusual, characterized by heavy and bizarre makeup and insistence on wearing sunglasses. She was dressed entirely in black, appeared anxious and sad, and described her mood as one of "panic and nerves." She denied hallucinations, but her thought content bordered on being delusional. She denied suicidal or homicidal ideation. Soon after admission, the patient adamantly requested discharge, claiming to be free of problems, yet she worried that her room was "bugged," slept on top of her bedclothes with her street clothes on, and displayed other unusual behaviors. She refused medications, and she refused to attend therapeutic activities or to attend the hospital school. Because of her clear illness but lack of insight, she was considered for longer-term hospitalization on a different unit specializing in the treatment of borderline and severely character-disordered patients. However, rather than accept a transfer, the patient accepted medications. Initial trials of antipsychotic medication proved ineffective, but antidepressive medication resulted in some amelioration of symptoms. In the context of continued psychotherapy and milieu therapy, the patient agreed to attend school, and her steady improvement led to her discharge to a residential school facility. Her persistent periods of resistance to aspects of treatment, however, turned the initial plan for brief hospitalization into a prolonged hospital stay; such a case illustrates the need for extended hospital care in some cases.

Therapy Session
T: How are you doing?
P: I've had a hard time since our last session. I get hostile easily and upset.
T: Did that relate to last time?
P: Yes. I revealed things too soon. It was upsetting. I felt pressured.
T: You seem to be feeling angry.
P: Yes. I want more feedback. More concern, more caring.
T: How would you want me to show it?
P: I don't know. I know you care. Just more feedback.
T: Do you feel that others are not concerned?
P: Yes. My parents. My mother said, you want me to cry? I now realize that she does care. But my brother doesn't care. It's too painful. My father cares; he's loving and warm.

T: Can you say more about that?

P: There are no problems with him.

T: And your mom?

P: She's warm and loving, too. Before I came I felt she was avoiding me; I feared I was too dependent.

T: How long have you known about their marital problems?

P: Only about a month before I came here. My mother told my grand-mother, who told my father, who told me. He didn't want a divorce, but my mother did.

T: How did you feel?

P: Anxious.

T: Where were you planning to live?

P: I don't know. They both say it's okay to live with them.

T: That must be upsetting.

P: Yes.

Comment:

After many weeks of resistance to discussing anything but her objections to being in the hospital and her objections to taking medications or attending therapeutic activities, the patient had in the last session, for the first time, begun to talk of some of her interpersonal anxieties. In this excerpt, she alternates between anger and her dependent wishes for caring and concern. The therapist focuses briefly on the transference but shifts quickly to question the patient about her relationship with her parents and about their marital problems. The supervisor felt that this approach was correct, in light of the persistent defensiveness that had characterized the patient's previous sessions. Thus the patient's ambivalence was explored in terms of her family circumstances, leading to her first brief acknowledgment of the family stress.

Therapy Session

P: I feel anxious and hostile. You don't understand. It's difficult to talk about feelings. I don't want to be called schizophrenic. My grandmother on my mother's side was. I don't want to have a label. I don't want medications; I'd be like a guinea pig. And they would have side effects.

Comment:

This sample demonstrates the flavor of this attenuated session, a brief one because of the patient's refusal to stay for the therapeutic hour. Again, after disclosing some fears, inching toward a more trusting relationship with her therapist, she retreats and attacks. She reveals her fears of being labeled schizophrenic and her implied fears that revealing more of herself would lead to a decision to medicate her. The supervisor felt that the patient's intense anxiety, related to being dependent on another person, in this case her therapist, leading to anxieties related to fusion fantasies, in all likelihood fueled the defensive stance. The therapist was unable to persuade the patient to discuss her feelings at greater length.

Therapy Session

T: How are you doing?

P: Not good.

T: What do you mean?

P: The same as before my nervous breakdown. I have a tight stomach, I feel tense, I'm thinking constantly. I want out. I don't have my parents here. People are supposed to care, but I want to leave.

T: Tell me more about those feelings.

P: I guess the staff cares; I'm not sure.

T: What would you do if you left?

P: I'm scared. I'm not sure.

T: Even here, you don't go to activities.

P: Well, I'm just not getting better here. I might as well go. At least I'd be in the fresh air.

T: What do you mean?

P: Well, the problems I have probably may never go away. If people had just listened to me a year and a half ago.

T: I don't understand.

P: Well, my parents, the doctor. Sometimes you have to be dying before people realize that you've got problems. Now, I'll never get better.

T: You know the things you have to do if you want to get out of the hospital, yet you reject them. It may be that in fact we may need to consider a long-term unit. Here, we aren't able to help with medications, because you are refusing them.

P: I am afraid of school and of the medications. The last time I took them they had bad effects on me. I'm afraid they'll take over my brain, and then I'll never stop them, even if they're not good for me. Can you guarantee that they will be successful?

T: No.

P: I'm still scared. I saw a patient have seizures on medications. I just recently learned that you're in training!

T: Does that concern you?

P: Yes. Who's supervising you?

T: I meet regularly with senior psychiatrists for supervision, and they and many other staff members and I meet together in team and discuss the patients and reach team decisions.

Comment:

In this next session, the patient is less angry, is more anxious, and begins to somatize. She alludes to her feelings of hopelessness and hints at extremes of behavior ("you have to be dying before people realize that you've got problems"). Instead of picking up on the patient's wish for her therapist to appreciate the insistent reality of her internal distress, the therapist attempts to confront the patient with her contradictory behavior. The supervisor had advised use of such confrontational techniques at this point in the treatment, but that confrontations should be followed by hypotheses about the reason for the patient's contradictory behavior. The therapist stops short of suggesting such a hypothesis and instead essentially tells the patient to shape up or ship out to another unit. Not surprisingly, the patient quickly retaliates by attacking the therapist for being inexperienced, and she demands to know the identity of the therapist's supervisor. The therapist's countertransference annoyance at the patient was discussed in supervision and seemed most likely to relate to the therapist's intolerance of the patient's profound dependency and her wish never to leave his side. From an object relations point of view, the patient was felt to defend against fusion anxiety, experienced when her needy part-self representation became strongly drawn to her nurturing part-object representation. The defense usually used was that of projective identification, where the aggressive part-self representation actively sought to control the projected attacking part-object representation.

Therapy Session
P: I still don't want to take the medications. I want my mom's opinion.
T: [Details of the medication reviewed] Are you still concerned about me being in training?
P: No. I'm just worried about the medications. You sound defensive about the medications. I think I'm hostile, and you're getting angry.

Comment:
    Here, the supervisor felt there was evidence for the defensive configuration outlined above, where the patient used a struggle with the therapist around the issue of medications as a framework within which to control him, thus keeping his transference-distorted and projected image at bay. At the same time, the patient unconsciously reassured herself that, by being "hostile" and getting her therapist angry, she needn't worry about a wish to depend on him forever.

Therapy Session
T: How are you doing?
P: I feel good. Actually I'm not bothered by things. I've been talking to my mental health worker about why I can't make decisions.
T: Can you give me an example of what you mean?
P: Well, the medications. And whether to stay here and take them or go to the long-term unit. Though I might have to take them there, too. That frightens me. I've been feeling stronger. I used to be disturbed. I wouldn't go out or go to school.
T: You're still not going to school. How are you different?
P: I'm confused. Last week I went to therapeutic activities. I did okay. I don't know why I didn't get a pass. I need reassurance from people. Either that I really need meds or that I'm not ill. I need to know if I have problems.
T: Can you say more about that?
P: I'm not sure.

T: Well, your difficulty going to school or activities may be an indication of your problems.

P: Maybe. I'm confused. There's not enough time to talk. These sessions stress me.

T: At first, you didn't want to meet.

P: I wish I could get better without the sessions. I'm confused. I don't know if I want longer sessions.

T: It does sound like you're confused about that.

P: I am. Anyone who talks about my problems confuses me. Let me go on a pass home and see if I'm okay.

T: That wouldn't answer what your problems are here.

P: Well I'm not sure about the medications.

Comment:

In this representative segment of a session, continued sparring occurs around issues of medications, school, and the patient's need for treatment. The therapist attempts to point out that the patient demonstrates her problems by her resistant behavior, but again he stops short of proposing a formulation. In fact, the therapist seems somewhat paralyzed by the patient, unable to pick up on the patient's invitation to be told candidly about her illness. In supervisory discussions, the therapist realized that he had again begun to feel ineffectual with this patient related to his own countertransference, leading him to unconsciously avoid stronger confrontations, secretly hoping that her uncooperativeness would persist and lead to a swift transfer to another unit. The patient may have at some level sensed this, for soon after this session she agreed to begin taking medications, perhaps to appear to be more cooperative and to stave off such a transfer.

Therapy Session

T: How are things?

P: Better. I'm not feeling like I did yesterday, nervous stomach, out of control, crazy thoughts, shaky.

T: Those are lots of problems. Do you think they're due to the meds?

P: I'm not sure.

T: What do you mean crazy thoughts?

P: Just anxious. What's the purpose of life. If death would be better.

T: Do you think so?

P: No.

T: Have you had thoughts about hurting yourself?

P: No. Just zooming around in my head.

T: Zooming?

P: What there is to enjoy in life.

T: But have you had thoughts about hurting yourself?

P: No. I'm not suicidal.

T: I'm confused.

P: Sometimes I wonder if I want to get better. Part of me doesn't.

T: What do you mean?

P: Part of me doesn't think I'll get better.

T: That's not the same as want?

P: Well, I don't get the words right always.

T: I don't understand.

P: If I feel like this, and I get better, you would send me out like I'm feeling now.

T: I'm confused. If you got better you'd only be feeling like you are now?

P: [giggle]

T: What made you laugh?

P: It's funny—that I'm confusing you!

T: Do you enjoy it?

P: I'm not sure.

T: It's not clear if *I'm* being difficult or if *your* thoughts are confused.

P: I'm confused. It happens with others, too.

T: What do you think is going on?

P: I'm not sure. I get frustrated and nervous with my parents and my brother. I wish I were normal.

T: In what way?

P: Just being happy instead of being sad. Understanding people. Things like that. With my family, something seems different.

T: What do you mean?

P: I want to be kind, but I can't anymore. There's something different with my mom and dad.

T: What do you think it is?

P: I don't know. They don't understand me or my difficulties.

T: Does it have anything to do with your father not being allowed to visit you in your room?
P: No.
T: Do you know why that decision was made?
P: No.
T: In order not to be on the bed with your father.
P: What are you worried about?
T: What do you think?
P: Incest!
T: Why do you think that might be a concern?
P: You're all so paranoid! In fact, my father and I were lying in the bed together. I said, we've got to cut this out. We were just fooling around. I was tickling him. But I told him things had to be different. It's not normal for a 16-year-old to tickle her father. Why not, though. I don't know.

Comment:

The therapist continues to respond sluggishly and awkwardly to the patient's thoughts, trying at first to assess her suicidal potential, and shortly thereafter attempting to confront her with her denial. The therapist explained to the supervisor, however, that he had been preoccupied during the first part of this session by the information he had learned at rounds about her behavior with her father on the unit during the previous day's visiting hours. He eventually, in a somewhat forced way, questions the patient about the incident. After attempting to joke about it, the patient admits her own concerns about the mutually seductive interaction between her and her father.

Therapy Session
P: I'm having an anxiety attack!
T: Why?
P: I think it's the medications. It was bad timing to give them to me when you did. I'm under a lot of pressure.
T: What do you mean?
P: Lots of difficulties with my family. Plus my friend [a male patient] who left.
T: What does that have to do with the meds?

P: I'm not sure. Maybe it does. I feel I'm choking, I feel hopeless. I feel I can't breathe. I feel overwhelmed. It's a choking feeling.

T: Why the meds?

P: I'm not sure. I *hate* the medicines!

T: Let's say for a minute it's not the meds; what else could be making you feel the way you are?

P: I don't know. I'd just like to stop them for a week. Then I'd be willing to go back on the medications if I didn't feel any different.

Comment:

Both the therapist and the supervisor agreed that the patient's intense anxiety in this session represented a reaction to the discussion in the previous session. However, the patient was adamantly unwilling to consider anything but her conviction that the medications were responsible for her anxiety. The therapist had hoped to suggest that she was displacing her anger at him onto the medications, but he felt that she was unable to listen to such a possibility. The supervisor suggested that the patient's anxiety might have been so intense because, again from an object relations viewpoint, her ambivalence about the manifestly sexualized behavior with her father likely represented a precocious oedipalization of more primitive ambivalence, more basic in nature, from preoedipal dynamics.

Therapy Session

T: How are you feeling?

P: Tired, nervous, anxious.

T: What do you think it has to do with?

P: My parents. And the school thing. I don't want to go. My parents agree that I don't have to. I don't want to.

T: Why?

P: I just don't want to! There's no need to. It's upsetting to be with people with problems. I don't want to go there.

T: You had problems before you were here.

P: I just don't want to go. Other people there have problems.

T: But *you* have problems.

P: My problems are different. I don't want to kill myself.

T: The others do?

P: Well, yea. I couldn't go out.

T: I don't understand.

P: I can't explain. I know one thing – I want to get out of here. I'll go to activities, so I can get out of here.

T: Why do you differentiate activities from school?

P: I don't know. I just want to get out of here. But I know I'm not ready.

T: What do you mean?

P: I'm not physically well.

T: Physically?

P: I have this nervous stomach.

T: Anything else?

P: Well, the medications give me problems, too.

T: Do you understand why I feel confused?

P: Yea.

T: Can you explain?

P: I can't. I don't know. You expect answers that are special. Some secret. Some major problem.

T: We seem to be going around in circles.

P: I understand that you feel that way.

T: Can you help me?

P: No. You don't understand. I don't want to go.

T: When you do leave the hospital, what do you think it will be like?

P: Like the way I felt when my father visited.

T: You mentioned before that you felt abandoned by your parents.

P: [sobbing] I feel alone. I feel that my parents deserted me. I can't stand my parents leaving me in the hospital. Kids suffer! Why did they have to get divorced! And you're such a great therapist. One of the best therapists I ever had. I am able to talk about these things. My parents have abandoned me, and I feel scared to be left alone!

Comments:

In the intervening weeks between this and the previous session, the patient demonstrated uneven progress, becoming more participatory in therapeutic activities and group therapy, but continuing to refuse school. The sessions had a desultory quality, often centered around the patient's complaints about the medications and the therapist's efforts to interpret the defensive aspects of these complaints. His attempts to focus on the patient's relationship with him led to her comment, "Oh, you think I'm in love with you!" followed by less flirtatious and more clinging behavior. Most important in this period was the decision of the parents to divorce, and the fact that the therapist learned of the mother's affair with a man who had frequented the family home and who had been interested in the patient as well. Again, the therapist was uncertain how to handle this new information and was preoccupied by the dilemma during this session. He chose to try to steer the focus to the family, and that tack alone elicited the patient's emotional outburst about both the parents and the therapist.

Therapy Session
T: How are you feeling?
P: Better than yesterday. I felt scared after taking the meds. The staff says I stay in my room too much. Sleeping. I am spending time in my room. I feel tired. The meds are tiring me.
T: Any other things besides the meds?
P: Possibly, but not likely. I did walk to activities, and I felt better, but I felt worn out.
T: The focus is so much on the medications that there is no time left to talk about other issues.
P: I just need to be reassured. My parents leave me here like a wet dog.
T: You're feeling angry?
P: They're out there and I'm in here, afraid to eat. I feel like I'm dying.
T: What do you mean?
P: I just feel rotten. I don't feel good.
T: In what way?
P: It's because of the meds.
T: You're sure?
P: Can I take all my meds at night?
T: Maybe. What else makes you feel not good?
P: I'm depressed. I want out of here. I have blurred vision, slurred speech.
T: You describe being depressed with physical symptoms.

P: I get afraid when I get physical symptoms.
T: Perhaps it's easier to talk about physical problems.
P: Yea. It's harder to talk about emotional issues. Probably they're tied up in it, too.
T: In what way?
P: I need someone to help. I need reassurance, to be certain that nothing will happen to me. If I'm on the right meds. I don't know. I don't seem too much different. I'm scared of the medications. I'm scared of dying.
T: Meaning?
P: Scared I have cancer! My grandmother had breast cancer. I know I don't but I'm just scared I might.
T: There's no evidence to suggest it; why do you feel fearful about it?
P: Because I feel a tightness in my chest, in my throat. And the other physical problems.

Comment:

Here, the patient's chronic depression is becoming more overt, having been previously masked behind her panoply of distracting behaviors. The therapist is for a brief moment successful in stimulating the patient to talk about her feelings and fears, which all take a depressive coloration. The therapist had been discussing in team rounds his growing conviction that perhaps the patient was right after all; ironically, the trial of antipsychotic medications, now of sufficient duration, did not seem to have been effective. There was general agreement to taper the antipsychotic medications and to initiate a trial of antidepressants.

Therapy Session
T: How are you feeling?
P: Better [giggling].
T: What's the laugh about?
P: Well, I feel better today. Just go with the flow!
T: I know your mother spoke to you about Jack and her relationship with him. [Mother informed patient of her affair with Jack, a man patient knew.]
P: I feel angry and sad about that. My mother lied to me. Jack was

supposed to be my friend. I feel used. Angry. Maybe I'll be angry about that when I leave. My father is, and my brother is. I don't know if I am.

T: You sound confused about your feelings about it.

P: I'm angry at them, but what good will that do? I'm not sure.

T: You say you may be upset when you leave; what makes you say that?

P: Well, I'm not outside. I thought it would happen but I didn't face it. Now I don't have to unless I leave.

T: It must affect you anyway.

P: I'm angry at my mother, but I don't have to deal with it here.

T: Like not dealing with the divorce?

P: Not with the reality of it. I cried when my mother told me.

T: What did she say?

P: He's a security guard. I thought he was my friend.

T: Was he interested in you sexually?

P: [giggle] My dad was worried about that. He said it wouldn't be good if we stayed in contact.

T: Do you want to?

P: I'm fond of him and feel he was a friend.

T: Can you say more?

P: There were all these hints. I had suspected something. My father had asked her; he had suspected. But I had accepted my mother's denial, and I told my father.

T: You seem relieved.

P: Yes! Now I know I'm not crazy. Plus I understand why my mother was avoiding me.

T: You know that I knew. Any feelings about that?

P: Good. This time somebody told her what was going on.

Comment:

Prior to this session, the therapist had insisted that the mother herself inform the patient of her affair with the man who was the patient's friend as well. As can be seen, the patient experienced relief, felt less "crazy," and felt entitled to the anger she had felt already toward her mother. The supervisor underlined the educational aspects of this experience for the therapist as to the importance of external reality, not just internal reality, in considering the psychotherapy material.

Therapy Session

T: How are you doing? [Antipsychotic medications had been discontinued]

P: Better off meds. I don't have blurred vision any more, and I'm not so tired. But the meds did help me sleep. But I was feeling different then.

T: I'm not sure what you mean?

P: Now you'll tell me my thinking is unclear!

T: Did you feel I was trying to make a case like that?

P: Maybe, I'm not sure.

T: I'm not, but I was interested in how you feel different.

P: I noticed since I started going off the unit that I didn't care what people thought.

T: What do you mean?

P: Oh, I used to be worried about the way they looked at me or talked. Like they thought I was ugly, or were thinking, "Who does she think she is."

T: Why do you think that worried you?

P: I'm not sure. Just the looks from people. They looked jealous. But I still want to be off the meds.

T: Are you nervous about it?

P: No. I'm so happy. I'm glad to stop. I do want to be better, not to go on like before.

T: Like how?

P: Depressed. Not able to go out except to school. I'm very scared of school, and you know why. I have bad memories of school. I spoke to someone, and they said I shouldn't have to go. Am I so monstrous you can't believe me?

T: Why do you think so?

P: I stand out! I look better than the others. Like an adult, not a kid!

T: You sound angry.

P: I'm angry that you didn't support me about the meds. You can't even see my eyes!

T: How does that relate?

P: You don't realize that I look like an adult.

T: Recently you said you're just a kid; now you say you're an adult.

P: Well it's both. But the decision to stop the meds . . . I usually like things gray. Now it's black and white. I'm making my own decisions. I guess I'm still a kid, but I'd like to be an adult. My *parents* put me here, and I didn't have much say about that!

Comment:

The patient clearly feels relieved by the discontinuation of the medications and, perhaps relatedly, seems more relaxed with the therapist in this session. Her primitive denial, however, continues to be obvious as she rapidly oscillates between self-referential fears that "they thought I was ugly" to statements like "they look jealous" and "I look better than others." For the first time, when the supervisor asked the therapist the meaning of the patient's statement, "You can't even see my eyes," the supervisor learned that the patient had always worn sunglasses in sessions. The therapist then realized how indicative his failure to deal with this was of his own continuing discomfort with closeness and intimacy with this patient. At this time he realized that his discomfort was not just related to the patient's profound dependency but also to her sexuality.

Therapy Session

P: I feel happy; I feel good. I don't know if I'm depressed or happy. I used to be depressed, but no one thought I was. People didn't know. I didn't let them. It has to do with the environment.

T: What about the environment?

P: If it's ugly . . . poverty is not nice to look at. I've seen it some here mostly, some in Europe.

T: Can you say more what you mean?

P: In town, everyone looked depressed. As if there's a lot of unhappiness or sadness.

T: What would be a good environment?

P: Lawrenceville, Cooperstown, they are nice.

T: What do you make out of the observation that the external environment makes you depressed?

P: It's scary. Reality, I don't want to face.

T: You describe the relationship of your feelings to the environment. Anything else?

P: Well, people. Poor people. Everyone should be equal.

T: Are you worried about being poor?

P: Yes. Everything has turned to shit. My father says business is okay, but I'm scared about it. What is depression?

T: I'm not sure what you mean.

P: People are unhappy, but people are all the time. Not just in the hospital.

T: Are you asking why you should be here?

P: Because of having problems like depression.

T: How much did the depression affect you, in terms of being able to function, eat and sleep okay, and things like that?

P: I felt hopeless. I feel good now.

T: What about when you leave?

P: I'm scared. I don't know if things will work out. My father says he's against my mother. My grandfather is against my father. My mother is not against anybody. She wants to be happy for herself.

T: You keep saying you want to leave, but you don't do things which you need to do to go. You always ask, "Do you think I'm crazy?" That's one thing that doesn't make sense.

P: It *sounds* like it's crazy but it isn't. Part of me *doesn't* want to leave. I fear depression, that I would be unhappy with my mother or father.

T: How far back do the problems go between them?

P: In Europe even. They argued more than usual. Lots of fights. Then they were all lovey dovey, so I thought they weren't problems any more [tearful]. I miss my parents. I'm angry about the divorce. And that I wasn't told about it. That I was put here. Then they separated. Both are out there having fun while I'm here in the hospital. Nobody really cares. Well . . . that's not true, but it's how I feel.

Comment:

The patient's continued affective symptoms are apparent, yet there appears to be more of an affective lability than a consistent depressive affect. The therapist's reminder that she still behaves in ways contradictory to her expressed desires brings, this time, a more rational and insightful response. The patient recognizes her own internal conflict.

Therapy Session

T: How are you doing?

P: Okay. Up, then down. The divorce is getting to me. I'd be going out there. The meeting with my mother and her boyfriend went okay. I got frustrated. He kept turning things into a joke. I went along. My mother and I were crying. My mother was fine. I don't want to be angry with them. But the anger is all bottled up. If it came out I worry they'd leave. I feel competitive with him for her love. I asked her about that. She said we're equal but different. That's hard to deal with. I don't understand why she doesn't love me more.

T: You said you have a lot of angry feelings?

P: Well, he's overjoyed with what he got. I was very serious but I laughed. He doesn't see me as upset. I went blank. It was all a joke to him. My mother was crying; he jokes. I don't know why I grinned. He thinks I'll get over it. Meanwhile back at the ranch I'm suffering. I wonder who you'd believe if you heard the story.

T: What do you think?

P: If you'd believe someone outside.

T: You clearly *have* been lied to. Do you feel you can trust me here?

P: I *hope* you'd believe me. You're a doctor. I do believe you would.

T: It would be easier for me to understand you if you took your glasses off.

P: I don't want to. I don't want you to know me. That's the way I feel. He joked about it.

T: Is it a laughing matter?

P: No. It's serious.

T: It interferes with my ability to communicate with you.

P: I wish someone had told me that when I came in. I might here, but not outside. It's something I have control over.

T: If it interferes with our communication, is being in control more important?

P: I guess you're right; it only hurts me. I'll think about it.

T: Do you understand why I think it's strange?

P: Yes. No other patients do it.

T: It's confusing. You complain about hiding your feelings, yet . . . .

P: I'll think about it. I might say yes here. My parents are all twisted. They take drastic steps. They called me crazy, sent me to a therapist, all because I expressed my feelings.

T: Therefore it's too difficult here.

P: Now I'm like an open book. It feels good. I do because nothing bothers me.

T: Is that true?

P: No. Sometimes I almost want to die. I'm tired of my mother and father and others.

T: Do you feel suicidal?

P: No. I do feel bad though. I'm worried you'd think I was suicidal.

T: Are you?

P: No. I have no such intentions.

T: Do you have a problem in using the phone?

P: No, not usually. It's just because it's greasy.

T: Don't you think it's unusual?

P: I don't use the public phones. I know people might think it strange. But I don't worry about it.

Comment:

   After several unsuccessful attempts to bring up the patient's sunglasses "disguise," the therapist here does so, as well as the patient's unusual way of handling the telephone. The therapist chose to present it as a problem interfering with communication and understanding, which the supervisor felt was a reasonable approach, one acceptable to the patient without producing excessive anxiety.

Therapy Session

P: I'm feeling good. The meeting Monday helped.

T: You said you were upset about it?

P: Well, this is the way it is; nothing can change it. Things are serious. It's not a joke.

T: I'm confused.

P: I want to meet with him again. My dad doesn't want me to be with him. But it's up to me. It's disturbing. If I'm with my mother I have to be with Jack.

T: How do you mean?

P: I'd like to live with my mother and my father but I can't. I'll live with my father. My room and my possessions are with my father. Maybe then I'll live with my mother.

T: Why are you feeling better today?

P: I spoke to my father. He gave me feedback. If I tell my mother I will live with her, it'll only be if Jack moves out.

T: Can you say more about that?

P: It seems I'm making her choose. But maybe I need to spend time with Jack to see if it would be okay.

T: Why are you feeling happy?

P: My dad said it's up to me. Having a choice is important. I always trusted my mother, though she lied to me. If you can never believe your *mother* you'd be in bad shape. I know it sounds confusing, but now that I have some choices, I don't like to be told what to do.

T: How do you feel about things you have to do here—activities, eating, going to meetings?

P: It's not fair. The Sustacal. No passes. It's like games.

T: What do you mean?

P: It's like being punished.

T: We don't see it as punishment. Why a game?

P: Well, I know it's probably good for me. Though I might have a different opinion from your judgment. It's a matter of trust.

T: Do you feel it here?

P: No. I do trust you; that's not an issue.

T: I'm confused.

P: I have faith you'll help me. But it's embarrassing and humiliating to be a patient. To be on the grounds. I do it because I have to. I don't like the fitness class. It's humiliating. Some of them look so much like patients. I only want to do things I want to do. Like a test of wills.

Comment:

The supervisor emphasized that, although the patient appeared to be more responsive to the therapist and more trusting to him, she persisted in suspending her therapeutic progress by her continued refusal to attend school. In the weeks that followed, the patient was placed on imipramine, was told of her therapist's upcoming two-week vacation, and at a stormy family meeting just before the next session was told that longer hospital treatment was being recommended. The patient was described to the family, in the patient's presence, as "not functioning," and the patient responded by saying, "I can function. I just don't want to." After the therapist said, "We don't see it," the patient stormed out of the family meeting.

Therapy Session

T: How are you doing?

P: How *should* I be doing? I'm fucking angry! Pissed. What you did to me! I don't know what you brought me there for. You don't listen. I tell the staff the way it is!

T: I understand why you're not feeling listened to but . . . .

P: Not listened to!

T: You're feeling isolated.

P: I don't know. If no one agrees with me!

T: It was a team decision, but I agree with it.

P: I was hoping for once I'd be listened to!

T: You never feel listened to?

P: I didn't say that!

T: What did you mean?

P: I don't want to talk to you. Everyone has to listen to what you say.

T: You feel betrayed.

P: I'm not in the mood to talk. I feel scared, and I get hostile. No I'm not. Forget it. I don't want to talk to you! Or are you going to make me do that, too!

T: I can't. But it might be useful to talk. Were you worried how I'd react to your being angry?

P: I don't give a shit!

T: You have felt abandoned before. Do you feel that I and the staff are doing that now?

P: What's new! Everybody does. My social worker, mother, father.

T: Me, too.

P: I don't know.

T: You're feeling lonely and angry.

P: *You* don't know what's best for me. You don't know how I feel. I haven't told you things.

T: Right. I can't read your mind, but we try on the basis of what we do see. I do appreciate that you don't feel understood.

P: Sometimes I do. I don't know if people give a shit. I just get threats. Eat. Or I'll force it down your throat.

T: You feel I don't care.

P: Just get me over and done with. Next victim. You didn't listen! I didn't agree! School, the divorce . . . . I'm tired of being bossed around.

T: You equate not caring with not agreeing with you.

P: They *are* the same. They *might* be different.

Comment:

The therapist felt quite discouraged at this point, feeling that the patient's angry eruption implied that all of the therapist's patience and carefulness and attempts to be sensitively responsive to the patient might have been a waste of time and that the current firm stand taken with the patient might have produced quicker results if done earlier. The supervisor cautioned the therapist about the pitfalls of hindsight and that an angry response such as this does not necessarily indicate prior lack of progress.

Therapy Session

P: I went to school. Every class.

T: How are you doing?

P: Good. I'm angry about school, you making me prove myself. You don't listen to me or trust me. My heart goes a mile a minute. I *said* I could go.

T: How did it go?

P: Very boring. Very basic. I'm angry. I'm too sensitive. I'm angry at my parents and at you. I'm sick of being humiliated. Of you all attacking me. All these threats and things.

T: Why have you not been going to school?

P: I told you. *I didn't want to leave the unit!* That's why I have not been going. Now I have an outside therapist. Why not leave the hospital? But I'm angry. The damned divorce. I've held a lot of anger in. I felt outraged at my parents at that meeting. And at you. I had a problem that I wanted to work on, but you made me leave. Now I'm ready to go.

T: If there are problems that you need to work on, how could you be ready to leave?

P: Well, it had to do with the divorce and things related to that.

T: I'm confused.

P: You're putting words in my mouth.

T: Look, either I'm crazy or you're crazy at this point.

P: I got myself in a hole. I was afraid to go to school all along. [Crying] I haven't told the truth. I didn't think I could do it. I am amazed I can. Will you trust me any more? I felt afraid because I'd lied. The divorce *is* upsetting, but, you know, I know my parents really love me.

Comment:

The patient's response to the recent confrontation had included arranging to attend the hospital school for the first time and arranging through her family to line up a private therapist to see after discharge. Here, she is candid about her clear wish not to leave the unit, reminding the therapist that she had tried to tell him that; neither of them corrects the wording to more accurately reflect her fear of leaving her therapist. After some contradictory statements from the patient, the therapist presses her to notice her confusion, and for the first time the patient admits her profound fear of school failure, masked by a bravado she feared would be seen as a lie.

Therapy Session

P: I feel okay, but I have these pains in my stomach. Do you think it could be gastritis? I was anxious before school. But it was okay when I was there. I was more comfortable than most of the kids. Now I know I can do it.

T: Last time you were angry and then worried about your family.

P: You were pushing me. But I didn't tell you everything.

T: You look anxious now.

P: I am.

T: Does it have to do with your not being at one class?

P: I'm scared about going to the long-term unit.

T: The long-term unit isn't directly related to the one class. Being in long-term treatment doesn't necessarily have to be in the hospital. It makes you afraid to think of going to the long-term unit?

P: Yea. You do have the power to do such things. I never thought I'd end up in the hospital. Things have been done without my control. The divorce. Decisions have been made without me. This is the first time I really do want to leave the hospital. Before I went to school, I was scared of my symptoms. Now I am interested in leaving the hospital.

Comment:

In this final session of this series, the patient again presents somatic complaints, but holds her gains and feels stronger. At that same time, the degree to which she had felt powerless and weak compared to her therapist—who, like her parents, had control over her—is clearer. The supervisor advised the therapist to help the patient understand her profound ego weakness, masked by both her defensive pseudo-independence and by her prolonged refusal to attend school. Such a maneuver had provided a sense of power and control over the therapist with the secondary gain of remaining at his side. His impending vacation along with the renewed decision to insist on longer-term hospitalization, which meant transfer to another unit and another therapist, catalyzed her to overcome her fears. As it turned out, she was able to stabilize at this point and was discharged shortly thereafter, without the need for transfer for longer hospital care after all. The therapist, the supervisor, and the patient agreed that by no means was the work all done, but the patient seemed to have made real gains and to be motivated within herself to work hard in outpatient psychotherapy. It was hoped that some consolidation of the patient's previously fragmented internal representational work had occurred, with some greater tolerance for the reality of both helpful and disappointing aspects of others.

Chapter 10

Acute Hospital Treatment of a Suicidal Borderline Patient

The patient was a 23-year-old single woman who presented for admission because of depression and suicidal feelings. She had a history of six prior psychiatric hospitalizations starting from age 16. Six months before this admission, she had finished graduate school in social work. She found temporary placement at an agency, but found the work too stressful and quit. She returned home to live with her mother, with whom she had a chronic hostile-dependent relationship. She contacted a former therapist – one of her previous instructors – who attempted to encourage her and provide support.

Over the ensuing months, she became increasingly dysphoric, had trouble staying awake, and gained weight. She described herself as being preoccupied with the hopelessness of her situation. She could not concentrate sufficiently to read or watch television, and she spent most of the month before admission in bed. Two days before admission, she impulsively and superficially cut her left forearm in an attempt to kill herself. She called her former teacher–therapist, who came over and insisted upon consultation the next day; the consultant recommended hospitalization. There was no recent history of alcohol or illicit substance abuse. The family history was positive for alcohol abuse in the mother; the father's whereabouts and history were unknown.

On admission the patient appeared dejected and was weepy. She presented as a pathetic, lost soul. Several nursing staff members immediately took a special interest in her. However, with her therapist she was hostile and negativistic. Her initial interview was characterized as being like "a dental interview—you had to pull teeth." She seemed to resent the need to ask questions about her, as if her therapist should know all the details of her history. Her wounds, now three days old, were superficial and healing, but she would intermittently pick at them. When asked by nursing staff members what she intended, she told them that she was intentionally trying to hurt herself. She frequently reiterated the belief that no one would be able to help her, in spite of the staff's obvious concern about her. One of the senior nursing staff members took a special interest in her and attempted to reassure her, but with little apparent effect. She had continued to receive a substantial dose of a tricyclic antidepressant from the time of the outpatient consultation.

Her depression gradually lifted, but in her psychotherapy, her critical attitude toward her treatment and her therapist persisted until she raised the possibility that she would be transferred to a state hospital. She went through a fairly typical course—devaluing others, splitting staff, idealizing her therapist—and she finally effected leaving the hospital by devaluing it and her treatment. With the assistance of friends, she was able to obtain meaningful and appropriate employment by the time of discharge. By devaluing her therapist and her treatment at the time of discharge, and concomitantly experiencing herself as an innocent victim in a process, she did not experience the loss of them as such a severe narcissistic mortification and was able to actually go to work. She had called her hospital therapist shortly after discharge and said that he was definitely the best therapist she had ever had and the only one who had ever understood her. Follow-up six months after discharge revealed that she was continuing outpatient treatment and performing adequately at work.

Therapy Session (Day 3 of hospitalization)
T: How are you feeling today? [silence] Can you tell me how you're
    doing now?
P: You know!
T: I can tell you're clearly not feeling well, but I was interested in the
    details, the specifics. [Silence] Can you tell me more specifically
    how you're feeling?

P: What for? You can't help me. I've got to help myself. But I'm just not able to. [Patient cries quietly] [Therapist offers tissues, which patient accepts]

T: It must be awful to feel that your therapist can't help you and that you can't help yourself.

P: [Silence] I never should have come into the hospital.

T: How's that?

P: *You* know! All you want is to make money. You're not interested in any of the patients.

T: What do I do that gives you that impression? [Silence] Is there something I did or said that suggested that to you?

P: There's no point talking about it. Can I have my status raised? There's no reason for me to be on CS [constant supervision].

T: Hold on. What about last night?

P: I was feeling desperate. There was no one around. I couldn't talk to Pauline [the person with whom she was on CS] so the only solution was to die.

T: Did you try to talk to anyone else? [Silence] Did you consider other things besides killing yourself? [Silence] I don't know what to make of your silence.

P: Never mind. I told Nancy [one of the nursing staff members who had taken a special liking toward her] that it was pointless – you don't understand.

T: Maybe I don't. I just don't think that I can recommend a liberalization of your status on the heels of attempts to hurt yourself. Maybe if I had some help understanding you.

Comment:

The therapist began this session with an intervention that is conventional, but classically subject to misinterpretation by borderline patients. That is, he inquired as to the current state of the patient. The patient is clearly aware of how she is presenting herself, so his question essentially fuels her indignation – the therapist can't see what's obvious! The patient's response as the therapist tries to pursue her description of her internal state – "you can't help me" – is the kind of response that often seduces therapists to offer reassurances, but the patient here cuts the therapist off by saying she needs to help herself but can't. The therapist attempts to empathize with the hopelessness and helplessness of the patient, but appears to collude with the patient in the change of subject to her status.

In the process, the patient appears to test the interest and capacity of the therapist to understand her and experience her state with her. She quickly challenges the therapist with her claim of his disinterest, and then throws in a diversion—her unit status. The therapist was nonplussed by her accusation, and was diverted from the more direct transferential material to the struggle over status. The therapist was advised that he needed to be sensitive to the transferential meaning of her statements and that he needed to deal directly with threats to the therapeutic relationship along with other matters. The failure of the therapist to bring the discussion back to her perception of him was a technical—but not irreversible—error.

Therapy Session
(Since the last session, there have been six incidents of the patient picking at her wounds or attempting to injure herself. These actions have included removing her bandages and picking at her wounds, or attempting to cut herself with a plastic knife [as a patient on suicidal precautions, she uses plastic silverware in the dining room]).

P: [Patient has tears in her eyes] I'm getting worse. [Silence] No one here can help me—only Janet [her former instructor and former therapist] can help. [Silence] I never should have come to the hospital.

T: Things seem to continue to be pretty bad. How do you understand that?

P: Are you saying that I'm not trying to help myself? You don't know what it's like to be depressed. All high and mighty!

T: Slow down! I don't think I said that you weren't trying. I simply asked how you understood that you're still feeling so bad.

P: Yeah, I know, it's all my fault. I'm the one who doesn't understand; you have all the right answers and I'm the sick one..

T: I'm sorry if that's the way I sound to you. I certainly don't intend it. Is there something in particular that leads you to think that I feel that way?

P: [Cries audibly] [Silence]

T: Can you tell me what I do?

P: [With occasional sobs] No, Carol [one of the favored nurses] told me
     that I should trust you, that I haven't given you a chance, and I
     guess she's right. It's just that I have a very difficult time trusting
     anyone, particularly men. But she said that I should talk to you
     about the problems that I've been having.

T: Uh huh.

P: I was doing okay for a while, until I began to have trouble with a
     guy at the office. He used to always come up to me and try to be
     friendly, you know, let's have lunch together and that sort of stuff.

T: Yeah.

P: Well, he's an okay kind of guy, but I was afraid that he'd want to get
     involved, and I just couldn't handle that. So I tried to be rather cool
     towards him, but it just didn't seem to work—he didn't seem to be
     able to take a hint.

T: And what happened?

P: I don't know. I just continued to feel depressed. [Silence] I hate my-
     self! [Cries]

T: It certainly seems like a complicated and difficult situation.

Comment:

   In the opening part of the session, the patient quickly takes the offense, possibly reading into something that the therapist had said, or
the way the therapist said it, but clearly missing the major thrust of the
therapist's intentions. It is difficult to think that the motivation for such
an attack on the therapist is anything but an attempt to distract the
therapist from the patient's persistent self-destructive behaviors.
When the therapist acknowledges the possibility that she had accurately perceived something the therapist had said to her, but that it was
not his intention to convey such an attitude and that he was sincerely
interested in addressing the possible problem in his actions towards
her, she becomes more open to him about other difficulties in her
life.

   In particular, she talks about her problems relating to men in general, and one would have to assume that the same concerns that she had
about the fellow in the office are relevant to her feelings about her therapist. The therapist took the wind out of her sails by acknowledging the

possibility of her perceptions. His nondefensive stance encouraged her to be more open with him. However, the therapist never took the patient back to the issue of her repeated self-destructive actions, which have punctuated the time from her admission. For the rest of the session, the patient and therapist talked about problems with men. The supervisor pointed out that the therapist was seduced into discussing this potentially erotic material and thus avoiding the more immediate issue of her self-destructive behaviors, with the probable tension that would accompany such a discussion. Minimally, the therapist should have acknowledged the issue of her self-destructive actions and probably should have saved some time for discussion of these acts. The failure to even acknowledge these acts represents a collusion with the patient to avoid the most significant fact of her current situation.

Therapy Session
(The patient has continued to pick at her dressings and wounds.)

T: What's with the picking at your wrists? [Silence] I understand that they had to put you in restraints last night. It seems that things aren't getting any better.

P: I just can't control myself. I want to, but I can't.

T: Tell me what happens?

P: What's there to tell? I can't control myself!

T: [Silence] Well, tell me what the experience is like? What goes through your head? What do you feel?

P: [Silence] I don't know. I get depressed and feel that I want to die, that I want to feel pain.

T: Does it hurt to pick at your wound?

P: No. I don't feel a thing. It's like I'm already dead. [Cries]

T: Tell me more about it.

P: I know I have to help myself, but I don't think I can. I don't want to go to a state hospital.

T: What do you think the alternatives are if you keep trying to hurt yourself?

P: [Angrily] You're not sending me to a state hospital! I'll put in a 72-hour notice! [A request to be discharged from the hospital, to which the hospital must respond within 72 hours by either discharging the patient or petitioning the court to retain the patient against the patient's will.]

T: I don't understand! You're the one that raised the issue of a state hospital. But, again, what do you see as your alternatives?

P: What do you mean?

T: Well, you say that you know that you have to help yourself, that no one can do this for you. Also, you say that you're not able to help yourself but that you don't want to go to a state hospital. If you were the social worker on your case, what would you be saying?

P: [Silence] I guess I'd be saying that you either have to get your act together or go for long-term treatment.

T: Is that an option then, long-term treatment?

P: I don't know, isn't it?

T: What do you think? If I told you that I had a patient who doesn't help herself, would that impress you that she was a candidate for long-term treatment?

P: [Cries softly.] I guess there's no hope. (Silence) I don't know what to do. You and the hospital can't help me. I never should have admitted myself.

T: It sounds to me that you're feeling pretty bad, but that you also have trouble facing the realistic aspects of your life. You can't stay here forever. This unit is a short-term unit. We'd ordinarily expect you to be discharged within about thirty days of when you were admitted. That's, let's see, you were admitted on Wednesday, a week and a half ago. We'd expect to have you out by three weeks from yesterday – that would be Thursday the 12th.

P: I don't know if I can do it.

T: You have about three weeks. You might be able to get a better hold on yourself by then. After all, the people in Admissions [the admissions office of the hospital, which makes all the decisions regarding admissions to the various units] must have thought you could do it or they wouldn't have placed you on this unit!

Comment:

In this session, the therapist seems to confront the issue of self-destructive acts directly, but seemingly in a fashion to make up for the earlier lapse. He should have seen if there were any issues of special note to the patient at the moment. However, from the flow of the session, this approach does not seem to have created excessive problems. The patient immediately disavows any responsibility for her actions while claiming great motivation to be better. Of note, the patient does not differentiate between the motivation to *be* different than she is from the motivation to *do* what is necessary to be different. The former is commonplace; the latter much rarer. Nevertheless, the raising of the spectre of the state hospital suggests an awareness, split off in consciousness, that continued self-destructive activity on her part will inevitably lead to state hospital referral. The therapist is able to tactfully explore this side of her fantasy, using a technique that dilutes some of the transferential aspects through the use of an imaginary other patient. This technique also tests the capacity of the patient to empathize with the viewpoint of others, a capacity seen by Kernberg as retained in patients with borderline personality organization (Kernberg 1975b).

Implicitly, a limit has been placed on the duration of the therapy on the acute unit—an expectation of discharge within thirty days. The therapist was quite specific and concrete regarding which day would be her expected discharge date. The therapist was advised to be liberal in the use of this date as a reminder to her, to help her organize her efforts. It would be anticipated that such organization and mobilization would be accompanied by a release of aggression, most probably directed toward the therapist and hospital staff.

Therapy Session
[Over the preceding weekend—days 11 and 12 of hospitalization—the patient had not made any self-destructive gestures. In the morning, the treatment team raised her status to SO (special observation), which affords her more freedom; the staff check her every 15 minutes instead of constantly accompanying her wherever she goes.]

P: My mother visited me this weekend. I can't believe her! I asked her to bring me some clothing to wear, and she brought me two pairs of slacks and four tops! You'd think that she would use her head. She knows that I don't like those slacks; I need jeans. She's such a pain in the ass. I'm sorry I ever talked to her about it.

T: She disappointed you again.

P: Yeah, I should have known it. She's never understood me. I always felt that she was sorry she had me, like I was a burden. She once told me that I was a mistake.

T: How did you feel about that?

P: Pretty shitty. Why would any mother say that to her kid? I mean, what are you to think?

T: What did you think?

P: I used to cry myself to sleep at night over it. For a while, I thought that I would really make her proud of me, make something of myself. When I went to social work school I thought she'd really like it.

T: What was her response?

P: She kept saying, "If that's what you want to do, then it's fine with me." It was as if *she* was doing *me* a favor in approving my going to grad school in social work! She gets me so mad! I don't know why.

T: Are there ever times when you don't feel mad at her, when you feel more warmly towards her?

P: Yeah, like when I first came home to live with her, after the job didn't work out. We got along okay for a while then. We didn't get into each other's hair.

T: How do you understand the difference now? Why are the two of you so often at each other's throats?

P: Well, she would say that it's my fault, that I ask too much of her and don't give anything in return. But let me tell you, she's not one to talk about that! Things were okay at home while I acted like her maid and servant. The moment I let up, she was on my case about it.

T: What do you mean? What happened?

P: One day I just felt too depressed to do anything. I stayed in bed all day, never got dressed. She came home from work, saw the dishes in the sink, me in my nightgown, and blew up! You'd have thought I'd committed a capital offense.

T: How did you think that she came to that reaction?

P: I don't know. I can't talk to her; she doesn't listen. Every other day I had taken care of things in the house, except maybe for a day or two. I just can't figure her out.

T: There had been some other occasions when you had felt too depressed to clean up and get dressed?

P: Not many, maybe once a week at most. I think what she expected was that just because I was staying at home that I would be like a live-in maid. But I was depressed and thinking about killing myself all the time.

T: Did you talk to her about how you were feeling?

P: No, you can't talk to her about things like that. She just gets all upset.

T: So, she had no idea that you were feeling so bad.

P: I guess.

T: She just saw you hanging out at home doing nothing.

P: But I was severely depressed then.

T: I take it that you're feeling a little better now?

P: Yeah, today isn't such a bad day. I slept better over the weekend, too.

T: But going back to getting along with your mother, she didn't know how bad you were feeling. You didn't think that she could hear that from you. On the other hand, she could see that you weren't doing very much, maybe one day a week, when you would stay in bed and not clean things up.

P: That's right. She would immediately start screaming at me about how lazy I was, that I didn't appreciate her. God, I was just about dying at home, and she was worried about her fucking coffee cups.

T: It's hard for you to see your mother as having any consideration for you.

P: She doesn't care about me. [Her eyes are teary.]

T: Hard for me to know. On the other hand, you didn't feel that you could tell her just how you felt, but that just made it so that she couldn't appreciate your pain. The two of you were trapped—you felt awful and desperately wanted some caring; your mother couldn't tolerate the idea of your feeling so bad, wanted you to feel and be okay, and couldn't understand why someone like you couldn't do simple things like housework. It's a set-up for conflict and bad feelings.

P: I think you're right. I never thought of it that way. I always thought that she just didn't care.

Comment:

Thus far, the prediction that when the patient organizes she will be more hostile toward her therapist has not been realized. She did get quite angry with her mother over the visit and bringing the wrong clothing. Her anger seemed to be inappropriate in that the articles of clothing the mother had brought were not unreasonable choices for wear in the hospital. One would hypothesize that the therapist in this session is perceived as the libidinally linked object while the mother is the aggressively linked object. This constellation is likely to change through the course of hospitalization, unless there are dramatic changes in her personality structure, a highly unlikely scenario.

Throughout the session, the patient seems able to take a more accepting view of her mother, in part the result of two low-level interpretations. Both interventions are followed by significant affective displays, the first, anger – when she curses at her mother's coffee cups – and the second, sadness – as she contemplates the state of her mother not loving her. If she gets into greater contact with the internal representation of the unlovable aspect of herself, and if she cannot tolerate this feeling, then she is likely to rage at the therapist as a way of fighting off these feelings. The therapist needs to know about these potential dynamics, since if this hypothesis turns out to be the case, the therapist may need some support to get through this phase of the treatment. The therapist was advised to pay close attention to the explicit and implicit views of the patient herself as revealed in whatever subject she discusses. These manifestations of the part-self representations will be critical elements in psychotherapeutic work with her.

Therapy Session
[The patient has not made any self-destructive gestures or acts since the last therapy session. She remains on SO status.]
P: Can I have my status changed?
T: How are you feeling?
P: Okay. I'm pretty bored on this unit. Much of what you do here is a waste of time. I'd like to be able to get off the unit, go to activities, maybe. Carol [one of the favored nurses] said that I should speak to you about it.
T: Do you think you'll have any trouble controlling your bad feelings?
P: I've been doing okay for a while. I'd speak to the staff if I was feeling suicidal, if that's what you're asking.
T: That's it. I wouldn't want you to feel that we couldn't handle hearing that you're feeling bad. Sometimes letting the staff know can not only help prevent an incident but can be helpful to someone, too.
P: So, can I have my status raised?

T: I'll talk to the other team members and, if they agree, we'll raise your status to CH [closed hall status, in which the patients are escorted in groups off the unit.]

P: Okay.

T: [Silence] What's been on your mind?

P: Nothing.

T: Really?

P: Yeah. I don't mind being in the hospital so much. [Silence] I've been concerned about what's happening with Diane [her roommate]. She's been having a rough time. I don't think that the care plan that keeps her in the Quiet Room works for her. She seems to be better when I talk to her.

T: Yeah.

P: Has the staff considered giving her more privileges and seeing if she can handle them? I don't know if I should say this, but I think that the aides provoke her, especially Jerry. A lot of the patients think he's really unfit to work in a hospital.

T: I know that the [other] treatment team has had many discussions about how to deal with Diane, including whether or not to let up on the restrictiveness of her care plan. Right now, they plan to stick with the nursing care plan as it is. You're not the only one who has questions about it, though, but frankly it's a tough call. It's too early to tell if the plan will work.

P: I just thought I'd tell you.

T: No, I appreciate your thoughts on it. On the other issue you raised, the one about Jerry, I'm surprised to hear you say that. My impression is that he's a pretty conscientious and thoughtful guy.

P: [Silence] I don't know what's going to happen to me. I feel that things are closing in on me. I got a call from Janet [her former instructor and therapist] last night. She said that she might be able to get me a job in the city.

T: How did you feel about that?

P: Nervous. I didn't do so well at my last job. [Silence] What did you say was my discharge date?

T: Let's see, it was the 12th, if I recall. [Silence] Why do you ask?

P: I'm afraid. What if I don't have things arranged by then? Will you send me to a state hospital?

T: Slow down. I thought you were talking about a job offer. Let's fin-
    ish with that first.

P: What's there to say?

T: How did you feel hearing that Janet might have a job for you?

P: [Silence] I don't know.

T: One thing is clear—you don't appear to feel particularly good about
    this news. How do you understand that?

P: I don't.

T: Well, what are your thoughts on it?

P: [Silence] I told you, I don't have any. This is a waste of time!

T: [Silence] I'm sitting here trying to think of how it is that a person
    could not feel good about what many other people might hear as
    great news. [Pause] The first thing that came to my mind was that
    you don't feel that you deserve a break, that you're unworthy of
    Janet's attention and interest. [Silence] What do you think?

P: [Mumbles something inaudible]

T: [Silence] I couldn't hear what you said. Could you repeat it?

P: I said you're an asshole. I want to leave! Can I go back to the unit?

T: How about staying? We don't have that much time left to meet any-
    way. [Pause] What do you think led to your being so angry with
    me?

P: You know, you think that you know everything. I wouldn't be an-
    gry with you if you didn't treat me the way you do.

T: Tell me how I treat you? I'm obviously not aware of what I do?

P: I'll say! You've got this high and mighty attitude, just because
    you're the doctor. You know you're not better than anyone else!
    [Pause] Can I leave now?

T: Okay. You can.

Comment:

The session begins with an administrative request—a status
change. This issue is dealt with reasonably well, and the patient appropriately senses that her request will be granted. One might reasonably
suppose that she would be pleased with the implicit recognition of her
progress by the staff in the granting of this request. She next moves the
subject to the issues of the treatment of another patient and criticism of
an evening staff member. In these two issues, one must wonder to what

extent she is really commenting on issues more directly affecting her. What does she think of her care plan? She has special relationships with two of the nurses now. Does she feel that they know how to deal with her and that their advice is going unheeded to her detriment? This is a likely internal scenario.

Although she has not made any recent self-destructive acts, and to that extent one could say that the plan has been quite effective, it is probable that she is ambivalent about the care plan. It is not a high order inference to suggest that she would like the limits that have been explicitly and implicitly placed on her to be replaced by a more "sympathetic" approach, more like what she experiences in her relationships with the specially selected nurses, such as Carol. However, such an approach is likely to be regressive and is likely to foster the very actions that one would like to contain and prevent. In fact, the mental health worker she has suggested as unfit is one of the more consistent limit setters among the staff, and her attack on him can be understood as the other prong of her assault on her care plan—divide and conquer. When her attempt to split the staff fails—her therapist doesn't support either her contention that Diane's care plan is ill-conceived or that Jerry is unfit—her mood shifts to a more dysphoric and apprehensive state. One would hypothesize that her attacks were attempts to ward off such feeling.

In a paradoxical way, the phone call from Janet further weakened her ability to ward off these feelings. The therapist assumes that it is the contradiction between the interest in her by Janet (that she so desperately wants but is incapable of accepting) and her devalued sense of self that fuels her dysphoria. She attempts to deny the dysphoria. When confronted with the contradiction between her observed state and the possible meaning of the news she had received—rather than attempting to integrate the devalued part-self representation with the valued part-self representation, activated by the realistic but intolerable positive interest of Janet—she immediately projects the negative feelings onto the therapist and perceives the therapist as contemptuous and uncaring. The supervisor, while not disagreeing with this formulation, suggested an alternative dynamic: perhaps the news about the job merely fueled the patient's fears of failure, fears linked to a fragile vulnerability to narcissistic injury. If so, then the patient may have become angry at the therapist because she felt misunderstood by him.

When the patient tries to flee the office, the therapist wisely encourages her to stay. However, shortly thereafter, and while still the object of her hostility, he permits her to leave rather than follow through on the exploration of the negative transference. This permission by the therapist clearly represented countertransference acting out. Such acting out is not uncommon even with experienced therapists when dealing with severely disturbed borderline patients. The therapist was able to see how he had acted out in this instance, noting that he had become furious with her and her abuse of him. That he was aware of feeling a sense of "Thank God I'm not like her" led to a sense of guilt which added to his difficulty in staying with her while being accused of being contemptuous. The therapist was reassured that borderline patients frequently provoke very strong reactions in therapists and that the therapist's responsibility is to be aware of such reactions in order to try not to act upon them, rather than to be without a reaction to the patient.

Therapy Session
[Three soda can tops had been found in the patient's room last night. She had not scratched herself with them.]
T: How are you feeling?
P: Okay. I'm sorry about storming out last time. I wasn't feeling very good then. Carol had told me that she was going on vacation after today, and I guess I was pretty upset.
T: But you're feeling okay now?
P: Yeah. [Pause] I called Janet last night. She said I should go to the agency next week for an interview. I'm a little scared about it. I don't know what they'll ask. What if they know about my being here?
T: I can understand why you'd be scared about a job interview, but how could they know about your being hospitalized?
P: Well, maybe Janet told them. No, she wouldn't do that. I don't know; you guys must find out things like that.
T: What if they did know? So what? Does being hospitalized mean that you can't be a social worker?
P: I don't know, does it?
T: It doesn't mean you can't be a physician. Why should it mean you can't be a social worker?

P: I don't know. I guess I'm just scared. I don't know what they'll ask.

T: I would imagine they would want to know what experience you have that is relevant to the kind of work they do, what you've done since graduation, things like that.

P: Yeah, I guess.

T: What do you think you'd say?

P: I don't know.

T: I'm confused. It seems to me that you could answer the question. The only explanation I can come up with is that you hold yourself in such low esteem that you don't feel any answer of yours is worthy. That I'd laugh at you or think that your answer was inane.

P: [Silence] I don't know. I'm scared that they won't take me. It's not easy getting a job now. I screwed up on the job I had before.

T: You seem to see yourself as incompetent, as if the only thing a job offer holds for you is another opportunity to demonstrate your incapacity. What do you think of that?

P: Well, I didn't do so well at my first job!

T: I know that. But that was a temporary job. Sometimes temporary positions are harder than permanent ones: they don't take the time to orient you.

P: That's what happened to me! They just put me in the office and made appointments for me with all these families without any instructions about what I was supposed to be doing!

T: I guess *you* expected yourself to figure it all out on your own, too.

P: I figured other people had done it; why shouldn't I be able to do it? You know that agency has a pretty good reputation.

T: So what? I bet they didn't get their reputation on the basis of temporary workers. Anyway, the issue isn't whether or not the agency has a good reputation; the issue is whether or not your orientation and instruction in the agency was adequate. It sounds to me like it wasn't. But in spite of that, you still expected yourself to have figured it all out. You've got pretty high expectations of yourself.

P: The job meant a lot to me. I felt like I was dying when I was there. There was no one to ask questions. Everyone was so busy. I was overwhelmed and eventually had to quit.

T: I get the sense that you somehow expected yourself to be able to do the job in spite of your lack of experience and their lack of proper supervision and instruction. You don't cut yourself much slack.

P: You're right. I really shouldn't have expected myself to do the job.
It really required a much more experienced worker, or at least
much more supervision.

T: What about the lead that Janet gave you? What's the story with
that?

P: It's a teaching hospital, so the supervision should be good. You do
the family work and discharge planning, working with the residents. It's like the social worker's job here, I think.

T: So you'd be doing things just like Ms. Smith [her social worker]?

P: I guess so. I've thought about that, but that's what I'd like to do. I
know you'll probably say it's not a good idea, that I'll get overin-
volved or something like that, but I want to help people.

T: You can read my mind. My point would be that there is a risk in it to
you—with overinvolvement and your problems with self-destructiveness. You couldn't find other ways to help people? My suggestion would be that you take a job a little further removed from hospital work. Then, after a few years of that, maybe reconsider and
then apply for hospital positions.

P: I knew you'd say that. I guess anyone in your position would say
that. But I want to try it out.

T: Well, good luck with the interview. Do you know when it is?

P: I'm supposed to hear from Janet later this afternoon. She said that
she thought they were fairly anxious to get someone and that she
would try to get me an interview for Monday morning.

T: Okay. I'll talk to the treatment team about that. That means you
would miss group psychotherapy. I'll touch base with you before I
leave this evening about it.

P: Okay.

Comment:

The session begins with the patient apologizing for having stormed
out of her last therapy session. Appropriately, that event is not explored, but the apology accepted. To have attempted to explore the
meaning of her leaving would have required a more stable and solid relationship with her therapist. For now, simply accepting the apology was
appropriate. There should have been some exploration of the meaning
of Carol's vacation. As it was left, the patient is left with the idea that
Carol's announcement fully explained the patient's behavior. This

incident could have been useful for exploring the patient's dependency on others and strong reactivity to losses. The next issue that is discussed is the lead for a job. The patient expressed apprehension about the interview situation, tinged with some paranoia, that the personnel will somehow know of her psychiatric history. The therapist didn't directly confront the paranoia, but diluted it with his statement that being hospitalized is acceptable. She seemed to be relieved by this suggestion but then proceeded to get blocked around the issue of what to say at the job interview. The therapist interprets this as evidence of low self-esteem, to which the patient responds by describing herself as incompetent.

In the context of the actual job situation, the therapist notes that her sense of incompetence was linked to her implicitly grandiose feelings that she could handle any position. She confounds the reputation of the agency with her job conditions at the expense of her self-esteem. This issue is clarified for her, which seems to bolster her self-confidence. The process would appear to be that the exploration of her low self-esteem initially worsened her already devalued part-self representation. The therapist's attempt to clarify her fundamental self-esteem deficit leads to her conclusion that she's incompetent. As the therapist checks this impression against reality, the poor supervision at work contrasted with the excellent reputation of the agency, rather than assisting in the integration of her part-self representations, the grandiose part-self representations seem to be activated, permitting her to ward off attempts to confront her with the reality of her choice for her next job. Thus, while discussing the position at a teaching hospital, she is able to maintain her stance that this choice is reasonable, in spite of the consistent advice she has received from unit and her therapist that this choice is ill-advised for now.

Therapy Session
[The patient had gone on her interview yesterday. Upon return to the hospital, she was described as tense and acting silly.]
T: [Silence] Will you tell me how the interview went?
P: It was nothing much. I was pretty scared, but they didn't ask me much. I told them that I had taken some time off after graduation, did some traveling. They seemed to accept that.
T: Anything else?

P: Well, they wanted to know when I could start? I told them any time. For a second, I thought that they knew I was in the hospital, but I decided that was ridiculous. Could I leave before the 12th if they give me the job?

T: I don't see why not, unless you mess around with your wrists again.

P: No, I'm not going to give you an excuse to send me to the state hospital. [Pause] We didn't get a chance to talk yesterday about my mother's visit over the weekend.

T: What about it?

P: I don't know. Carol said I should talk to you about it.

T: Yeah.

P: [Silence] I don't know. She said we should discuss it.

T: [Silence] I take it that you don't really agree.

P: I don't know. I don't understand my mother. I told her about the discharge date, and she seemed so pleased! It doesn't seem to dawn on her that that may be the date I go to the state hospital. Anyway, she came at 8 P.M. [one-half hour before the end of visiting]! I sat and waited all afternoon and evening, and with less than an hour left to visit she comes parading in as if I should be glad to see her!

T: How did you feel about that?

P: I mean, why bother to come at all?

T: Did you talk to her about it?

P: No, there'd be no point. She said she had been shopping for some shoes and just couldn't find a pair. She said that she had planned to come in the afternoon, but got delayed.

T: Uh huh. But how did you feel about that?

P: How would *you* feel if you were kept waiting all day? I'm sure you wouldn't feel so good.

T: I'm *certain* I wouldn't feel good about it. I'd probably be pretty pissed off.

P: Well, that's the way I felt. I felt like telling her to go to hell.

T: I take it that you didn't. How come?

P: And be put in the Quiet Room? No way!

T: You felt that if you told your mother how you felt that you'd lose control and end up in the Quiet Room.

P: I know how you operate around here. Don't tell *me* that's not what would happen!

T: It seems that what you're saying is that if you verbalized to your mother how you felt, that you'd actually let loose such a tirade that the staff would feel that you need to be placed in the Quiet Room.

P: I said that! [Says this annoyingly.]

T: I just wanted to make sure I understood. What strikes me about it is that you can't tell someone like your mother that you're very angry with her without enacting the anger right there and then.

P: Yeah. I guess that's true. But I was really pissed at her.

T: I wonder if it wasn't the extent of your anger at your mother, and the difficulty that you have controling it that led Carol to suggest that we talk about the visit from your mother?

P: I don't know. You'd have to ask her.

T: [Silence] Is there anything to learn about yourself from this?

P: I don't know. That I don't get along with my mother!

T: Sure, that's true. But it does seem that you have this idea that if you talk about how angry you are, that you'll enact that anger. That seems to me to be a big problem. After all, it's not all that unusual to get angry with people—even very angry. If you can't talk about it—and when you're really getting angry is when it'll count— then you're stuck: either enact it with a temper tantrum or attempt to bury it inside you, and apparently that doesn't work for you.

P: So what am I supposed to do?

T: I just wonder whether or not you're right, that to talk about it means that you'll enact it. Maybe that idea isn't right.

P: I don't know.

T: Well, perhaps you could think about that. After all, a lot of people do learn to talk about many feelings without letting loose. It's not clear to me that you couldn't be one of them.

Comment:

The session starts with a fairly perfunctory discussion of the job interview. The therapist might have pursued the issue in greater depth. Clearly the patient must have many complicated feelings about the process of the interview as well as the implications of her getting a job while being an inpatient. Nevertheless, it was probably wise for the therapist not to pursue those issues. The issue that the patient obliquely raises—she disavows any personal responsibility by invoking the name of a staff member—is that of her recent visit from her mother. The patient has regularly reminded herself of the potential threat of transfer to the state hospital if she doesn't conform her behavior to reasonable standards. However, she talks of this potentiality as if the staff is constantly lording this over her head. Rather than focus on her probable dyscontrol, she focuses on the probable response of the staff to a tempter tantrum, placement in the Quiet Room. In both instances, she clearly uses projection to defend against an awareness of her extremely strong and intolerable feelings of destructiveness and despair.

Her capacity to hear from the therapist that her lack of differentiation between the enactment of a feeling and talking about the feeling suggests that she is making some progress. One would hypothesize that with the diminution of some of her depression—through the use of the antidepressant—combined with the various psychotherapies, she is experiencing less polarized views of herself and others. Hopefully, one of the results of her individual and group therapies would be broader, more complete, but still part-self and part-object representations that permit greater integration of complex attitudes and attributes. As the therapy is progressing, she does not seem to be shifting into a negative view of the therapist, but is maintaining a reasonably positive view. In so far as she idealizes the therapist, this positive transference will have to be addressed. One has to address idealization since it occurs concomitantly with devaluation of the self—the patient is good only in relationship to this therapist. If the idealization is not addressed, then upon discharge the patient's self-esteem will precipitiously drop, and she will be forced to seek readmission. So far, there are not elements in the therapy to suggest such idealization. However, the therapist was advised to be alert to such a turn of events.

Therapy Session
[The previous evening another patient became violent on the unit and was restrained by eight staff members. The patient had become visibly upset by this incident and was calmed after being talked to by two staff members.]
T: [Silence] How are you feeling?
P: Okay.
T: [Silence] Can you say more? [Silence] Can you elaborate on how you're feeling?

P: Okay!

T: Well, it sounds like things were fairly rough last night.

P: I got over it.

T: Can you tell me what happened and how you felt?

P: There's really nothing to say.

T: From what I heard at the community meeting, it sounded quite scary. Is that the way you felt?

P: [Silence] I guess I got pretty upset. I thought I might get killed! It took a whole bunch of guys from other units to restrain him. What if they weren't on last night? What would have happened?

T: You were afraid for your personal safety?

T: *You* would be too if you were there! He was throwing those big chairs! Shit, he could have killed someone!

T: That sounds even more scary than what they said at the community meeting! How come you didn't tell people what you'd seen and what you felt?

P: Oh, there's no point in talking in those meetings. Nothing important ever gets said or done. And I didn't think anyone really wanted to hear it.

T: Wait a moment. You've said a lot. I don't think I can agree with you about the community meetings, but getting back to you, what made you think that no one would want to hear it?

P: Oh, come on! You know that Steve [the patient who had become violent] was ready to blow—it was just a matter of time. The staff let him do what he wants—they've been afraid of him.

T: The staff saw him as a time bomb?

P: Of course! He used to smoke anywhere he wanted to. If *I* light up a cigarette at the fruit bowl [just outside the smoking area] I get on cigarette restriction for 24 hours, but he can go up and down the halls with a cigarette!

T: How do you feel about all that?

P: I don't know. I was glad that Carol wasn't on last night. She could have gotten hurt by Steve.

T: Well, it certainly sounds like quite a frightening scene. As you describe it, even more frightening than I had originally heard. On the other hand, you seemed particularly affected by the incident. I wonder what your thoughts are on that?

P: Uh. I don't know. It was scary.

T: [Silence] I may be off, but I wonder if when you get angry you're not afraid of what you might do?

P: Like kill someone? I'd die before that!

T: What do you mean?

P: You really don't know me at all! I could never kill anyone.

T: Uh huh. But you do get quite angry at times.

P: Yeah, but there's a big difference between getting angry and doing what Steve did.

T: How do you see that?

P: He really lost control. I've never seen anyone so out of it. All from a phone call from his parents, I think.

T: You don't think that being in control of your feelings and impulses is a central issue for you?

P: [Silence] I guess you could see it that way. But I don't think I'd ever be like Steve. Hell, I couldn't even lift one of the end tables!

T: Maybe you ought to think more about why you were so particularly affected by the incident. Maybe you could learn something about yourself.

P: All right.

Comment:

The parallel between what apparently happened to the other patient and to our patient is striking. Both have had severe conflicts with parents leading to poorly tolerated feelings. It would be hard to deny the parallel and not to think that her sense of her own potential for rage was not exemplified by Steve's violent outburst. However, the patient is not able to discuss this parallel at this point. In fact, she must deny that her reaction was significantly deviant from that of her peers. Clearly she identified with Steve and was frightened of the potential of her rage as enacted by Steve. The connection between her rage and suicidal acts is suggested through her comment about "dying" before she'd assault someone else. To follow up her comment with an attempt to interpret that connection would have been premature. It is unclear from the session just how available the connection would be, though the therapist might have explored this connection, both to assess her current suicidal state and her awareness of the link. Considering the glib way in which she links them, it was a technical error not to have pursued her statement about killing herself before killing someone else. Had her mental status at the moment of the session and since the incident not been as stable as it appeared, it would have been a potentially serious error of omission. Hostile-dependent suicidal patients may not provide many signals about imminent suicidal acts; one needs to have a low threshold for the exploration of suicidal ideas, plans, and contingencies.

Therapy Session
[The patient heard yesterday that she has been offered the job, to begin in ten days (a week from the coming Monday).]

P: I'm doing okay. Janet said that I'm lucky to get the job – they chose me over a lot of other social workers, some with a good deal of experience.

T: Uh huh. How do you feel about it?

P: Okay, I guess.

T: Yeah.

P: I'm not really excited about it, if that's what you mean.

T: Really? Just how are you feeling about it?

P: Well, I know it's not easy to get a job now. And I'm pretty lucky to get this job. I guess that I'm scared. My other job didn't work out at all, you know, and I'm afraid I won't make it again. Do you really think I can do it?

T: Sure. I'm not sure I understand your doubts. We'd spoken about some of the problems with your other job. I don't see why you'd use that as a baseline.

P: That's what Janet said, too. I don't know. I'm worried about whether or not I can make it. I'm not sure I'm ready.

T: You don't see yourself as capable?

P: Well. [Silence] Do you think that I'm ready?

T: I think you'll be ready by the time of your discharge.

P: Really?

T: Sure. I have no doubt that it'll be rough going for a while. You're not going to instantly feel comfortable at a new job. There's a lot to learn about social work in a hospital, but if you have good supervision and support you should be able to do it. Janet said that you'd done quite well at your placements.

P: Yeah, but she didn't know what I had to go through all the time. It was a helluva struggle!

T: I'm certain it was. Even more than I know. But there's no real alternative that I can see to it.

P: I just hope you're right that I'll be ready to go by Thursday.

T: You seem to persist in seeing yourself as not competent. I think that represents part of your problem—you don't have a good grasp of your capabilities or limitations.

P: Carol had said that to me, too. She said I had to trust myself before I can trust others. Do you think that's true?

T: I think there's certainly some truth to it.

P: I'm sorry that I've been such a pain. It's been really hard for me. I know that I didn't trust you before. I realize now that it's me that causes my problems and that I have to be willing to talk about them, but it's hard. Does the hospital have a rule about whether therapists can follow patients on discharge?

T: It sounds like you'd like to continue therapy with me after discharge.

P: Well, yeah. If it was okay with you.

T: I'd have to talk to the team about that. But there is the issue of geography. I wonder whether it would be wise to have a therapist in another county. It's not a great commute from the city up here.

P: I know. But I need a therapist who really understands me. And you've seen me through my worst—when I came into the hospital.

T: Well, as I said, I will need to talk to the team about that on Monday. In the meanwhile, you ought to think about what motivates your request other than the idea that I've seen you through this hospitalization. Maybe you could learn something about yourself.

P: Okay.

Comment:

This session begins with an attempt to elicit the patient's reaction to hearing about her employment offer. The patient's reaction is unenthusiastic, and this is explored. She is aware of her anxiety about her ability to function at the job. Quickly, her devalued part-self representations are articulated. The therapist attempts to provide support and reiterates his link to Janet, a good part-object, by reporting to the patient that which Janet had said about the patient. Later, the patient links the therapist to her other good part-object, Carol. By the end of the session, the patient is implying that only this therapist can understand her, evidence of idealization. The supervisor suggested that the therapist should have explored the meaning of the changes in her attitude towards him, first by clarifying what the current perception was and then what the previous perceptions were. He seems to be distracted from the task by her request to be followed in outpatient therapy by him.

The therapist admitted to the supervisor that he was not inclined to follow her, so that this distraction, and his subsequent deferral of the decision to the team, probably represented countertransference acting out. The therapist was seduced by her idealization of him. He was unaware that he was arranging to disappoint her by saying that the team—and his supervisor—did not think it in her best interests for therapy to continue with him. Even the therapist's earlier reassurance about her ability to handle the job, while basically supportive, probably concealed his discomfort with the patient's regressive, aggressive, and dependent tendencies; he did not appreciate his relief at the idea that she would "graduate" from the hospital to a different location and a different therapist.

Therapy Session
[The patient had two passes over the weekend. She found an apartment with a reasonable commute to her new job. She arranged to share the apartment with a friend she had known from graduate school. On return from her second pass, she was reported to have two valium pills. Her room was searched and her pockets and pocketbook searched but no pills were found. She said that she had flushed them down the toilet.]

P: I'm really excited about my apartment. It's on the West Side, near my school.I can take the subway down to work. Cynthia [her former classmate and future roommate] has all the stuff we need. I'll need to get a bed, but her uncle said he had one he could give me. So, I'm pretty much set and happy about it.

T: Sounds like pretty good plans.

P: Yeah, Mary [Ms. Smith, her social worker] had suggested that I look at the school bulletin board for someone looking for a roommate. I was pretty lucky in finding Cynthia. The rent isn't bad either. Cynthia said she could help me until I got paid.

T: That's pretty nice of her.

P: Yeah, that's like her. She's a very giving person. We're sort of similar that way.

T: You're that way, too.

P: Yeah, that's what gets me into trouble. I do too much for others.

T: Tell me about it.

P: I don't know. We don't really have enough time to get into it.

T: We may as well use the time we have.

P: Well. [Silence] That's where I get into trouble with guys. Relationships always seem to mean more to me than to them. Like, I knew at the Agency [her first job] that Eric [the man at the Agency mentioned previously] was interested in me and I sort of liked him. But I was afraid that it would be the same old shit.

T: Uh huh. But I still don't know what you mean by the same old shit.

P: I guess I feel used. That's what happens. You get involved with someone and they take advantage of you.

T: How do you mean that?

P: You know what I mean!

T: I'm not certain. You said that you give too much, that you're taken advantage of. But that's still pretty vague.

P: You know, they have lots of time and interest when it's convenient for them, but when you need them, pffffft!

T: So you feel you meet their needs but when it comes to your needs they're ignored.

P: Yeah!

T: Can you give me an example of it?

P: Well, I dated this guy last year for about two months. He worked at my placement – he was an OT [occupational therapist]. He seemed really nice – fun to be with, very good with the patientts. He asked me out very shortly after I started work there. We got involved pretty quickly.

T: Yeah.

P: Well, it wasn't long before he was telling me that we couldn't go out Friday night 'cause he had to go out with some of his friends.

T: You felt that you had a proper claim on his time?

P: He'd said that he really liked me – and it seemed that he did. It just didn't make sense. If he liked me so much, why didn't he want me to be with his friends.

T: I get the feeling that you felt quite close to him and wanted a more exclusive relationship with him than he was ready for.

P: That's what I said!

T: That's what you mean by you give too much, that you experience relationships more intensely than others and then feel – properly so, I suspect – that your feelings aren't reciprocated.

P: Exactly!

T: What do you make of that?

P: Of what?

T: Of the fact that you seem to feel a greater intensity in relationships than others do and then find yourself feeling that you're taken advantage of, that you give too much.

P: I don't understand your question. I said that.

T: It just seems that there must be something to learn from this. I was hoping you could think out loud about it.

P: I think it's pretty straightforward. I have bad taste in men! [patient laughs nervously]

T: I guess that's a possibility. But another possibility is that you too quickly develop specific expectations that are unrelated to the guy but more related to you and your needs.

P: What do you mean?

T: That you have fairly strong needs for other people in your life – guys and girls. And when you get into a relationship, those needs get activated pretty quickly, almost regardless of what sort of signals you might get from the guy.

P: I don't know. Maybe that's true. I'd have to think about it.

T: I think that's a good idea. Certainly things don't go right for you. You've got to be able to learn something about it. But there's another unrelated issue: what was the story with the valium?

P: What do you mean?

T: I was told that you had brought back some valium?

P: Look, I've been getting fairly anxious, and frankly I was afraid you'd ignore me. So when Jeff [a patient on the unit] offered me some valium, I took them. But then I figured that with my luck, I'll get caught, and then you'd have the excuse to send me to the state hospital. So I flushed them down the drain.

T: I see. I'm glad you got rid of them. You're a set-up for getting addicted to pills. You're the sort of person for whom one is too many; you find yourself anxious too often.

P: Yeah, I think you're right. I think that's why my mother drinks.

Comment:

For the better part of the session, the patient appears to have a rather dependent and positive transference. She seeks support from her therapist and seems willing to explore her troubles in dealing with men. The therapist, however, too quickly attempted to move to deeper levels of understanding with the patient. He ran into her lack of understanding, as a defense against certain part-self representations that were most probably related to feeling unlovable, unworthy, and defective. He too quickly attempted to reframe her experience with his term of intensity in relationships. The supervisor suggested that a more helpful approach might have been a more patient, if seemingly tedious, exploration of her notions of what occurs in her relationships. In this case, the pressure of short-term work and the wish to help the patient resolve the issue, combined perhaps with the implicit erotic aspects, contributed to premature attempts to resolve the problem. The patient's inability to understand the intervention of the therapist, however, was more likely defensive than an indication that it was incorrect. The change in subject to the incident with the pills was reasonable.

The therapist should have explored her expectations about what he would prescribe for her rather than so quickly taking an educative stance. This incident could have provided some insight into the hostile side of the transference. Again, it seemed that countertransference forces colluded with the patient's ostensible ignorance of the risks of sedative abuse, to result in avoidance of exploration of the negative transference. The therapist should have explored her expectations of him, assessed the reality as well as the distortions, and then provided education as needed.

Therapy Session

[The patient is scheduled for discharge tomorrow. A private therapist in the city, reasonably accessible to the patient, had been found for her. This session is the last scheduled individual session.]

P: I'm scared. I don't think that I can make it.

T: Tell me about it.

P: [Patient cries softly] I don't know what to do!

T: How do you mean that?

P: Can't you understand anything? I'm *scared*!

T: I can see that. I'm trying to understand your scaredness better.

P: I just know that I can't make it.

T: How are you so certain?

P: I don't know. I just don't think that I can make it. I failed at the agency, and now you're throwing me out of here. I'm just not ready.

T: You feel that we're just tossing you out.

P: Well, aren't you? You said it was either out to the apartment or to the state hospital. That's being thrown out!

T: You feel that the staff and I don't really appreciate the depths of your problems. How impaired you are.

P: You don't! I don't think that you have the least fucking idea about any of your patients!

T: You seem particularly pissed at me. What gives?

P: Sometimes I think you're stupid! I *told* you! I'm afraid that I can't make it. And you and the rest of the goddam staff don't give a shit! You'd probably laugh if I died!

T: Hold on a minute. I hear that you feel that you can't make it. On the other hand, one of your persistent problems is that you're not the best assessor of your capacities. There are two possibilities here: either you're right, and we're idiots, sadists or simply wrong, or we're right, and your assessment is off again.

P: You know it doesn't pay to talk to you. You just don't listen!

T: It seems to me that you have a hard time confronting the possibility that your fears of leaving the hospital have increased your anxiety, fueled your own sense of inadequacy and, rather than dealing with those anxieties, you go on the attack.

P: [Crying] There's no point. No one cares about me, not even my own mother. She was saying that if the doctors gave you the date, then you must be ready. No one cares!

T: I guess that's one way of looking at things—no one cares. Another way might be that people *do* care but that doesn't mean you'll be feeling real good. I don't think there could be any way by which you could leave the hospital and not be pretty damn scared.

P: You'd be scared too if you'd been through what I've been through.

T: But you don't tolerate feeling scared real well. That's a problem in itself. Medications are a risky alternative for you. So that leaves you with your fears. But when you experience those fears, you think that we're callously indifferent. I don't think that's true, that the staff is indifferent to your plight. It seems that the way you measure caring is through what you experience — "If I feel anxious then the staff doesn't care."

P: Well, what else am I supposed to do?

T: I don't have any easy formulas. You need to be willing to look at yourself and see how you operate. Then you need to correct things on the basis of a better understanding of yourself. None of these tasks is easy.

P: You certainly haven't helped me with them here. I think that coming to the hospital was a waste.

T: I'm sorry that you feel that way. Hopefully your outpatient therapy will be more successful. Hope things go okay on the job. I'm certain that the adjustment period will be trying and you'll feel no less anxious. But I think if you stay with it — both your therapy and your job — that you'll do all right. Good luck!

Comment:

The session starts with two critical facts that are linked: the therapy and the hospitalization are terminating. As suggested earlier, there has been a mobilization of her aggression directed towards the therapist and staff concomitant with termination. Attempts to explore her fears regarding discharge are dismissed by the patient as evidence of the therapist's insensitivity and stupidity. She describes the staff as callously throwing her out of the hospital and launches into curses and invectives against the therapist and staff. Her statement that no one would care if she died is of particular interest. It implies two things: that dying is on her mind but that gratifying retaliation would not be possible through dying. That dying is an issue on her mind at such a time is not unusual. It is reassuring, however, that her implicit message is that she won't kill herself for spite. Although she is describing her intense doubts and fears, she is going along with the recommendations of the staff. She describes her feelings of anxiety and fears of incompetence.

It is highly speculative, but consistent, to suppose that her anger at the staff and her therapist is her only means of separating from them without feeling a loss of self-esteem, and that her anger serves to organize her part-self representation as a more positive and competent image. The evidence for this assumption is in her behavior, not in her words. She is acting competently while describing her incompetence. She is verbally describing her incapacity to tolerate her affective states while she is, in fact, tolerating them. One would eventually need to confront her with this discrepancy between her statements about herself and her actual behavior. At the moment, splitting and denial support this contradiction. The therapist needed support during this time as well, since he felt hurt by her parting vilification of him. The fact that the supervisor had earlier predicted such a turn of events made it possible for the therapist not to respond punitively or impulsively, but his overintellectualized style kept him, on his side, at a defensive distance from her.

Some of the staff felt the patient's caustic criticism of the staff represented serious regression that meant she needed continued hospitalization at the state hospital, but such a view did not make dynamic or phenomenological sense. Her neurovegetative signs and symptoms had remitted. There was no clinical evidence of untreated depressive disorder. Dynamically, her response seemed to represent an attempt to restore her self-esteem as she left a fairly supportive environment.

Chapter 11

An Example of an Object Relations Approach to Group Psychotherapy

This example illustrates the use of the object relations conceptualization of conflict and its integration with group psychotherapy. Although we again recognize that one cannot fully appreciate the significance of events in the group without addressing the systems implications, those issues are deliberately not discussed here in order to highlight our point.

The group is composed of eight patients and two therapists—a nurse and a psychiatrist. There are four observers: a psychiatrist, a psychiatric resident, a mental health worker, and a social worker. The group begins on time; there is a new male patient, Mr. A., 27 years old. The diagnoses of the patients are: chronic undifferentiated schizophrenia—two patients; borderline personality—one teenage girl and one 23-year-old man; a manic patient in partial remission; a depressed middle-aged woman; a chronic paranoid schizophrenic; and the new patient (diagnosis unknown to the therapy staff at the time).

The therapists open the group with the observation that there is a new group member. They request that the group members orient the new member. The teenage girl states with a bored tone that this meeting is the small group psychotherapy that meets three times a week from 8:30 A.M. to 9:15 A.M., that the purpose of the meeting is to discuss

the problems that brought you into the hospital as well as the problems
that you have in leaving the hospital. The new patient is obviously angry
from the moment the group starts. He asks, "Who are the people sitting
behind me?" "Why is that guy taking notes?" The nurse–therapist
quickly responds that the people sitting outside the group are members
of the treatment team; that the person taking notes is a psychiatrist;
that the notes are taken in order to help the team and the leaders conduct the group more effectively; and that the observers are *silent* observers. The other patients chime in that they, too, were concerned
about the observers at first, but that they quickly became accustomed
to them. The manic patient notes that it helps since all the team members know all about you.

The psychiatrist–therapist tells the new patient that it is usual for
the new patient to introduce himself to the group by describing what led
to his hospitalization. The new patient then begins a long harangue
against his family. He describes his family as being condescending,
unsupportive, and duplicitous. He tells the group that his family under-
mines all of his activities – his attempts to set up a business, "to make important contacts." His description of how his parents told him that the
family was simply going to "see someone" when he was brought to the
hospital is vivid. He alludes to other times when he was "tricked" into
the hospital by his family. He makes it clear that his only problem is his
state of being hospitalized. His anger diffuses over to an attack on the
nursing staff for their inadequate, unfeeling care that he received over
the preceding weekend. The nurse–therapist notes that Mr. A is having
a hard time adjusting to being in the hospital and that he doesn't feel
that the staff is able to do right by him. The other patients have little
room to either interrupt his barrage of complaints and criticisms or
agree with him. The 23-year-old borderline man squirms uneasily in his
seat as the new patient's criticisms of the staff persist.

One of the chronic schizophrenic patients gets up, stating that she
has to go to the bathroom; the female mental health worker follows her
down the hall. They return in about a minute. The psychiatrist-
therapist offers the observation that the patients in the group seem to
be intimidated by the complaints and protestations of the new patient.
The old patients continue to make timid attempts to interrupt the new

patient's harangue but retreat quickly. The psychiatrist–therapist notes that Mr. A. seems to have had a fair amount of trouble prior to admission, yet to listen to his story he is not in need of hospitalization and has no problems! "It doesn't add up," the therapist adds. The borderline man agrees and asks how come he gets into such conflict with the staff since they aren't all that bad, although he does agree that "the night staff is bad." Mr. A. responds condescendingly and angrily, "You don't understand." The borderline girl snaps back, "Then explain it to us." One of the chronic schizophrenic patients fills a brief pause with a comment of how she misses her pet dog. No one follows up on this comment, and the new patient continues. The psychiatrist–therapist interrupts, saying that it seems difficult for Mr. A to acknowledge that he needs help, even though it is obvious to other members of the group that he needs help. The therapist continues that it also seems to be difficult for Mr. A to accept help from staff members. Other patients attempt to change the subject but always pick subjects of little obvious interest or concern to others. The therapists intervene to clarify that the new patient seems to perceive many situations as "always dangerous – with people being malevolent," and then the therapist attempts to encourage other patients to explore, question, and reflect upon what the new patient stated. The group members gradually begin to fall silent, not asking for any clarifications or attempting to introduce new subjects. The new patient appears to be experienced by the members of the group as domineering and threatening. His monopolization of the group is clear.

The psychiatrist–therapist intervenes:

It seems that the group is having as much trouble dealing with Mr. A as Mr. A is having accepting his hospitalization; Mr. A acts as if we are dangerous. He implies that he doesn't have any problems and that since we don't understand that, it makes sense to him to be mad at us and suspicious of us. On the other hand, it is possible that Mr. A, at some level, knows that he has problems and needs to be in the hospital; it is certainly obvious to us that that's true. Maybe it is just this feeling – that he needs someone else – that is hard for Mr. A to admit, so he avoids it by going on the attack. Sort of the best defense is a good offense.

Mr. A responds, acknowledging that he needs help but not from the hospital. The nurse–therapist suggests that he give other people a chance to talk. A discussion ensues about how difficult it is to get help. There is substantial discussion about how many ways others have tried to get help and have been offered help, but it is sometimes inadequate. Mr. A picks up at the end of the discussion with less vehemence. Nevertheless, he is still protesting and complaining. He now restricts his complaints about staff to night staff and their checking him. The therapists begin to feel irritated by the patient and sense that this irritation is shared by the patient members, too. Other group members fall silent again. A therapist interrupts the new patient and makes the observation that something unhelpful seems to be occurring in the group again. The group members remain silent. Mr. A expresses, with some irritation, that he agrees with the observation, but then continues with his complaints. The nurse–therapist interrupts again, noting that the group is having difficulty talking with Mr. A, the group retreating to silence. (It appears to the silent observers that the members of the group seem incapable of acknowledging their anger at the new patient, as if to meaningfully confront him would be to kill him. The patients seem to be concomitantly furious with the group psychotherapists for not protecting them from such a person.) At this point, the teenage girl justifies her atypical silence with the statement that she just doesn't "have anything to say." A therapist asks if other members of the group feel the same way, and two other patients nod in agreement. The group remains silent.

The group therapists experience the group members as sulking. The psychiatrist–therapist intervenes:

It seems that at first the group saw that Mr. A needed help and tried to be supportive, but got turned off by the angry rejections you received in return. You changed your view of him from "being one of us" to that of someone who is himself dangerous, so dangerous, in fact, that the only safe thing to do seemed to be to say nothing or make small talk. As we have seen in this group before, this pattern is a typical one for all the old members of the group; probably for Mr. A, too. That is, you withdraw, feel helpless, and then want the therapist to bail you out.

A discussion ensues which centers upon their feelings of helplessness and inability to function. The initial thrust of the discussion, fueled by the partially treated manic patient, is in the direction of the need for an expert therapist to "cure" them. This attitude receives substantial support from most of the group members.

Both therapists attempt to redirect the discussion to views of the patients themselves, clarifying that they are perceiving themselves as being inadequate and dependent, especially vis-á-vis the therapists. The psychiatrist–therapist states:

> Every one of you in the group is struggling with feelings about yourself that you don't like. The choices are then either to deal with those feelings and obtain the help that you need, or to somehow avoid the feelings but then not to get the help either. No doubt you feel angry not only with Mr. A but with us – the therapists too – for not doing something. This may be yet another way of trying to deal with stresses that members of the group use that doesn't work very well. You end up feeling hopeless, see other people – here us the therapists – as having abilities, yet cruelly refusing to help you. A vicious cycle begins involving selling yourselves short here and then overvaluing us, the therapists, both way out of proportion from what's really true. You don't give yourselves a chance.

The teenage girl quickly responds, saying that it is not easy to get help and sometimes it doesn't pay. She talks about her despair over her ambiguous discharge plans. She knows that if her placement does not materialize soon, that she will have to return home. She looks over at the new patient and informs him that her problems came from her being at home and her inability to get along with her mother. The depressed middle-aged woman talks about how even when you do ask, no one ever bothers to help you out and how uncaring her children are. The borderline man gently confronts the middle-aged woman about how she expects too much of her children and needs to do things herself.

A discussion follows in which several members discuss how hard it is to get along with family members. Mr. A elaborates on his difficulties with his family. This time other patients speak, too; Mr. A's descriptions are less distorted. The members obtain a clear understanding of how

Mr. A's paranoid attitude is maintained and aggravated by actions of his parents. The nurse-therapist notes that there clearly are ways for getting help, which doesn't imply that one is terrible or that others have all the answers. Discussion continues, with a much reduced sense of tension in the group, centering around the idea of how people have to pull together to ensure that they have their best care and discharge plans.

In the rehash that immediately followed the group meeting, there was agreement that, after the series of interventions centering around the group's perception of Mr. A. and Mr. A's self-concept, the group became more organized and productive. Mr. A's hostility dropped significantly; the members rose out of their sulking silence. The interactions that followed, including Mr. A's willingness to participate as an equal, were seen as a response to the interventions. The therapists viewed Mr. A as predominantly interacting with others in the group on the basis of the "negative" self-object unit, with projection of his rage in a near-paranoid fashion. Their assumption was that this interpersonal configuration represented both a defensive projection of internalized rage and a defense against awareness of Mr. A's feelings of helplessness and wish for gratification, as well as fears of merger and fusion. Concomitantly, the therapists viewed the group as having begun with reasonable commitment to its task. The initial challenges by Mr. A were received without disruption; in fact, group members collectively attempted to support and validate Mr. A and his perceptions. However, Mr. A's monotonous perception of danger and his response of constant raging in and at the group moved the group from a work orientation into resistance.

The group was able to tolerate the raging of Mr. A to a substantial extent. The last collective effort by the group to work with the challenge that Mr. A presented seemed to have been the unification with Mr. A against the night staff, but even that failed. Attempts by the therapists—to clarify and confront the process within the group while the group reacted with withdrawal and anger—failed. The group members avoided past painful feelings of helplessness and weakness by not confronting those feelings in Mr. A; it was as if he were the sole repository of such feelings. Uncertain of their own new-found self-esteem, they avoided the underlying issue of Mr. A's helplessness as if they risked losing their own self-esteem in the process of trying. The interventions of the therapists served to clarify and confront the process apparent in the group and contrasted it with the reality of the situation. Rather than the fantasied mutual destruction (the old group members feel helpless and weak, and Mr. A is crushed), the group became more organized and functioned with less tension as the issue was confronted.

Chapter 12

An Example of a
Community Meeting

The community meeting is held in the living room area adjacent to the nursing station. At about 8:25 A.M., patients and staff members begin to congregate in the living room area. Some staff members bring extra chairs from the dining room into the living room; two patients assist. Some chairs are set up in rows, facing the front of the room where the leader sits. The remaining chairs are arranged along the sides of the room, also facing the leader. About a minute before the meeting is scheduled to begin (8:30 A.M.), the leader of the meeting, Dr. Clark, enters the living room and takes his seat, which faces the auditorium-style section. He has a sheet of paper with the names of the patients who were admitted since the last meeting as well as the names of those patients who are about to be discharged. The leader notes that many of the patients are not present and asks a mental health worker (Mr. Lewis) if all the patients have been invited to attend. Mr. Lewis says that he does not know, and leaves the meeting to check with other staff members. It is now 8:30 A.M.

Staff Scheduled for Attendance

Dr. Clark = Leader
Dr. Adams = Unit Chief

Ms. Anderson = Head Nurse
Ms. Becker = Charge Nurse

Dr. Black = Assistant Unit Chief
Drs. Diamond, Evans and Fields = Second Year Residents
Mrs. Harris, Miss Grant, and Mr. Johnson = Social Workers
Miss David, Mr. Ellis = Staff Nurses
Mr. Lawrence, Mr. Lewis, and Miss Hansen = Mental Health Workers
Ms. Hunter = Occupational Therapist
Ms. Cohen = Psychology Intern

Dr. Clark:	It's now 8:30 and time to begin. I'm Dr. Clark. I don't believe that all the patients are here. Mr. Lewis, who are we missing?
Mr. Lewis:	Misses Jackson, Kane, Lane, and Lee are still in the ladies' room. Mr.'s Baker, Campbell, Daniels, and Edwards said they are coming. Mr. Walsh is in his room per his nursing care plan. [Misses Jackson and Lane arrive and take seats, as do Mr.'s Baker, Campbell and Daniels.]
Miss Farrell:	Is Mr. Walsh dying? Why were there so many doctors in his room yesterday? What are you doing to him?
Miss Gardner:	Yeah! What's happening to him? Why doesn't he talk?
Dr. Clark:	Hold on for a moment. In this meeting if you'd like to speak, please raise your hand and wait to be recognized by me. Now Mr. Walsh is okay. His illness interferes with his ability to communicate well with others or to take nourishment. He is receiving fluids by vein because he is not able to drink or take food right now. He is receiving medications, and we expect that he'll do all right. Why don't we finish with the other people who are supposed to be here, and, since Mr. Walsh's condition is a concern, we can put it on the agenda. Now, that accounts for all the patients, what about the staff? Miss Anderson?
Ms. Anderson:	Dr. Diamond called and said that she would be in late this morning. We can expect her after the Team Meeting.
Mr. Hall:	Did I hurt Dr. Diamond? I mean I asked her a question yesterday.

Dr. Clark:	No, Dr. Diamond called and said she would be in late. She's okay; you did not hurt her. She won't be at this meeting today.
Mr. Hall:	Oh, I see.
Dr. Clark:	Are there other staff not present, not accounted for?
Ms. Anderson:	No, I think that covers everyone.
Dr. Clark:	Okay, before I proceed, let me tell the new members of the community that this is our community meeting where we discuss issues of concerns to the entire community. I'm Dr. Clark. We meet Tuesday and Thursday mornings in the living room here, from 8:30 A.M. until 9:15 A.M. Because we have so many people in this meeting, we don't permit smoking. We use an agenda that is developed during the meeting; we'll be doing that in a moment. As I mentioned before, if you'd like to speak, please raise your hand and wait until I call on you. Let's see, we have three new patients. When I call your name, perhaps you could raise your hand—Miss Smith and Mr. Thomas. [The patients raise their hands as their names are announced.] Mr. Walsh was admitted yesterday, and we have already said a few words about him. Let me welcome both of you. I hope that your stays here are comfortable and useful. We have four patients about to be discharged—Miss Martin, Mr. Edwards, Mrs. Grant, and Miss Nelson. We'll get back to you in a moment. Let's collect the rest of the agenda items. Can I hear from the President of the Patient Committee?
Mr. London:	We just have a few items: we need more diet soda, especially Diet Coke; there aren't enough towels; we'd like a change in the snacks; and the stereo is broken.
Dr. Clark:	Okay. Other items besides the discharges? Mr. Thomas?
Mr. Thomas:	I want to be discharged. I don't need to be here.
Dr. Clark:	Mr. Thomas, that sounds like an issue you should discuss with your individual therapist. We discuss items here that concern all of the community. When you are

	to be discharged is a personal issue, to be worked out between you and your treatment team. We discuss the impact of people's discharges here, but don't decide them. Other items? Miss Becker?
Miss Becker:	No one has mentioned that Miss Lane had some problems last night. We need to talk about it—she submitted a 72-hour notice [written request to leave the hospital which must be responded to within 72 hours by state law]. Also, there was an incident last night involving Miss Jackson and Mr. Reid.
Dr. Clark:	Okay. Anything else? [Pause] We have the item from before about Mr. Walsh [Pause] All right. The first item is the discharge of Miss Martin. Could you tell the community what your experience in the hospital was like and what your plans are for the future?
Miss Martin:	This morning I'll be leaving after three weeks of therapy and medication. I'll be going to the day hospital near my home and seeing a therapist there. This hospitalization has helped me more than any of the three others I've had. I think that I can accept the need to take my medications better, even though I still don't like the side effects. If the day hospital works out all right, I'll then look for a job. I'd like to thank my doctor, Dr. Evans, who helped me through some rough times, as well as Miss David who always seemed to listen and really care. My social worker, Mrs. Harris, was a big help to me and my family. I want to thank the other patients, especially my roommate Nancy [Marks].
Dr. Clark:	Any comment or reactions to what Miss Martin said? Miss Marks?
Miss Marks:	You've been a great roommate. Good luck!
Dr. Clark:	Miss Able?
Miss Able:	I'll miss you. Hope things go well.
Dr. Clark:	Dr. Evans?
Dr. Evans:	Miss Martin, your stay in the hospital was not smooth. Initially you had a lot of questions about whether or

	not the stay would be useful. In fact, you submitted a notice to leave early on. However, I think that your perseverance in your treatment has paid off for you. I believe that you have a better appreciation of your need for medication and continued treatment. I think that the discharge plans are good, and I wish you well.
Miss Martin:	Thanks, Dr. Evans.
	[Miss Lane arrives and sits in the back. She is accompanied by a staff member.]
Dr. Clark:	Other comments or reactions? Miss David?
Miss David:	I've worked closely with you during this stay, Miss Martin. I know that you've struggled and worked hard. Hope all goes well for you. Good luck.
Miss Martin:	Thanks.
Dr. Clark:	Mrs. Harris?
Mrs. Harris:	I really can't add to what's been said—best wishes!
Miss Martin:	Thanks.
Dr. Clark:	Any other comments or reactions? [Silence] Okay, let's move on. The next item is the discharge of Mr. Edwards. I see that he is still not here. Were people aware that he was to be discharged? Miss Kane?
Miss Kane:	No, I wasn't.
Dr. Clark:	What about others? Miss Able?
Miss Able:	I knew about it.
Dr. Clark:	Mr. Baker?
Mr. Baker:	He doesn't want to go there!
Dr. Clark:	It sounds like not everyone is aware of what's occurring. Maybe, Dr. Fields you could fill us in on what the situation is with Mr. Edwards.
Dr. Fields:	Mr. Edwards was admitted as an involuntary patient about 5 weeks ago because of troubles controlling his aggressive impulses. Hospitalization was essential for his welfare at the time, but he's had a hard time accepting his need for treatment—I think that his absence from this meeting is evidence for some of that, in addition to the incidents that we have talked about at previous community meetings [assaults on both pa-

	tients and staff]. He'll be going to another private hospital for long-term treatment. His family told him that he could not come home. He'll be leaving tomorrow afternoon.
Dr. Clark:	Any comments or reactions about what Dr. Fields said? [Silence]. Any feelings about Mr. Edward's discharge? [Silence]. It's hard to know what to make of the silence. [Silence] Miss Able?
Miss Able:	I hope that he gets the help he needs.
Dr. Clark:	Mr. Baker?
Mr. Baker:	Is he going there against his will?
Dr. Clark:	Dr. Fields?
Dr. Fields:	He's still not able to control his temper and has been told by his parents that he cannot go home. He has no means of support. As long as he continues to have problems with his temper, won't regularly take his medications, and sees no need for treatment, his and the staff's hands are forced: he needs inpatient care. He signed the releases of information to other hospitals, which might be a clue that he has some realization that he has problems that require treatment.
Dr. Clark:	Mr. Baker?
Mr. Baker:	I see. I hope it works out. He's basically a nice guy.
Dr. Clark:	Other comments, reactions or feelings? [Silence] If not, let's move on. The next item is the discharge of Mrs. Grant. Could you tell us about your stay in the hospital and your discharge plans?
Mrs. Grant:	I was brought to the hospital four weeks ago by my husband. He's a crazy and jealous man. Every time he gets upset about things, I end up in the hospital! I really didn't need to be here, but I got a good rest. I'll miss all the patients and wish you all well. I'm leaving the day after tomorrow.
Dr. Clark:	Could you tell the community about your plans?
Mrs. Grant:	Oh yeah, I forgot. I'm going to go home and take care of my house.
Dr. Clark:	Any comments or reactions? Dr. Adams?
Dr. Adams:	What about treatment plans after discharge?

Mrs. Grant:	I'll be seeing a therapist at the clinic in my neighborhood. I'm taking medication, and he'll give it to me.
Dr. Clark:	Reactions, feelings about Mrs. Grant's leaving? Miss Martin?
Miss Martin:	Good luck, I'll miss you.
Dr. Clark:	Mr. Campbell?
Mr. Campbell:	Good luck.
Dr. Clark:	Dr. Black?
Dr. Black:	I'm sorry that Dr. Diamond is not here this morning, but as a member of your treatment team, I know that this has been a difficult stay for you, Mrs. Grant. Nevertheless, I think that it has been useful, although perhaps you'd disagree with that opinion. I hope that you continue to take your medications and attend the clinic; perhaps it will forestall future admissions. I wish you well.
Mrs. Grant:	I'll never come back to any hospital. It's my husband who needs to be here!
Dr. Clark:	Other comments, feelings? [Silence] If not, let's move on. The next item on the agenda is the discharge of Miss Nelson. Could you tell us something about your stay here and your plans after discharge?
Miss Nelson:	When I was admitted three weeks ago, I thought seriously about committing suicide. I was under a lot of stress; things were falling apart around me. I felt depressed, anxious, and suicidal. I let my outpatient therapist talk me into coming into the hospital, but I really didn't think that anything could be done for me. I went through about two weeks of hell, but then things seemed to take a turn for the better. I feel more confident now, although I realize that I still have a way to go. I'd like to thank my doctor, Dr. Diamond, even though she's not here, because I think that she saved my life. Also Miss David and Mr. Ellis for putting up with me. He's not here, but Mr. Lawrence gave me a lot of support. I don't want to leave off the patients, because they made me see that there was more to my life than what I could see. My plans are to

	continue in outpatient treatment, take the medication that I was started on, and to return back to work on Monday.
Dr. Clark:	You've said quite a bit! Comments or reactions? Miss Able?
Miss Able:	I'm going to miss you. You're the best!
Dr. Clark:	Mr. Baker?
Mr. Baker:	Good luck. I'm glad we met.
Dr. Clark:	Miss Lane?
Miss Lane:	Thanks for all the advice. Good luck!
Dr. Clark:	Miss Becker?
Miss Becker:	Good luck. You've worked really hard in the hospital.
Dr. Clark:	Mrs. Harris?
Mrs. Harris:	I'm sorry that Dr. Diamond isn't here, but I know that she would agree that you've worked very hard during your stay here, and that the success is more a reflection of your efforts and perseverance than of those of the staff. If you had not permitted the staff to help you, and you had not stuck it out through that difficult period in the beginning, you wouldn't have achieved the result. I think that your plans are good, and I wish you well.
Dr. Clark:	Other comments, feelings? Miss Kane?
Miss Kane:	Lots of luck.
Dr. Clark:	Other comments? [Silence] If not, let's move on. The next item on the agenda is about sodas. Could we hear about it? Mr. Daniels?
Mr. Daniels:	Yeah, I put it on the agenda. We ran out of diet soda two days ago! We need another case of soda for the unit.
Dr. Clark:	Can we hear from others? Mr. Miller?
Mr. Miller:	I don't see it as such a big problem. There was still some diet soda in the refrigerator last night.
Dr. Clark:	Mr. Daniels?
Mr. Daniels:	I think that we need more Diet Coke. All they have is that orange soda.
Miss Able:	But it is diet orange soda!

Dr. Clark:	Hold on for a minute. We should raise our hands and wait to be recognized. What about others? Mrs. Parker?
Mrs. Parker:	Most often we get enough soda. However, many of us have favorite ones, and they get used up fast.
Dr. Clark:	Miss Becker?
Miss Becker:	In the past dietary has said that they cannot guarantee us the specific brand of soda. We can get more diet soda, but we cannot be sure which one we'll get. I'm still uncertain – do we need more diet soda, or is it just a preference for Diet Coke?
Dr. Clark:	Mrs. Parker?
Mrs. Parker:	It's really the preference for Diet Coke.
Dr. Clark:	In that case, I don't think we can do anything about it. We can make sure that there are diet sodas; we cannot deal with the personal preferences. We will not be able to get more Diet Coke unless that's what is delivered by chance. We'll have to go to the next item. We have the item about the towels, but let's go to the incident last night with Miss Lane. Can we hear about what people observed? Miss Able?
Miss Able:	At about 9 P.M. last night, Kathy [Lane] was on the phone with her boyfriend, and they had a fight. After that I talked to her for at least an hour. She was pretty shaken up – crying, feeling that she had made a big mistake in coming into the hospital. She talked a little about putting in her 72-hour notice, but I thought that she was feeling a bit better after we had talked. The next I knew, people were rushing down the hall. I didn't know that she actually submitted her notice.
Dr. Clark:	Miss Martin?
Miss Martin:	She said to me that she was feeling okay, but I was a little worried and told Mary [David] that Kathy seemed to be pretty upset by the phone call. That must have been after you [Miss Able] had spoken to her. Mary spoke to her after that.
Dr. Clark:	Miss David?

Miss David:	I spoke with her for a short while. She said that she and her boyfriend had broken up. She felt it was because she had come into the hospital, that she should sign out. I told her that didn't seem like such a good idea, that perhaps she should talk to her therapist today about it. She said that that was a good idea. At that point, she didn't seem especially upset. She ended the meeting without protest. I went back to the nursing station after that.
Dr. Clark:	Miss Ingram?
Miss Ingram:	I went into the bathroom at a little after midnight. I saw the blood on the floor in her stall. I asked who was in there. No one answered, and I ran to tell the staff. They pushed the buzzer, and in a minute or two there were a whole bunch of people here.
Dr. Clark:	Ms. Anderson?
Ms. Anderson:	She was found in the stall with cuts on both her wrists. The doctor on call examined her and determined that she needed to be sutured. There were pieces of a light bulb next to her. She was alert and could move her fingers. She was escorted to the local Emergency Room where her wrists were sutured. On return to our hospital, she submitted a 72-hour notice. She is currently on CS [constant supervision] status.
Dr. Clark:	Maybe we could hear from Miss Lane about her experience of it?
Miss Lane:	I don't have anything to say. I don't want people to talk about it! It's my private business.
Dr. Clark:	Dr. Adams?
Dr. Adams:	When someone does something like this it affects the entire community, and we must talk about it; it no longer is a private affair. Cutting one's wrists in the unit bathroom and submitting a 72-hour notice is of community concern!
Dr. Clark:	Comments or reactions regarding Miss Lane's cutting her wrists or her 72-hour notice?
Mr. Hall:	I didn't cut her!

Dr. Clark:	We know that, Mr. Hall. Let me remind you that we raise our hand in this meeting and wait to be recognized if we want to speak. Other comments or reactions? Miss Martin?
Miss Martin:	I was pretty upset last night. I thought that Kathy was doing okay. It was pretty scary with all those people on the unit last night. They did a great job, although I thought she had died at first.
Dr. Clark:	Other comments? Mr. Oliver?
Mr. Oliver:	I don't understand why the bathroom is unlocked at night. Shouldn't it be locked at midnight? How do you know what's going to happen?
Dr. Clark:	Others feel that way? Miss Marks?
Miss Marks:	Yeah, what's going to stop someone from cutting themselves in the bathroom. You can't see what goes on in there. It's unsafe.
Dr. Clark:	What about others? How do others feel? Miss Martin?
Miss Martin:	I don't know. The staff can't watch every move we make. Some of it is up to us.
Dr. Clark:	[gestures to Miss Able]
Miss Able:	I agree. I was pretty upset by what Kathy did, but I think that we need to talk straight to people about our problems.
Dr. Clark:	[gestures to Miss Martin]
Miss Martin:	Kathy, when I first came here I couldn't stand it. I thought that my biggest problem was that I was hospitalized here and forgot all the troubles I had had before. With a lot of encouragement, I decided to stay, and I think that was a tough but good decision. You really should take out your notice.
Dr. Clark:	Mr. Daniels?
Mr. Daniels:	I want to know what you're going to do about the bathrooms. I think that the staff should check them every 10 minutes.
Dr. Clark:	Dr. Adams?
Dr. Adams:	It sounds like people are concerned about their safety here in the hospital. Some wish that all responsibility

be taken over by the hospital, guaranteeing that they will be safe and secure. However, an environment that would be that safe would be pretty restricted and uncomfortable. There is a limit to how much the staff can do for people; we are dependent upon patients to let us know how they are feeling and to clue us in as to when to provide more supervision. It certainly is uncomfortable for me as staff member to hear of what occurred with Miss Lane. Patients need to tell us directly of their needs, and even then we may not hear the requests as well as we ought. Repeated messages may be necessary, but will hopefully result in a reasonable response.

Dr. Clark: Comments or reactions? [gestures to Miss Able]

Miss Able: I think that Dr. Adams is right. I wouldn't want the bathrooms locked. We're supposed to get used to living at home while we are here. No one has locked bathrooms at home.

Dr. Clark: Any other comments or reactions? [Silence] Reactions to what Dr. Adams said? [Silence] If not, perhaps we can move on to the item about Miss Jackson and Mr. Reid. Could we hear about what the incident entailed? Were people aware of a problem?

Miss Lane (interrupting): It's no one's damn business!

Dr. Clark: Is that the way others feel? Actually, I'm not sure just what this item is about. Am I the only one who doesn't know? Miss Becker?

Miss Becker: It was reported that Miss Jackson and Mr. Reid were found in bed together during a room check at 1 A.M. When they were discovered and reminded that sexual contact was not permitted on the unit, they became abusive, but Mr. Reid then returned to his own room. I think that a number of patients were awakened by it.

Dr. Clark: Miss Marks?

Miss Marks: I was woken up by the commotion last night. I didn't

	know that they were in bed together, but Peggy [Jackson] told me that she wanted to marry George [Reid].
Dr. Clark:	Others have comments, questions, or observations? Mr. Thomas?
Mr. Thomas:	I don't think that it's such a big thing. I'm sure the staff has PC [physical contact, generic phrase used on the unit to indicate sexual contact which is prohibited] outside, so why can't we?
Dr. Clark:	Other reactions or comments? Miss Able?
Miss Able:	Sometimes I find it upsetting to see Peggy and George on the couch near the stereo. It's not fair to the other patients; we have own problems to work on.
Dr. Clark:	Uh huh. Other feelings? [Silence] No other feelings about it? Maybe we could hear from Miss Jackson and Mr. Reid about their perspectives. Miss Jackson?
Miss Jackson:	I think that the rule is stupid, just like most everything else here! There's nothing wrong with PC between George and me.
Dr. Clark:	We'll get back to that in a minute. Mr. Reid?
Mr. Reid:	I don't have anything to say.
Dr. Clark:	Dr. Adams?
Dr. Adams:	This issue is obviously a difficult one for the community to talk about – sexual behavior between patients. Nevertheless, it is important to understand that we have a rule prohibiting such activity and that there are reasons for this rule. Patients who are admitted to the hospital have difficulties with many feelings including sexual feelings. We ask all the patients to be open with one another and to use these experiences in the hospital to learn about themselves as well as others. In the course of this we expect patients to feel closer to each other and to feel better about themselves. Our experience has been universal in that when these relationships take on the quality of a romance as opposed to part of the work of the hospitalization, that the attention and energy needed to com-

plete the work of the hospitalization is diverted away from such work and into the romance. When the staff then tries to get the patients to redirect their energy, we often find ourselves in a struggle in which the patients feel they need to justify the legitimacy of their relationship, while their hospital time dwindles down and no therapeutic process occurs. Discharge of one of the patients occurs, and the inevitable confrontation with the lack of therapeutic progress results in a catastrophic situation. Typically we are told, "This relationship is different. I can tell." However, the rule is nonnegotiable. All patients are expected to abide by it.

Dr. Clark:	Comments or reactions to what Dr. Adams has said? [Silence] No other comments? [Silence] If not, perhaps we can move on to the issue of the towels. Could we hear what the problem has been?
Mr. London (interrupting):	I forgot who brought it up. I've been on pass lately.
Mrs. Grant (interrupting):	I brought it up. There aren't enough towels. I keep running out of them. I know that I'm being discharged soon, but something has to be done.
Dr. Clark:	How do others see the problem? Miss Farrell?
Miss Farrell:	I think that it's real. It's especially bad on weekends.
Miss Gardner (interrupting):	Can anything be done about it?
Dr. Clark:	Let's first see the extent of the problem. Who has had problems recently with obtaining towels? Raise your hand. Let's see; there are eleven hands raised. That's a lot of people. What's the story with towels? Miss Becker?
Miss Becker:	Towels are sent up daily from the laundry. If we are running short, we can order some more.
Dr. Clark:	Okay, the last item on the agenda has to do with Mr. Walsh. At the beginning of the meeting some people had some concerns about him and his situation. Is that a concern of the community? Miss Gardner?

Miss Gardner:	No, I think that you answered the question before.
Dr. Clark:	Mr. Hall?
Mr. Hall:	Who is Mr. Walsh?
Dr. Clark:	He's the new patient in the room opposite the nursing station.
Mr. Hall:	Oh, that guy.
Dr. Clark:	Are there still concerns about Mr. Walsh? Miss Farrell?
Miss Farrell:	What makes a person like that? Why isn't he in a medical hospital?
Dr. Clark:	Mr. London?
Mr. London:	Wouldn't he be better cared for in an ICU? This hospital is for people with mental problems.
Dr. Clark:	It sounds like people are unsure if the staff can handle a problem like Mr. Walsh's. Miss Farrell?
Miss Farrell:	Well, so many people were in his room last night and this morning, too. No one's going to have the time to speak to us.
Dr. Clark:	Is that a concern of others? Miss Able?
Miss Able:	I was a little concerned about that.
Miss Kane (interrupting):	So was I. Is he schizophrenic? Is that what causes him to not talk?
Mr. Oliver (interrupting):	Schizophrenia means "split personality," not that you don't talk!
Dr. Clark:	Wait a moment. That's actually a very common idea of what schizophrenia is, but it's incorrect. Let's keep the focus more on our reactions to Mr. Walsh's situation. Mr. Lawrence?
Mr. Lawrence:	I know that I get a bit more concerned when we have people as ill as Ray [Walsh] is. We don't often have patients here with IV's running.
Dr. Clark:	Other reaction or comments? . . . Feelings about the situation? . . . Thoughts about it? Dr. Adams?
Dr. Adams:	It's understandable that both patients and staff would be concerned seeing someone in Mr. Walsh's condition. It is certainly not common, but on the other hand it's also a situation that I and many of the staff have

managed before. Sometimes it's hard to accept that an emotional illness can so profoundly affect someone, and, when we see it in this fashion almost wish the person away—to another unit or hospital. Mr. Walsh has a mental illness which led him to stop eating, drinking, and talking. We have instituted treatment including IV's and medication, and we expect he will feel more comfortable and thus be able to talk, take fluids and food soon. However, I don't expect this to occur in a day or two, nor do I expect this progress to be smooth and steady. It's likely to be more up and down for a while. In the meantime, we will closely monitor him.

Miss Able: Is there any way we can help him?

Dr. Adams: That's hard to say right now. The staff will be watching him constantly. Most patients like this are pretty aware of what is going on around them, even though they seem oblivious to their surroundings. When he is feeling more comfortable, we'll let you know.

Dr. Clark: Other concerns or questions? If not, it's 9:15 and time to end the meeting. Thank you.

References

Abramczuk, J. (1972). The type of leadership and the topics of discussion in a large open group: observations on community meetings. *International Journal of Social Psychiatry* 18:53–60.

Abroms, G. M. (1968). Setting limits. *Archives of General Psychiatry* 19: 113–119.

_____ (1969). Defining milieu therapy. *Archives of General Psychiatry* 21: 553–560.

Action for Mental Health, Final Report of the Joint Commission on Mental Illness and Health (1961). New York: Basic Books.

Adler, G. (1979). The psychotherapy of schizophrenia: Semrad's contributions to current psychoanalytic concepts. *Schizophrenia Bulletin* 5:130–137.

Akhtar, S., and Byrne, J. P. (1983). The concept of splitting and its clinical relevance. *American Journal of Psychiatry* 140:1013–1016.

Almond, R. (1975). Issues in milieu treatment. *Schizophrenia Bulletin* 13:12–26.

Arons, B. S. (1982). Effective use of community meetings on psychiatric treatment units. *Hospital and Community Psychiatry* 33:480–483.

Arriaga, K., Espinoza, E., and Guthrie, M. B. (1978). Group therapy evaluation for psychiatric inpatients. *International Journal of Group Psychotherapy* 28:359–364.

Arthur, R. J. (1973). Social psychiatry: an overview. *American Journal of Psychiatry* 130:841–849.

Bailine, S. H., Katch, M., and Golden, H. K. (1977). Minigroups: maximizing the therapeutic milieu on an acute psychiatric unit. *Hospital and Community Psychiatry* 28:445–457.

Battegay, T. (1974). Group psychotherapy as a method of treatment in a psychiatric hospital. In *The Challenge for Group Psychotherapy: Present and Future*, ed. S. DeShill, pp. 173–230. New York: International Universities Press.

Beck, A. T. (1976). *Cognitive Therapy and Emotional Disorders*. New York: International Universities Press.

Bernard, H. S. (1983). Anti-therapeutic dimensions of a community meeting in a therapeutic milieu. *Psychiatric Quarterly* 55:227–235.

Bernardez, T. (1969). The role of the observer in group psychotherapy. *International Journal of Group Psychotherapy* 19:234–239.

Beutler, L. E., Frank, M., Schieber, S. C., et al. (1984). Comparative effects of group psychotherapies in a short-term inpatient setting: an experience with deterioration effects. *Psychiatry* 47:66–76.

Bion, W. R. (1961). *Experiences in Groups and Other Papers*. New York: Basic Books.

Bjork, D., Steinberg, M., Lindenmayer, J., and Pardes, H. (1977). Mania and milieu: treatment of manics in a therapeutic community. *Hospital and Community Psychiatry* 28:431–436.

Bloom, V., and Dobie, S. I. (1969). The effect of observers on the process of group therapy. *International Journal of Group Psychotherapy* 19:79–87.

Bolten, M. P. (1984). Short-term residential psychotherapy: psychotherapy in a nutshell. *Psychotherapy and Psychosomatics* 41:109–115.

Borriello, J. F. (1976). Group psychotherapy in hospital systems. In *Group Therapy*, ed. L. R. Wolberg and M. L. Aronson, pp. 99–108. New York: Stratton Intercontinental.

Bouras, N., Chilvers, C., and Watson, J. P. (1984). Estimating levels of disturbed behavior among psychiatric in-patients using a general linear model. *Psychological Medicine* 14:439–444.

Bouras, N., Trauer, T., and Watson, J. P. (1982). Ward environment and disturbed behaviour. *Psychological Medicine* 12:309–319.

Brabender, V., Albrecht, E., Sillitti, J., et al. (1983). A study of curative factors in short-term group psychotherapy. *Hospital and Community Psychiatry* 34:643–644.

Brenner, C. (1973). *An Elementary Textbook of Psychoanalysis*. New York: International Universities Press.

——— (1976). *Psychoanalytic Technique and Psychic Conflict*. New York: International Universities Press.

Brodsky, C. M., and Fischer, A. (1964). Therapeutic programming for the non-psychotic patient. *American Journal of Psychiatry* 120:793–797.

Brown, L. J. (1981). A short-term hospital program preparing borderline and schizophrenic patients for intensive psychotherapy. *Psychiatry* 44: 327–336.

Burgoyne, R. W., Kline, F., Goin, M. K., et al. (1978). Observed psychotherapy: what the patients say about it. *Journal of Psychiatric Education* 2:83–92.

Bursten, B. (1973). Decision making in the hospital community. *Archives of General Psychiatry* 29:732–735.

Cameron, N. (1963). *Personality Development and Psychopathology*. Boston: Houghton Mifflin.

Carpenter, W. T., McGlashan, T. H., and Strauss, J. S. (1977). The treatment of acute schizophrenia without drugs: an investigation of some current assumptions. *American Journal of Psychiatry* 134:14–20.

Carr, V. (1982). The state concept and inpatient psychotherapy. *Journal of Nervous and Mental Disease* 170:324–331.

Caudill, W. (1958). *The Psychiatric Hospital as a Small Society.* Cambridge: Harvard University Press.

Ciompi, L. (1983). How to improve the treatment of schizophrenics. In *Psychosocial Intervention in Schizophrenia*, ed. H. Stierlin, L. C. Wynne, and M. Wirsching, pp. 53–66. New York: Springer-Verlag.

Clark, D. H., (1964). *Administrative Therapy, The Role of the Doctor in the Therapeutic Community.* Philadelphia: Tavistock Publications, JB Lippincott.

———— (1977). The therapeutic community. *British Journal of Psychiatry* 131:553–564.

Colby, K. M. (1951). *A Primer for Psychotherapists.* New York: Ronald.

Cooperman, M. (1983). Some observations regarding psychoanalytic psychotherapy in a hospital setting. *The Psychiatric Hospital* 14:21–28.

Cory, T. L., and Page, D. (1978). Group techniques for effecting change in the more disturbed patient. *Group* 2:149–155.

Crabtree, L. H., Jr., and Cox, J. L. D. (1972). The overthrow of a therapeutic community. *International Journal of Group Psychotherapy* 22:31–41.

Cumming, J., and Cumming, E. (1962). *Ego & Milieu, Theory and Practice of Environmental Therapy.* New York: Atherton.

Dain, N. (1976). From colonial America to bicentennial America: two centuries of vicissitudes in the institutional care of mental patients. *Bulletin of the New York Academy of Medicine* 52:1179–1196.

Daniels, D. N., and Rubin, D. S. (1968). The community meeting. *Archives of General Psychiatry* 18:60–75.

Davanloo, H., ed. (1978). *Basic Principles and Techniques in Short-Term Dynamic Psychotherapy.* New York: SP Medical and Scientific.

Davis, D. M. (1977). An implementation of therapeutic community in a private mental health center. *Diseases of the Nervous System* 38:189–191.

Denford, J., Schachter, J., Temple, N., et al. (1983). Selection and outcome in inpatient psychotherapy. *British Journal of Medical Psychology* 56:225–243.

Dincin, J., and Witheridge, T. F. (1982). Psychiatric rehabilitation as a deterrent to recidivism. *Hospital and Community Psychiatry* 33:645–650.

Dorpat, T. L. (1976). Structural conflict and object relations conflict. *Journal of the American Psychoanalytic Association* 24:855–874.

———— (1981). Basic concepts and terms in object relations theories. In *Object and Self: A Developmental Approach*, ed. S. Tuttman, C. Kaye, and M. Zimmerman, pp. 149–178. New York: International Universities Press.

Dreikurs, R. (1955). Group psychotherapy and the third revolution in psychiatry. *International Journal of Social Psychiatry* 1:23–32.

Edelson, M. (1970a). *Sociotherapy and Psychotherapy.* Chicago: University of Chicago Press.

_____ (1970b). *The Practice of Sociotherapy*. New Haven: Yale University Press.

Ellsworth, R. B. (1983). Characteristics of effective treatment milieus. In *Principles and Practice of Milieu Therapy*, ed. J. G. Gunderson, O. A. Will, and L. R. Mosher, pp. 87–123. New York: Jason Aronson.

Ellsworth, R., and Ellsworth, J. (1970). The psychiatric aide: therapeutic agent or lost potential. *Psychiatric Nursing* 8:7–13.

Ellsworth, R., Maroney, R., Klett, W., et al. (1971). Milieu characteristics of successful psychiatric treatment programs. *American Journal of Orthopsychiatry* 41:427–441.

Engel, G. L. (1977). The need for a new medical model: a challenge for biomedicine. *Science* 196:129–136.

Erickson, R. C. (1981). Small-group psychotherapy with patients on a short-stay ward: an opportunity for innovation. *Hospital and Community Psychiatry* 32:269–272.

Farrell, D. (1976). The use of active experiential group techniques with hospitalized patients. In *Group Therapy*, ed. L. R. Wolberg and M. L. Aronson, pp. 44–51. New York: Stratton Intercontinental.

Feinsilver, D. B., and Gunderson, D. B. (1972). Psychotherapy for schizophrenics: is it indicated? A review of the relevant literature. *Schizophrenia Bulletin* 6:11–23.

Fenichel, O. (1941). Problems of psychoanalytic technique. *The Psychoanalytic Quarterly*. New York.

_____ (1945). *The Psychoanalytic Theory of Neurosis*. New York: WW Norton.

Filstead, W. J., and Rossi, J. J. (1973). Therapeutic milieu, therapeutic community and milieu therapy: some conceptual and definitional distinctions. In *The Therapeutic Community, A Sourcebook of Readings*, ed. S. S. Rossi and W. J. Filstead, pp. 3–13. New York: Behavioral.

Frances, A. (1982). Categorical and dimensional systems of personality diagnosis: a comparison. *Comprehensive Psychiatry* 23:516–527.

Frank, A. F., and Gunderson, J. G. (1984). Matching therapists and milieus: effects on engagement and continuance in psychotherapy. *Psychiatry* 47:201–210.

Frank, J. D. (1975). Group therapy in the mental hospital. In *Group Psychotherapy and Group Function*, ed. M. Rosenbaum and M. Berger, pp. 465–482. New York: Basic Books.

Friedman, H. J. (1969). Some problems of inpatient management with borderline patients. *American Journal of Psychiatry* 126:299–304.

Fromm-Reichmann, F. (1950). *Principles of Intensive Psychotherapy*. Chicago: University of Chicago Press.

Gedo, J. E. (1979). Theories of object relations: a metapsychological assessment. *Journal of the American Psychoanalytic Association* 27:361–373.

Gedo, J. E., and Goldberg, A. (1973). *Models of the Mind*. Chicago: University of Chicago Press.

Glick, I. D., & Hargreaves, W. A. (1979). *Psychiatric Hospital Treatment for the 1980s: A Controlled Study of Short Versus Long Hospitalization.* Lexington, MA: Lexington Books, D. C. Heath.

Glick, I. D., Klar, H. M., and Braff, D. L. (1984). Guidelines for hospitalization of chronic psychiatric patients. *Hospital and Community Psychiatry* 35:934–936.

Glover, E. (1931). The therapeutic effect of inexact interpretation: a contribution to the theory of suggestion. *International Journal of Psycho-Analysis* 12:397–411.

Goffman, E. (1961). *Asylums, Essays on the Social Situation of Mental Patients and Other Inmates.* Garden City, NY: Anchor Books, Doubleday.

Goforth, E. M., Mowatt, M., and Clark, N. (1978). Effect of the presence of an observer on the defensive patterns of an ongoing group. *International Journal of Group Psychotherapy* 28:55–71.

Greben, S. E., Berger, D. M., Book, H. E., et al. (1981). The teaching and learning of psychotherapy in a general hospital. *Canadian Journal of Psychiatry* 26:449–454.

Greenblatt, M., Solomon, M., Evans, A. S., and Brooks, G. W. (1965). *Drug and Social Therapy in Chronic Schizophrenia.* Springfield, IL: Charles C Thomas.

Greenblatt, M., York, R. H., and Brown, E. L. (1955). *From Custodial to Therapeutic Patient Care in Mental Hospitals: Explorations in Social Treatment.* New York: Russell Sage.

Grinspoon, L., Ewalt, J. R., and Shader, I. (1972). *Schizophrenia: Pharmacotherapy and Psychotherapy.* Baltimore: Williams & Wilkins.

Gruber, L. N. (1978). Group techniques for acutely psychotic inpatients. *Group* 2:31–39.

Gunderson, J. G. (1974). Management of manic states: the problem of fire setting. *Psychiatry* 37:137–146.

_____ (1978). Defining the therapeutic processes in psychiatric milieus. *Psychiatry* 41:327–335.

_____ (1980). A reevaluation of milieu therapy for nonchronic schizophrenic patients. *Schizophrenia Bulletin* 6:64–69.

_____ (1983). An overview of modern milieu therapy. In *Principles and Practice of Milieu Therapy,* ed. J. G. Gunderson, O. A. Will, and L. R. Moser, pp. 1–13. New York: Jason Aronson.

Gunderson, J. G., and Carroll, A. (1983). Clinical consideration from empirical research. In *Psychosocial Intervention in Schizophrenia,* ed. H. Stierlin, L. C. Wynne, and M. Wirching, pp. 125–142. New York: Springer-Verlag.

Gurel, L. (1964). Correlates of psychiatric hospital effectiveness. In *Intramural Report 64-5: An assessment of Psychiatric Hospital Effectiveness,* ed. L. Gurel, pp. 1–18. Washington, DC: Veterans Administration Psychiatric Evaluation Project.

_____ (1974). Dimensions of the therapeutic milieu: a study of mental hospital atmosphere. *American Journal of Psychiatry* 131:409–414.

Guttentag, M., and Struening, E. L. (1975). *Handbook of Evaluation Research* Vol. 2. Beverly Hills: Sage.

Guze, S. B. (1978). Nature of psychiatric illness: why psychiatry is a branch of medicine. *Comprehensive Psychiatry* 19:295–307.

Hargreaves, W. A., and Attkisson, C. C. (1978). Evaluating program outcomes. In *Evaluation of Human Service Programs*, ed. C. C. Attkisson, W. A. Hargreaves, M. J. Horwitz, and J. E. Sorenson, pp. 303–339. New York: Academic.

Harris, M., Bergman, H. C., and Greenwood, V. (1982). Integrating hospital and community systems for treating revolving-door patients. *Hospital and Community Psychiatry* 33:225–227.

Henisz, J. E. (1981). *Psychotherapeutic Management on the Short-Term Unit*. Springfield, IL: Charles C Thomas.

Hertzman, M. (1984). *Inpatient Psychiatry*. New York: Human Sciences.

Herz, M. I. (1972). The therapeutic community: a critique. *Hospital and Community Psychiatry* 23:69–72.

——— (1979). Short-term hospitalization and the medical model. *Hospital and Community Psychiatry* 30:117–121.

Herz, M. I., Endicott, J., and Spitzer, R. L. (1977). Brief hospitalization: a two year follow-up. *American Journal of Psychiatry* 134:502–507.

Herz, M. I., Wilensky, M., and Earle, A. (1966). Problems of role definition in the therapeutic community. *Archives of General Psychiatry* 14:270–276.

Horowitz, M. J., and Weisberg, D. S. (1966). Techniques for the psychotherapy of acute psychosis. *International Journal of Group Psychotherapy* 16:42–50.

Hyde, R. W. (1957). Current developments in social psychiatry in the United States. In *Symposium on Preventive and Social Psychiatry*, pp. 419–429. Washington, DC: Walter Reed Army Institute of Research.

Imber, S. D., Lewis, P. M., and Loiselle, R. H. (1979). Uses and abuses of the brief intervention group. *International Journal of Group Psychotherapy* 29:39–49.

Jacobson, G. F., Strickler, M., and Morley, W. E. (1968). Generic and individual approaches to crisis intervention. *American Journal of Public Health* 58:338–343.

Janowsky, D. S., Leff, M., and Epstein, R. S. (1970). Playing the manic game. *Archives of General Psychiatry* 22:252–261.

Johnson, D., and Howenstine, R. (1982). Revitalizing an ailing group psychotherapy program. *Psychiatry* 45:138–146.

Johnson, J. M., and Parker, K. E. (1983). Some antitherapeutic effects of a therapeutic community. *Hospital and Community Psychiatry* 34:170–171.

Jones, M. (1956). The concept of a therapeutic community. *American Journal of Psychiatry* 112:647–650.

_____ (1957). The treatment of personality disorders in a therapeutic community. *Psychiatry* 20:211–220.

_____ (1968a). *Beyond the Therapeutic Community: Social Learning and Social Psychiatry.* New Haven: Yale University Press.

_____ (1968b). *Social Psychiatry in Practice.* Baltimore: Penguin.

_____ (1976). *Maturation of the Therapeutic Community: An Organic Approach to Health and Mental Health.* New York: Human Sciences.

_____ (1983). Therapeutic community as a system for change. In *Principles and Practice of Milieu Therapy,* ed. J. G. Gunderson, O. A. Will, and L. R. Moser, pp. 177–184. New York: Jason Aronson.

Jones, M., Baker, A., Freeman, T., et al. (1953). *The Therapeutic Community: A New Treatment Method in Psychiatry.* New York: Basic Books.

Kahn, R. L., Wolfe, R. P., Quinn, R. P., et al. (1964). *Organizational Stress: Studies in Role Conflict and Ambiguity.* New York: Wiley.

Kanas, N., and Barr, M. A. (1983). Homogeneous group therapy for acutely psychotic schizophrenic inpatients. *Hospital and Community Psychiatry* 34:257–259.

Karasu, T. B., ed. (1984). *The Psychiatric Therapies.* Washington, DC: American Psychiatric Association.

Karasu, T. B., Plutchik, R., Conte, H. R., et al. (1977). The therapeutic community in theory and practice. *Hospital and Community Psychiatry* 28:436–440.

Katz, G. (1983). The noninterpretation of metaphors in psychiatric hospital groups. *International Journal of Group Psychotherapy* 33:53–67.

Kaufman, E., and Sporty, L. (1983). A modified milieu for acute patients. *Hospital and Community Psychiatry* 34:384.

Kennard, D. (1979). Limiting factors: the setting, the staff, the patients. In *Therapeutic Communities: Reflections and Progress,* ed. R. D. Hinshelwood and N. Manning, pp. 181–193. London: Routledge and Kegan Paul.

Kernberg, O. F. (1975a). A systems approach to priority setting of interventions in groups. *International Journal of Group Psychotherapy* 25:251–275.

_____ (1975b). *Borderline Conditions and Pathological Narcissism.* New York: Jason Aronson.

_____ (1976a). *Object Relations Theory and Clinical Psychoanalysis.* New York: Jason Aronson.

_____ (1976b). Technical considerations in the treatment of borderline personality organization. *Journal of the American Psychoanalytic Association* 24:795–820.

_____ (1978). Leadership and organizational functioning: organizational regression. *International Journal of Group Psychotherapy* 28:3–25.

_____ (1980). Psychotherapy with borderline patients: an overview. In *Specialized Techniques in Individual Psychotherapy,* ed. T. Karasu and L. Bellak. New York: Brunner/Mazel.

———— (1984). *Severe Personality Disorders*. New Haven: Yale University Press.

Kibel, H. D. (1978). The rationale for the use of group psychotherapy for borderline patients on a short-term unit. *International Journal of Group Psychotherapy* 28:339–413.

———— (1981). A conceptual model for short-term inpatient group psychotherapy. *American Journal of Psychiatry* 138:74–80.

Kirshner, L. A. (1982). Length of stay of psychiatric patients. *Journal of Nervous and Mental Disease* 170:27–33.

Kisch, J., Kroll, J., Gross, R., and Carey, K. (1981). In-patient community meetings: problems and purposes. *British Journal of Medical Psychology* 54:35–40.

Klass, D. B., Growe, G. A., and Strizich, M. (1977). Ward treatment milieu and posthospital functioning. *Archives of General Psychiatry* 34:1047–1052.

Klein, R. H. (1977). Inpatient group psychotherapy: practical considerations and special problems. *International Journal Group Psychotherapy* 27:201–214.

———— (1981). The patient-staff community meeting: a tea party with the mad hatter. *International Journal of Group Psychotherapy* 31:205–222.

Klerman, G. L., Weissman, M. M., Rounsaville, B. J., and Chevron, E. S. (1984). *Interpersonal Psychotherapy of Depression*. New York: Basic Books.

Krasner, J. B., Feldman, B., Liff, F., et al. (1964). Observing the observers. *International Journal of Group Psychotherapy* 14:214–217.

Kreeger, L., ed. (1975). *The Large Group: Dynamics and Therapy*. Itasca IL: Peacock.

Kritzer, H., and Phillips, C. A. (1966). Observing group psychotherapy: an affective learning experience. *American Journal of Psychotherapy* 20:471–476.

Langsley, D. G. (1985). Community psychiatry. In *Comprehensive Textbook of Psychiatry/IV*, ed. H. I. Kaplan and B. J. Sadock, pp. 1878–1884. Baltimore: Williams & Wilkins.

Lax, R. (1983). Discussion: critical comments on object relations theory. *The Psychoanalytic Review* 70:423–433.

Leeman, C. P. (1980). Involuntary admissions to general hospitals: progress or threat? *Hospital and Community Psychiatry* 31:315–318.

Leeman, C. P., and Berger, H. S. (1980). The Massachusetts Psychiatric Society's position paper on involuntary admissions to general hospitals. *Hospital and Community Psychiatry* 31:318–324.

Lehman, A. F., and Ritzler, B. (1976). The therapeutic community inpatient ward: does it really work? *Comprehensive Psychiatry* 17:755–761.

Lehman, A. F., Strauss, J. S., Ritzler, B. A., et al. (1982). First-admission psychiatric ward milieu. *Archives of General Psychiatry* 39:1293–1298.

Leopold, H. S. (1976). Selective group approaches with psychotic patients in hospital settings. *American Journal of Psychotherapy* 30:95–102.

Levine, H. B. (1980). Milieu biopsy: the place of the therapy group on the inpatient ward. *International Journal of Group Psychotherapy* 30:77–93.

Levinson, D. J. (1959). Role, personality, and social structure in the organizational setting. *Journal of Abnormal and Social Psychology* 58:170–180.

Lewis, D. J., Beck, P. R., King, H., and Stephen, L. (1971). Some approaches to the evaluation of milieu therapy. *Canadian Psychiatric Association Journal* 16:203–208.

Lin, I. F., Spiga, R., and Fortsch, W. (1976). Insight and adherence of medication in chronic schizophrenics. *Journal of Clinical Psychiatry* 33:1443–1446.

Lloyd, C. (1980). Life events and depressive disorder reviewed. *Archives of General Psychiatry* 37:529–548.

Lothstein, L. M. (1978). Human territoriality in group psychotherapy. *International Journal of Group Psychotherapy* 28:56–71.

Ludwig, A. M., and Othmer, E. (1977). The medical basis of psychiatry. *American Journal of Psychiatry* 134:1087–1092.

Main, T. F. (1946). The hospital as a therapeutic institution. *Bulletin of the Menninger Clinic* 10:66–70.

———— (1975). Some psychodynamics of large groups. In *The Large Group: Dynamics and Therapy*, ed. L. Kreeger, pp. 57–86. Itasca, IL: Peacock.

Malan, D. H. (1976). *The Frontier of Brief Psychotherapy*. New York: Plenum.

Mann, J., and Goldman, R. (1982). *A Casebook in Time-Limited Psychotherapy*. New York: McGraw-Hill.

Margolis, P. M. (1973). *Patient Power: The Development of a Therapeutic Community in a Psychiatric Unit of a General Hospital*. Springfield, IL: Charles C Thomas.

Martin, P. A., Tornga, M., McGloin, J. F., and Boles, S. (1977). Observing groups as seen from both sides of the looking glass. *Group* 1:147–161.

Maves, P. A., and Schulz, J. W. (1985). Inpatient group treatment on short-term acute care units. *Hospital and Community Psychiatry* 36:69–73.

Maxmen, J. S. (1978). An educative model for inpatient group therapy. *International Journal of Group Psychotherapy* 28:321–338.

———— (1984). Helping patients survive our theories: the practice of an educative model. *International Journal of Group Psychotherapy* 34:355–368.

Maxmen, J. S., Tucker, G. J., and LeBow, M. (1974). *Rational Hospital Psychiatry: The Reactive Environment*. New York: Brunner/Mazel.

May, P. R. A. (1968). *Treatment of Schizophrenia: A Comparative Study of Five Treatment Methods*. New York: Science House.

May, P. R. A., and Simpson, G. M. (1980). Schizophrenia: evaluation of treatment methods. In *Comprehensive Textbook of Psychiatry/III*, ed. H. I. Kaplan, A. M. Freedman, and B. J. Sadock. Baltimore: Williams & Wilkins.

May, P. R. A., Tuma, A. J., and Dixon, W. J. (1981). Schizophrenia: a follow-up study of the results of five forms of treatment. *Archives of General Psychiatry* 38:776–784.

McEvoy, J. P., Aland, J., Wilson, W. H., and Guy, W. (1981). Measuring chronic schizophrenic patients' attitudes toward their illness and treatment. *Hospital and Community Psychiatry* 32:856–858.

Meissner, W. W. (1985). Theories of personality and psychopathology: classical psychoanalysis. In *Comprehensive Textbook of Psychiatry/IV*, ed. H. I. Kaplan and B. J. Sadock, pp. 337–418. Baltimore: Williams & Wilkins.

Menninger, W. C. (1936). Psychiatric hospital therapy designed to meet unconscious needs. *American Journal of Psychiatry* 93:347–360.

Moos, R. H. (1974). *Evaluating Treatment Environments: A Social Ecological Approach.* New York: Wiley.

Moos, R., Shelton, R., and Petty, C. (1973). Perceived ward climate and treatment outcome. *Journal of Abnormal Psychology* 82:291–298.

Mosher, L. R., and Gunderson, J. G. (1979). Group, family, milieu, and community support systems treatment for schizophrenia. In *Disorders of the Schizophrenic Syndrome*, ed. L. Bellak, pp. 399–452. New York: Basic Books.

Mosher, L. R., and Keith, S. J. (1979). Research on the psychosocial treatment of schizophrenia: a summary report. *American Journal of Psychiatry* 136:623–631.

Mosher, L. R., and Menn, A. Z. (1978). Community residential treatment for schizophrenia: two-year follow-up. *Hospital and Community Psychiatry* 29:715–723.

_____ (1983). Scientific evidence and system change: the Soteria experience. In *Psychosocial Intervention in Schizophrenia*, ed. H. Stierling, L. C. Wynne, and M. Wirsching, pp. 93–108. New York: Springer-Verlag.

Oldham, J. M. (1982). The use of silent observers as an adjunct to short-term inpatient group psychotherapy. *International Journal of Group Psychotherapy* 32:469–480.

Oldham, J. M., and Russakoff, L. M. (1982). The medical-therapeutic community. *Journal of Psychiatric Treatment and Evaluation* 4:347–353.

_____ (1984). Suicide at a training center. *Journal of Psychiatric Education* 8:97–104.

Oldham, J. M., Russakoff, L. M., and Prusnofsky, L. (1983). Seclusion: patterns and milieu. *Journal of Nervous and Mental Disease* 171:645–650.

Oldham, J. M., Sacks, M. H., Nininger, J. E., et al. (1983). Medical students' learning as primary therapists or as participant/observers in a psychiatric clerkship. *American Journal of Psychiatry* 140:1615–1618.

Pardes, H., Bjork, D., Van Putten, T., and Kaufman, M. (1972). Failures on a therapeutic milieu. *Psychiatric Quarterly* 46:29–48.

Parloff, M. B., and Dies, R. R. (1977). Group psychotherapy outcome research. *International Journal of Group Psychotherapy* 27:281–319.

Paul, G. L., and Lentz, R. J. (1977). *Psychosocial Treatment of Chronic Mental Patients: Milieu Versus Social-Learning Programs.* Cambridge: Harvard University Press.

Pepper, B., Kirshner, M., and Ryglewicz, H. (1981). The young adult chronic patients: overview of a population. *Hospital and Community Psychiatry* 32:463–469.

Pines, M. (1975). Overview. In *The Large Group: Dynamics and Therapy*, ed. L. Kreeger. Itasca, IL: Peacock.

Pinney, E. L., Wells, S. H., and Fisher, B. (1978). Group therapy training in psychiatric residency programs: a national survey. *American Journal of Psychiatry* 135:1505–1508.

Quitkin, F. M., and Klein, D. F. (1967). Follow-up of treatment failure: psychosis and character disorders. *American Journal of Psychiatry* 124:499–505.

Rabiner, E. L., Wells, C. F., and Zawel, D. (1975). The assessment of individual coping capacities in a group therapy setting. *American Journal of Orthopsychiatry* 45:399–413.

Rapoport, R. N. (1960). *Community as Doctor: New Perspectives on a Therapeutic Community*. Springfield, IL: Tavistock Publications, Charles C Thomas.

Rapoport, R., and Rapoport, R. (1959). Permissiveness and treatment in a therapeutic community. *Psychiatry* 22:57–64.

Rappaport, M., Hopkins, H. K., Hall, K., et al. (1978). Are there schizophrenics for whom phenothiazines may be unnecessary or contraindicated? *International Pharmacopsychiatry* 13:100–111.

Raskin, D. E. (1971). Problems in the therapeutic community. *American Journal of Psychiatry* 128:492–493.

——— (1976). Milieu therapy reexamined. *Comprehensive Psychiatry* 17: 695–701.

Robbins, L. L. (1980). The hospital as a therapeutic community. In *Comprehensive Textbook of Psychiatry/III*, ed. A. M. Freedman, H. I. Kaplan, and B. J. Sadock. Baltimore: Williams & Wilkins.

Rogoff, J. (1986). Individual psychotherapy. In *Inpatient Psychiatry: Diagnosis and Treatment*, ed. L. I. Sederer, pp. 240–262. Baltimore: Williams & Wilkins.

Rubin, R. S. (1979). The community meeting: a comparative study. *American Journal of Psychiatry* 136:708–712.

Russakoff, L. M., and Oldham, J. M. (1982). The structure and technique of community meetings: the short-term unit. *Psychiatry* 45:38–44.

——— (1984). Group psychotherapy on a short-term treatment unit: an application of object relations theory. *International Journal of Group Psychotherapy* 34:339–354.

Rutchick, I. E. (1986). Group psychotherapy. In *Inpatient Psychiatry: Diagnosis and Treatment*, ed. L. I. Sederer, pp. 263–279. Baltimore: Williams & Wilkins.

Sacks, M. H., and Carpenter, W. T. (1974). The pseudotherapeutic community: an examination of antitherapeutic forces on psychiatric units. *Hospital and Community Psychiatry* 25:315–318.

Sacks, M. H., Sledge, W. H., and Rubinton, P., eds. (1984). *Core Readings in Psychiatry*. New York: Praeger.

Sandler, J., Dare, C., and Holder, A. (1973). *The Patient and the Analyst*. New

York: International Universities Press.

Schaffer, C. B., Campbell, R., and Abramowitz, S. I. (1983). Inpatient community meeting as an aid to psychiatric diagnosis. *International Journal of Social Psychiatry* 29:199–204.

Schiff, S. B., and Glassman, S. M. (1969). Large and small group therapy in a state mental health center. *International Journal of Group Psychotherapy* 19:150–157.

Schoonover, S. G., and Bassuk, E. L. (1983). Deinstitutionalization and the private general hospital inpatient unit: implications for clinical care. *Hospital and Community Psychiatry* 34:135–139.

Schwartz, C. G. (1957). Problems for psychiatric nurses in playing a new role on a mental hospital ward. In *The Patient and the Mental Hospital: Contributions of Research in the Science of Social Behavior*, ed. M. Greenblatt, D. J. Levinson, and R. H. Williams, pp. 402–426. Glencoe, IL: The Free Press.

Sederer, L. I., ed. (1986). *Inpatient Psychiatry: Diagnosis and Treatment.* Baltimore: Williams & Wilkins.

———— (1984). Inpatient psychiatry: what place the milieu? *American Journal of Psychiatry* 141:673–674.

Sheets, J. L., Prevost, J. A., and Reihman, J. (1982). Young adult chronic patients: three hypothesized subgroups. *Hospital and Community Psychiatry* 33:197–203.

Sifneos, P. E. (1972). *Short-Term Psychotherapy and Emotional Crisis.* Cambridge: Harvard University Press.

Silver, D., Book, H. E., Hamilton, J. E., et al. (1983). Psychotherapy and the inpatient unit: a unique learning experience. *American Journal of Psychotherapy* 37:121–128.

Skynner, A. C. R. (1975). The large group in training. In *The Large Group: Dynamics and Therapy*, ed. L. Kreeger. Itasca, IL: Peacock.

Soloff, P. H., Gutheil, T. G., and Wexler, D. B. (1985). Seclusion and restraint in 1985: a review and update. *Hospital and Community Psychiatry* 36:652–657.

Spadoni, A. J., and Smith, J. A. (1969). Milieu therapy in schizophrenia: a negative result. *Archives of General Psychiatry* 20:547–551.

Spensley, J., and Langsley, D. G. (1977). Interdisciplinary training of mental health professionals. *Journal of Psychiatric Education* 1:75–84.

Spruiell, V. (1978). Report of panel: current concepts of object relations theory. *Journal of the American Psychoanalytic Association* 26:599–614.

Standish, C. T., and Semrad, E. V. (1975). Group Psychotherapy with psychotics. In *Group Psychotherapy and Group Function*, ed. M. Rosenbaum and M. Berger. New York: Basic Books.

Stanton, A. H., and Schwartz, M. S. (1954). *The Mental Hospital: A Study of Institutional Participation in Psychiatric Illness and Treatment.* New York: Basic Books.

Stein, A. (1975). The training of the group psychotherapist. In *Group Psycho-*

therapy and Group Function, ed. M. Rosenbaum, and M. Berger, pp. 684–704. New York: Basic Books.

Stein, A., Hulse, W. C., Lulow, W. V., and Kaufman, M. R. (1955). Group psychotherapy on the psychiatric ward of the general hospital. *Journal of Mt. Sinai Hospital* 22:104–111.

Steiner, H., Haldipur, C. V., and Stack, L. C. (1982). The acute admission ward as a therapeutic community. *American Journal of Psychiatry* 139:897–901.

Sternbach, D. (1983). Critical comments on object relations theory. *The Psychoanalytic Review* 70:403–421.

Stewart, R. L. (1985). Psychoanalysis and psychoanalytic psychotherapy. In *Comprehensive Textbook of Psychiatry/IV*, ed. H. I. Kaplan and B. J. Sadock. Baltimore: Williams & Wilkins.

Stone, W. N. (1975). Dynamics of the recorder-observer in group psychotherapy. *Comprehensive Psychiatry* 16:49–54.

Strauss, J. S., and Carpenter, W. T. (1981). *Schizophrenia*. New York: Plenum.

Struening, E. L., and Guttentag, M. (1975). *Handbook of Evaluation Research*. Vol. I. Beverly Hills: Sage.

Sullivan, H. S. (1931). Socio-psychiatric research: its implications for the schizophrenia problem and for mental hygiene. *American Journal of Psychiatry* 10:979–991.

Talbott, J. A., ed. (1978). *The Chronic Mental Patient in the Community*. Washington, DC: American Psychiatric Association.

———— (1981). The national plan for the chronically mentally ill: a programmatic analysis. *Hospital and Community Psychiatry* 32:699–704.

Turquet, P. (1975). Threats of identity in the large group. In *The Large Group: Dynamics and Therapy*, ed. L. Kreeger. Itasca, IL: Peacock.

Tuttman, S. (1981). A historical survey of the development of object relations concepts in psychoanalytic theory. In *Object and Self: A Developmental Approach*, ed. S. Tuttman, C. Kaye, and M. Zimmerman. New York: International Universities Press.

Ullmann, L. (1967). *Institution and Outcome*. New York: Pergamon Press.

Van Putten, T. (1973). Milieu therapy: contraindications? *Archives of General Psychiatry* 29:640–643.

Van Putten, T., Crumpton, E., and Yale, C. T. (1976). Drug refusal in schizophrenia and the wish to be crazy. *Archives of General Psychiatry* 33:1443–1446.

Van Putten, T., and May, P. R. A. (1976). Milieu therapy of the schizophrenics. In *Treatment of Schizophrenia: Progress and Prospects*, ed. L. J. West and D. E. Flinn, pp. 217–243. New York: Grune & Stratton.

Waxer, P. H. (1977). Short-term group psychotherapy: some principles and techniques. *International Journal of Group Psychotherapy* 27:33–42.

Weiner, H. (1978). The illusion of simplicity: the medical model revisited. *American Journal of Psychiatry* 135:27–33.

Weissman, M. M. (1979). The psychological treatment of depression: evidence for the efficacy of psychotherapy alone, in comparison with, and in combination with, pharmacotherapy. *Archives of General Psychiatry* 36:1261–1269.

Wendt, R. J., Mosher, L. R., Matthews, S. M., and Menn, A. Z. (1983). Comparison of two treatment environments for schizophrenia. In *Principles and Practice of Milieu Therapy*, ed. J. G. Gunderson, O. A. Will, and L. R. Mosher, pp. 17–33. New York: Jason Aronson.

White, N. F. (1972a). The descent of milieu therapy. *Canadian Psychiatric Association Journal* 17:41–50.

———— (1972b). Reappraising the inpatient unit: obit milieu. *Canadian Psychiatric Association Journal* 17:51–58.

Whitely, J. S. (1975). The large group as a medium for sociotherapy. In *The Large Group: Dynamics and Therapy*, ed. L. Kreeger, pp. 193–211. Itasca, IL: Peacock.

Wilmer, H. A. (1958). Toward a definition of the therapeutic community. *American Journal of Psychiatry* 114:824–834.

———— (1981). Defining and understanding the therapeutic community. *Hospital and Community Psychiatry* 32:95–99.

Winer, J. A., and Lewis, L. (1984). Interpretive psychotherapy in the inpatient community meeting. *Psychiatry* 47:333–341.

Wolf, M. S. (1977). A review of literature on milieu therapy. *Journal of Psychiatric Nursing and Mental Health Services* 15:26–33.

Yalom, I. D. (1983). *Inpatient Group Psychotherapy*. New York: Basic Books.

Youcha, I. Z. (1976). Short-term inpatient group: formation and beginnings. *Group Process* 7:119–137.

Zeitlyn, B. B. (1967). The therapeutic community – fact or fantasy? *British Journal of Psychiatry* 113:1083–1086.

Zilboorg, G. (1941). *History of Medical Psychology*. New York: WW Norton.

Index

227